As One

Individual Action · Collective Power

Mehrdad Baghai & James Quigley

with Ainar Aijala, Sabri Challah & Gerhard Vorster

PORTFOLIO
PENGUIN

PORTFOLIO / PENGUIN

Published by the Penguin Group
Penguin Books Ltd, 80 Strand, London WC2R 0RL, England
Penguin Group (USA) Inc., 375 Hudson Street, New York, New York 10014, USA
Penguin Group (Canada), 90 Eglinton Avenue East, Suite 700, Toronto, Ontario, Canada M4P 2Y3
(a division of Pearson Penguin Canada Inc.)
Penguin Ireland, 25 St Stephen's Green, Dublin 2, Ireland (a division of Penguin Books Ltd)
Penguin Group Australia Ltd, 250 Camberwell Road, Camberwell, Victoria 3124, Australia
(a division of Pearson Australia Group Pty Ltd)
Penguin Books India Pvt Ltd, 11 Community Centre, Panchsheel Park, New Delhi – 110 017, India
Penguin Group (NZ), 67 Apollo Drive, Rosedale, North Shore 0632, New Zealand
(a division of Pearson New Zealand Ltd)
Penguin Books (South Africa) (Pty) Ltd, 24 Sturdee Avenue,
Rosebank, Johannesburg 2196, South Africa

www.penguin.com

Published simultaneously in the United States of America by Portfolio / Penguin,
a member of Penguin Group (USA) Inc. and in the United Kingdom by Portfolio Penguin,
a member of Penguin Books Ltd 2011

1 3 5 7 9 10 8 6 4 2

Printed in China

ISBN for UK and Commonwealth edition: 978-0-241-95400-3
ISBN for USA edition: 978-1-59184-415-0

We dedicate this book to people all over the world and from all walks of life who labor tirelessly — some in highly visible roles and many others without due recognition — to enable groups of people to work "As One" in pursuit of noble goals. We believe that the future of civilized society depends on their success.

Join the global community on the As One website and get immediate access to:

- A fully searchable library of more than 80 case studies from the book as well as a growing set of new cases contributed by As One community members.

- A collection of over 130 research notes that led to the formulation of the concepts in the book as well as a growing set of links and papers on collective leadership.

- Handy archetype summaries as well as the automated "classifier" tool which can help you to quickly determine the archetype of any group.

- Links to download the very useful As One iPhone and iPad apps as well as to stay connected by subscribing to the RSS feed.

- A complete set of endnotes and annotations for the book including links to websites and referenced citations on the Internet.

- Special offers and promotions including advance notice for special As One events around the world.

Contents

NOTE

Endnotes for this book are published online at: **www.asone.org**
Images are supplied by Bridgewater Associates, Construction Photography, Corbis,
CSIRO, Getty Images, W.L. Gore & Associates, IDEO, Medco Health Solutions,
Mondragon Corporation, PatientsLikeMe.com and Press Association Images.
For full picture credits, please visit the As One website.

We began speaking about the idea of collective leadership three years ago. We had, however, been thinking about it separately for a very long time before that. We realized that we were all focused on the same thing but had been thinking about it from two very different perspectives.

Mehrdad is a management thinker and writer. He has been advising leaders of large global organizations on their growth strategies for nearly twenty years, first as a partner at McKinsey & Company, and later as the leader of his own boutique firm. Over the years, he has come to appreciate more and more that strategy is executed through people; yet getting them to work "As One" to deliver strategies is easier said than done. Experience has taught him that generating collective behavior seems to be a nearly universal challenge for leaders in all kinds of organizations.

Jim is the chief executive officer of Deloitte Touche Tohmatsu Limited, the world's largest private professional services network. Deloitte comprises more than 170,000 people who provide audit, tax, consulting, and financial advisory services to public and private clients in 147 countries. Jim's biggest challenge is getting all those people to work "As One" global organization despite belonging to relatively strong practice areas in different member firms. He has been in a leadership role for many years and experience has taught him that the true challenge of leadership is not simply addressed by relying on the right structures and incentives. It is a far deeper issue.

Ainar, Sabri and Gerhard have a foot in both worlds. They are leaders in the Deloitte network but they have also been lead advisors to chief executives around the world. All three have been dealing with the challenges of getting large numbers of people to work together for the past three decades.

We all believe that leaders from all walks of life are searching for a pragmatic and tested approach that can help them to realize the full potential of their people to work together. Yet looking across the scores of management books on offer, we were hard-pressed to find insights and advice that were underpinned by rigorous analytical research. In many ways, the subject matter seemed to us to be a domain suitable for the development of "next practice" approaches. We joined forces to make a contribution to advancing the thinking in this space.

The ideas we express in this book are derived from a Deloitte Flagship Project aimed squarely at the challenges of working "As One." As leaders of this initiative, we intentionally pursued a global orientation in our research.

From the outset, we drew on the best resources from the US, UK, Canada, Netherlands, Australia, South Africa and Japan. Despite the challenging logistics, the five of us held regular face-to-face meetings, convening for two- to three-day working sessions at least every three months. As a result, we believe our ideas apply across a broad range of geographies and cultures.

This book attempts to equip leaders with the ability to connect their strategies with the people in their enterprise. The suggested ideas and approaches are applicable to businesses, and business units, of all sizes and in all locales, from the C-suite to individual project teams. They are intended to provide practical advice to all levels of business leaders. But not just business leaders: our ideas are equally applicable to the public sector or the non-profit world. Quite simply, we are hoping to help leaders turn individual action into collective power.

We have been able to try out our ideas with many large organizations around the world. The most exciting aspect of these market tests of our ideas over the past two years has been the positive reaction of senior leaders and their broad applicability to many different industry and geographic contexts. Several of the world's largest corporations as well as organizations in the public sector have started to use the "As One" frameworks with great commitment. The concepts have proven to be intuitively appealing and helpful. The new diagnostic tools have provided a new common vocabulary to discuss engagement and alignment in strategic execution.

Each time we apply these ideas in a new setting or country, we discover more about their power and usefulness. Indeed, it is our universally positive experience within Deloitte and with our clients that has moved us to share our ideas with a broader audience.

Our personal aspiration in writing this book is not to offer the final word on the subject; far from it. We believe a huge amount of work needs to be done in this emerging field. Our hope is to make a contribution by shifting the discourse from loosely-defined, theoretically appealing concepts to a much more analytically rigorous and pragmatic footing. We need real research in order to enhance the capacity of leaders to generate "As One behavior" in their organizations.

We also realize that many of the economic, political and social challenges now confronting our planet are variations of the same collective action dilemma. We hope that our work will also contribute in some constructive and possibly unimaginable ways to their resolution over time. We believe our future security and prosperity depends on our collective ability to act "As One."

As One

It's a short phrase. Only five letters. But those five letters are filled with meaning and inspiration. They make all the difference between a group of individuals and a unified team. Those five letters symbolize the culmination of individual action into collective power. They describe how individuals can collaborate to achieve extraordinary results – together.

As One in our world

Every day, millions of people around the world collaborate. We join, share and cooperate with others from different countries and backgrounds, across organizations and industries. The world continues to advance because people are problem solving, innovating and collaborating to make things happen. Some even argue that, throughout history, our very survival and progress have depended on working together.

Some collaborations may be unintentional; others are quite deliberate. Some are modern and supported by web-enabled technology; others are traditional and draw on community beliefs and customs. Yet despite significant studies into human behavior, our knowledge of deliberate collaborative endeavors is still formative, especially as it applies to large organizations and corporations. Furthermore, the study of collaboration may be about working together, but it isn't necessarily about working as one.

Adding the phrase "as one" to another word changes its entire meaning. Working *versus* Working As One. Winning *versus* Winning As One. Stronger *versus* Stronger As One. Think of the possibilities. The sources of inspiration are endless. Believing As One. Succeeding As One.

"As One behavior" represents something entirely different and distinctive – but not formulaic. We often look for strong and dominant leaders in our working world, but based on what we are learning about collaboration, leadership can come in many different shapes and sizes. It can sometimes be about creativity, empowerment, top-down direction, emergent strategy, strength in numbers, precision, autonomy, as well as hierarchy. It is all about further defining the different shapes and sizes and applying them to your unique situation. Consider the differences among these eight examples:

Creating As One

When it was unveiled in 2007, Apple's iPhone was a marketer's dream: instantly iconic, category shaping, with a launch that itself became a cultural event. More than a quarter of a million handsets were sold in the first two days. Three years later, Apple scored an even bigger win with the launch of the iPad. However, the bigger story behind both is the innovative App Store, a virtual store dedicated to promoting the range of iPhone and iPad applications. As of mid-2010, the App Store had published more than 300,000 applications, and not just from software professionals; many of them created by amateurs and enthusiasts keen to share an idea or innovation, and some hoping to unleash the next iPhone craze. Apple allows this extended developer community to take home the bulk of the generated revenues through a 30/70 split. No single company, not even Apple, could have developed anywhere close to the number and variety of applications generated by this creative network.

Pioneering As One

The early 1990s saw the start of a revolution in the IT industry: a challenge to the hegemony of the software giants. It came in the somewhat unlikely form of Finnish engineer, Linus Torvalds, who developed the core component of the Linux operating system and then – via a posting on the Internet – asked fellow enthusiasts to help him perfect it. Unlike proprietary software such as Windows, Linux is open source, based on principles put forward by pioneer Richard Stallman in the early 1980s. You can make money out of it and you can sell it, but you must offer access to the source code for free. Today, Linux is a thriving multi-billion dollar organic community, whose collaborators and distributors include Dell, Red Hat, Sun Microsystems and Nokia.

Smarter As One

In healthcare, detail, accuracy, and precision are, literally, vital. Yet, in 2006, an estimated 1.5 million preventable serious medication errors occurred in the US, with over $200 billion in associated costs. For example, there are too many points in the prescription dispensing process where mistakes can happen. How can you be sure that you're receiving the medication your doctor prescribed? Medco Health Solutions, named one of the most innovative companies of 2008 is reinventing US healthcare with a new type of dispensary. It combines rigid protocols and standardized processes with innovative technologies to reduce human errors in pharmacy care. And it's succeeding. Medco's 3,000 pharmacists continue to deliver more than 100 million prescriptions per year with Six Sigma accuracy.

Transforming As One

Over the past 25 years, Guy Laliberté has reinvented the circus. He, his company of 4,000 employees and the 20,000 or so dedicated performers on his books, create memorable shows that combine extraordinary talents and skills with spectacular effects. Cirque du Soleil is not about recycling stage-worn tricks. It's about putting on performances the world has never seen before. Each show is several years in the making. Though imaginative and fantastical, Laliberté's circus harnesses creativity and talent using a remarkably structured process. The initiation and training process for each member of the Cirque family is rigorous and long. To belong to the company, you must let yourself be transformed; and the transformation allows a collective dream to take shape over time.

Working As One

The hours are challenging, the tasks are often menial, the pay tends to be poor... What's the hospitality industry ever done for its workers? In the case of global hotel chain Marriott, the answer is quite a lot. For decades, the company has run a program to help foreign entry-level workers learn English and adapt to their new countries. A family business, Marriott wants its people to feel they belong – and, crucially, provides these workers with optimistic career prospects and the chance of promotion. Some housekeepers even go on to become general managers. It's a policy that's paid off: staff turnover is extremely low by industry standards giving Marriott a competitive advantage in a difficult industry setting.

Innovating As One

Ratan Tata, the CEO of the Tata Group, had a seemingly impossible dream: to build a car for just 1 lakh ($2,500). The only way to realize it was to convince the most innovative automotive suppliers to commit to the project. Together, they would re-invent many traditional car components, continuously integrate each other's innovations into the design process, and, through aggressive project management, keep everyone on the same page. He promised the world that he would deliver a 1-lakh car, and through the creative collaboration of the band of suppliers that believed in his Tata Nano, the Indian people's car was born. Thanks to him, car ownership is now within the reach of millions more in India and beyond.

Operating As One

The dabbawalas, the lunch box delivery men of Mumbai, deliver more than 200,000 hot meals a day in an operation of Six-Sigma precision. Of every six million deliveries, only one fails to arrive on time. If one dabbawala is injured and unable to complete the task, another can be instantly called in to ensure that the lunch still gets to its hungry recipient. The system runs not on technology but on agility, adaptability and commitment. Since most of the dabbawalas are illiterate, they follow color-coded symbols on the dabbas (lunch boxes) to make sure they reach their final destinations. Paid well by Indian standards, dabbawalas are bound by a shared sense of pride in their work and a culture of mutual support.

Managing As One

Engineering company W.L. Gore & Associates, inventor of GORE-TEX® the revolutionary fabric treatment, is regularly listed as one of the best companies to work for. But in many ways, it represents the antithesis of traditional management: there are few job titles, no job descriptions, no defined organization charts. Employees work in small, fluid and adaptive teams with minimal structure. Yet Gore continues to be one of the world's most innovative companies, producing more than 1,000 products across aerospace, automotive, medical, military, and pharmaceutical industries. Its employees form a collective; they're self-motivated and pro-active associates who are committed to their team members and to the greater good of the company.

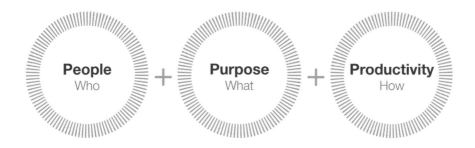

People
Who
+
Purpose
What
+
Productivity
How

A new definition of collective leadership

The previous stories point to the evolving nature of the definition of leadership. Some say leadership is all about productivity. They think a leader's job is to get people to be on the same page so they work together efficiently. They say a great leader should get people to have a common interpretation around how to work together.

Many say leadership is all about people. They say a leader's job is to develop people's sense of belonging to their group. They believe a great leader should get people to have a strong shared identity or sense of who they are.

Others say leadership is all about purpose. They feel a leader's job is to drive people's commitment to act on the goals of the organization. They say a great leader gets people to have a strong sense of directional intensity around what they need to do together.

We believe real leadership involves all these things. We call it working "As One" and we think it represents the pinnacle of collective leadership, or leadership that results in a cohesive group of people working together effectively toward a common goal or purpose.

The need for a common language

The marketplace is constantly – and for the most part efficiently – selecting winners. Whether the competition is for capital, talent or market share, the winning edge can almost always be determined by the organization that is best able to work together as one. Collective power is a powerful competitive force.

Frequently the case studies on leadership point to the enterprise as a whole, and its leader, generally the CEO. The winning edge that the "As One" approach can provide, is clearly available to an entire enterprise and its CEO – but these leadership concepts also cascade throughout an organization. Business unit leaders, product managers, and account team leaders that are able to work as one will perform at a higher level. Whether as a team of five or a team of 50,000, the aspiration to work as one is the timeless leadership challenge.

We do not espouse collaboration for its own sake. Leadership should be much more strategic and deliberate. The initial difficulty lies in identifying which people need to be involved (the Who) and what purpose they need to satisfy (the What). We call this a leader's "As One Agenda" because it outlines the "Who–What" information that is most critical for the organization's success.

The As One Agenda clearly identifies where in the organization collective leadership is most valuable. A better understanding of this agenda, and how to obtain, and then sustain, the power of As One using collective leadership is the purpose of this book.

We have developed tools to help leaders assess the strength of the Who and What dimensions. But the greater challenge is this: how do leaders ensure they share with their team a clear understanding of what working together productively means? People often have different interpretations of "working together" or how they need to collaborate to achieve their priorities (the How) ranging from effective communication processes to a sense of belonging created through culture or other means to incentives to motivate behavior.

A common language, framework or taxonomy has not been developed and widely accepted that accurately describes how different people think about working with those around them. So how can leaders possibly test whether their people have the same understanding? We need to develop a more precise understanding of the different ways that individuals collaborate. We have discovered that there is a rich taxonomy for how people can work together, but mapping it in detail is much more difficult than anyone has really imagined.

It involves a great many factors: hierarchy, decision making, incentives, communication, control, or technology. It involves separate and multiple parties – leaders, followers, partners, and organizations – with varying agendas, interests, and environments – all working toward a common goal. If leaders could equip themselves and their teams with the right language to align all of these disjointed pieces, they – and their organizations – would deliver greater impact.

Our mission has been to take all these factors into account and still manage to create a common language or taxonomy that can be accessible to most people.

The thinking behind As One behavior

Almost anything can be classified – organisms, stars, cultures, events, and places. In fact, the leading naturalists of the eighteenth and nineteenth centuries spent most of their lives identifying newly-discovered organisms. They not only discovered and categorized new organisms, but they also made attempts to determine similarities, differences and patterns among them.

Similarly the core ideas about the different forms of collaboration have been around for hundreds of years. But it wasn't until the 1960s that academics, economists, and political theorists, such as Tom Schelling, Mancur Olson, Robert Axelrod, and Albert Hirschman, began serious study and classification of collective action, or what we call "As One behavior." These and other thinkers laid a strong theoretical foundation for understanding collective action and how people work together for common goals.

Around the same time, scientists began discovering how complex adaptive systems in nature, such as bee hives and ant colonies, often display very strong collective characteristics. Based on these reinforcing strands of research, huge strides were taken in our understanding of cooperation and conflict in large, group behavior.

Although the theoretical foundation behind collective action is not new, its practical application to modern management and leadership is still developing. Management gurus have latched on to the concept of collective action and have attempted to apply it to modern organizations and leadership practices.

As expected, these early "translations" of the academic thinking to management have been primarily directional in nature. They have put very intriguing ideas and concepts on the table, but have not yet delivered the right tools, with the right precision, to make them actionable by leaders.

The traditional perspective

For the most part, management thinkers have approached the world by suggesting a very limited taxonomy, with two ways to generate collective leadership:

1. The traditional "command-and-control" model.
2. A new "agile-and-adaptive" model (basically, everything else).

Many of these thinkers and writers tend to regard command-and-control as past its use-by date. But they've overlooked the fact that the command-and-control model is highly effective in situations such as emergencies, where a high degree of direction and authority is required. Equally, their description of the new model has encompassed a disparate array of elements, some of which are inconsistent. Moreover, the new model is considered unequivocally good, but we all know that things are never that categorical.

A new perspective

In a world that is so diversified, why should there be only two modes of collective behavior? Common sense alone says there ought to be numerous variations, each with unique characteristics. And why should one be considered new and innovative while the other, which has worked well in many situations, be deemed obsolete?

Clearly, we need to have greater granularity and depth in the way we classify different approaches to collaboration. With a few notable exceptions, such as the MIT Center for Collective Intelligence, most people have been content with subjective and qualitative perspectives about the changing nature of collective behavior. Thomas W. Malone, the renowned organizational theorist and head of the MIT Center, states in his book, *The Future of Work* that "To be successful in the world we're entering, we will need a new set of mental models. While these new models should not exclude the possibility of commanding and controlling, they need to encompass a much wider range of possibilities."

We agree that a new, richer taxonomy is required, and that we need to move away from a simplistic bimodal view of the universe to a taxonomy that captures more of the distinguishing features of different mental models. This is not an impossible task. It's just that forms of collaboration have yet to be categorized or classified in an analytically rigorous and actionable way.

The As One Flagship Project

For the past two years, Deloitte has been investing in the As One Flagship Project, a global knowledge initiative to study the next practice in collective leadership. The project had the goal of further developing a systematic understanding of As One behavior and of bridging the gap between collective action theory and practical management thinking.

Deloitte commissioned this Flagship Project due, in part, to the seismic shifts that were occurring in the business environment. Business leaders were challenged by the continued globalization of the economy and the rapid expansion of the emerging markets. The talent pool was being redefined by major demographic shifts, the pace of technological developments was accelerating, and the manner that people were convening, collaborating, and communicating had also shifted. The time was right for a fresh look at collective leadership.

Our methodology

The initial research consisted of the following two components:

1. An academic review of hundreds of perspectives on collaboration and collective action drawn from disciplines such as science, history, economics, psychology, and popular culture.

2. A set of 60 detailed case studies – representing a balance across 19 industries and many geographies – that analyzed successful examples of As One behavior in corporations, government agencies and non-profit-making organizations. Each case represented a single powerful example of As One behavior inside an organization, rather than an organization itself.

Specifically, each case study examined more than one hundred factors ranging from organizational structure, systems and processes to leadership mechanisms, and communications. An extensive list of questions relating to each of the factors was compiled. These included:

- What kind of formal and informal structures are used to channel individuals into the As One behavior?
- How are individuals recruited and trained?
- What kinds of incentives are used for reward or punishment to foster As One behavior?
- To what extent is the idea or purpose aligned to a charismatic leader or a group of leaders?
- What leadership mechanisms are used to attract the individuals into the collective?

Once all of these factors had been analyzed, the challenge was to identify distinct models or archetypes, as well as the key characteristics that defined each. But when you're dealing with human behavior, how do you: 1) decide which characteristics are most critical for classification purposes, and 2) distinguish different types of As One behavior?

To answer this question in an objective way, we used an advanced forensic data analytic technique called a self-organizing map (SOM).

The power of the SOM

Self-organizing maps (SOMs) are an advanced statistical technique used in forensics research for making sense of highly dimensional and complex information. They:

- Find relationships in data where the number of variables makes the analysis complex.
- Divide complicated data into groups of similar items so that you can understand what makes them similar.

The SOM figures out what is occurring by looking for the best statistical "fit" for the data. This is not driven by hypotheses provided by researchers. The SOM identifies the relationships by considering all variables in all records simultaneously. It generates a model that is akin to a map where similar observations are closer to each other and dissimilar ones farther apart. In the As One project, this allowed us to find groups of cases which were very similar and to see what led to groups of cases being seen as different from each other.

The SOM was able to identify distinct modes of As One behavior based on the classification of each case across all factors. It also identified which of our dozens of data points were the key defining characteristics for each mode.

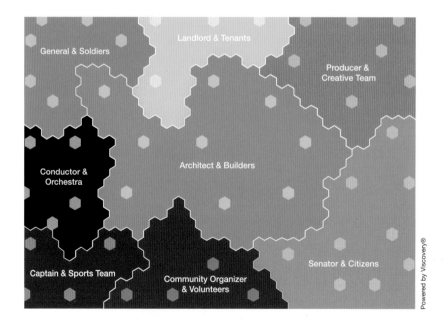

Introducing the eight archetypes

The SOM helped uncover at least eight distinct models of As One behavior. For simplicity, the eight clusters were described around two primary dimensions, or axes, within the SOM.

Although it is a simplification and abstraction of the overall analysis, the two-axes framework helps us to visualize – and therefore explain – the groupings.

The vertical axis is a direction-setting component that describes how power is exercised in the organization, from centralized and top-down to decentralized and bottom-up.

The horizontal axis conveys the nature of individuals' tasks and outlines how work is organized, from highly scripted and uniform to highly creative. Four clusters of cases sit at the end points of the axes and four more hybrid clusters sit between the axes.

These clusters were defined as "archetypes" and each assigned a "leader and followers" label, which was representative of eight different ways that organizations can operate.

Some archetype labels reflect strong, top-down market mechanisms. Some reflect bottom-up, democratic participation and creativity. Other labels have traits that are similar to those of superorganisms such as ant or honey bee colonies.

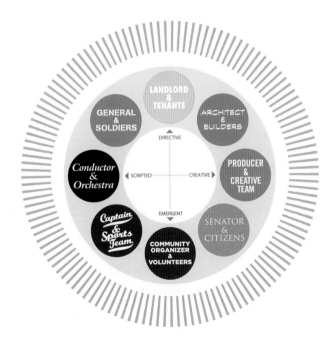

The main archetypes

At the beginning of the introduction, we summarized eight different cases that capture the essence of an archetype in action. Each story clearly demonstrates specific characteristics for their respective archetype:

The first two pairings sit at the extremities of the vertical direction-setting axis.

 The **Landlord & Tenants** pairing is based on landlords' top-down driven strategy and power: they control access to highly valuable or scarce resources. Landlords decide how to generate the most value for themselves and dictate the terms of participation for the tenants. Tenants voluntarily decide to join landlords, and it's usually in their best interests to do so. However, once they do, landlords define the rules of participation. Landlords maintain their power by ensuring the best tenants are rewarded, so that, over time, as the number of tenants grows, the landlords' power increases.

 The **Community Organizer & Volunteers** pairing is based on volunteers' bottom-up, autonomous, independent, decision-making ability and their desire to voice their opinions. Community organizers ignite volunteers' interest through compelling storytelling and opportunities for volunteers to join in. They may have little direct power over the volunteers, but they can tap into volunteers' interests by gaining their trust, promoting a strong brand, and understanding their motivations. Volunteers themselves are drawn together by a rallying cry, or out of a sense of enlightened self-interest; they gain their power through a strength-in-numbers approach.

The popularity of Apple's App Store is a great example of the Landlord & Tenants archetype.

The Linux operating system phenomenon is a great example of the Community Organizer & Volunteers archetype.

The second two pairings sit at the extremities of the horizontal "nature of the task" dimension.

The **Conductor & Orchestra** pairing is based on highly scripted and clearly defined roles that focus on precision and efficiency in execution as defined by the conductor. The orchestra members, who have similar backgrounds, need to be fully trained to comply with the requirements of the job, and, therefore, must be carefully selected to ensure they fit the strict culture and scripted tasks. Belonging to the orchestra provides members with the best way to make a living while focusing on tasks at which they excel.

The **Producer & Creative Team** pairing is typically about producers providing their creative team with the freedom to do their best work and reach their natural potential. This pairing is led by legendary, charismatic producers who bring together a team of highly inventive and skilled independent individuals to achieve the producers' objective. Producers guide the vision and overall progress, while the creative team develops ideas through frequent meetings and interactions using an open culture of collaboration. Dissent is used to push creative boundaries. To maintain longevity in their industry, producers and creative teams need to continuously produce new and innovative ideas.

Medco Health Solutions' protocol-driven pharmacy is a great example of the Conductor & Orchestra archetype.

Cirque du Soleil's show creation process is a great example of the Producer & Creative Team archetype.

The hybrid archetypes

There are also four hybrid archetypes, which combine the characteristics of the adjacent pairings and occupy the spaces between the axes. Some of the traits are similar, but they exist to different degrees and in combination with other characteristics in the hybrids.

 The **General & Soldiers** pairing has a command-and-control-type culture combined with a multi-level hierarchy organized around the general's clear and compelling mission. Soldiers' activities focus on clearly defined and scripted tasks. They are motivated by advancing up the hierarchy through well-defined roles at all levels. Soldiers undergo extensive training to understand the army and its culture, and to learn specific skills. They are committed to the mission, the overall institution, and each other, while the general provides strong top-down authoritarian direction to motivate and direct them.

 The **Architect & Builders** pairing focuses on the creative, even ingenious, collaboration between groups of diverse builders that have been recruited by visionary architects to bring a seemingly impossible dream to life. Their visions are so innovative and ambitious that they can't be achieved simply by using conventional means, so builders often need to reinvent and rethink ways to achieve them. Builders strive to meet ambitious deadlines and milestones mapped to deliberate work cycles. As each milestone is completed, the builders become one step closer to bringing the architect's dream to reality.

The career advancement that Marriott provides for its entry-level hospitality workers is a great example of the General & Soldiers archetype.

The development of the world's cheapest car, the Tata Nano, is a great example of the Architect & Builders archetype.

The **Captain** *&* **Sports Team** pairing operates with minimal hierarchy and acts like a single cohesive and dynamic organism, adapting to new strategies and challenges with great agility as they appear. Members of the sports team have a strong shared identity. They have extensive and networked communication channels, and carry out the same highly scripted, repeatable tasks. There is strong camaraderie and trust among the sports team – the collective good outweighs the needs of the individual – while captains are there, on the field as part of the team, to motivate and encourage.

The **Senator** *&* **Citizens** pairing is based on a strong sense of responsibility to abide by the values or constitution of the community, which have been outlined by the senators. Sovereignty is held by both senators and citizens, and the citizens thrive on the values of democracy, freedom of expression, and autonomy. Since citizens are autonomous, the community structure is flexible. There is no set framework or direction organizing the citizens. Instead, much of their direction is emergent as they gather ideas and collaborate with other citizens. Senators are the guiding intelligence for the citizens and oversee decision making for the community.

The low-tech adaptability of the dabbawalas of Mumbai is a great example of the Captain & Sports Team archetype.

The flexible structure and unique culture of W.L. Gore & Associates is a great example of the Senator & Citizens archetype.

Classifying As One

The power of the As One taxonomy stems from its ability to divide the simplistic "traditional" binary groupings – command-and-control and agile-and-adaptive – into eight different categories. Our eight stories, as well as the other examples provided, represent a diverse range of organizations and their modes of working across countries and cultures, which further demonstrate the richness of the As One taxonomy. Command-and-control is comprised of three categories and agile-and-adaptive spans five different categories as shown below.

Our goal in sharing these findings is to provide leaders with a practical tool and a common or universal language for discussing the different ways they can effectively ignite collaboration in their organizations.

However, just as importantly, this book represents a fundamental shift forward in the theoretical discourse on collective leadership. It also provides the tools for a richer understanding and more precise thinking in order to both generate and shape effective collective behavior.

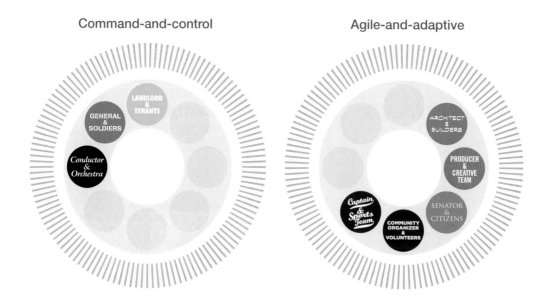

Command-and-control

Agile-and-adaptive

How to use this book

This book has eight chapters that correspond with the eight As One archetypes. Understanding the archetype is the first step, but the critical thing is to understand how to use each archetype effectively. Each chapter is divided into four key sections that help bring the archetype to life:

1. An "inspirational" story based on the inspiring lives and careers of actual leaders and the challenges they faced. The story sets the stage for the naming of the archetype.
2. A more detailed version of one of the "archetype in action" stories described at the beginning of this introduction. Based on an in-depth business case study, this story helps create a good general sense of how the archetype can work well.
3. A description of each of the archetype's six key characteristics, using examples to illustrate each of them, offering real detail around the nature of the archetype.
4. An applicability section describing when and how to use the archetype and a variety of tools for doing so effectively.

On pages 20 and 21, you'll find a simple decision tree, which will help you determine your default archetype. Do you tend to lead in a more top-down directive, scripted way or a creative or participative way? Once you've completed the short questionnaire, go to the relevant chapter to find out more in-depth information on your As One working style.

However, understanding your default archetype is only part of the story. The checklist at the end of each chapter will help you determine whether your default is actually suitable and effective for your situation. In other words, are you using the archetype that is most effective for your organization and its current situation, or simply the one that is most natural for your own leadership style?

You will also find it helpful to study the conclusion which explains how to put the As One archetypes into practice. A word of warning: you will not find this a paint-by-numbers exercise. There is no precise wiring diagram or recipe book with detailed instructions for you. You will need to exercise judgment and discretion. Still, we do offer a proven approach that will guide you to ask the right questions and consider your options as you reflect on your own collective leadership challenges.

There is no prescribed way to read this book. However, you will find that once you've identified your current and most effective archetypes, certain aspects of adjacent archetypes will also be relevant. As you'll discover, some archetypes are more applicable in certain situations where authority and direction are required, while others are better suited for open and emergent decision making. To gain the most from this book, read the chapters that fall under your current and most effective archetypes but keep in mind the impact of the situation you're facing.

Where to begin

Wondering how you should read this book?
Use this classifier to figure out the archetype
that is closest to your current situation.
Start with that chapter.

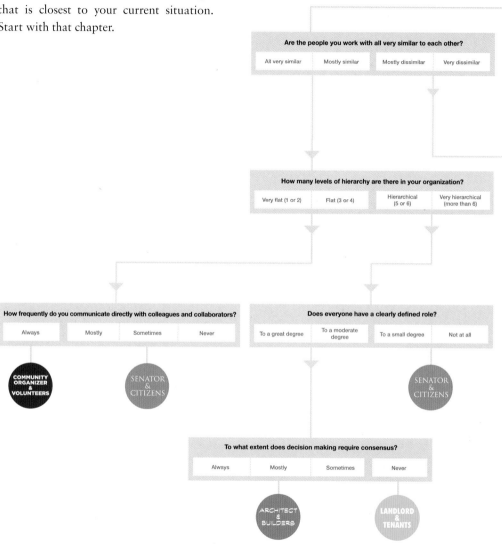

Our future – As One

As One may seem primarily applicable to leaders and their teams, but it doesn't just have to be about interactions inside organizations. It's much more than that. The concept is a starting point for all leaders to understand how they can apply specific collective leadership techniques to best fit the situations and challenges they face.

For the first time, we have the beginnings of a rigorous toolkit for leaders to understand and decide what it means to work As One. We have a common language for collective leadership. People need not only to be on the same page but also to be reading the same words.

Around the world, examples of inspirational As One leadership continue to present themselves. As you'll see, regardless of where you are, the real power of As One happens when the positive one-on-one activities of individuals culminate as something bigger and better. Imagine what we could accomplish if we could unlock the power of As One on a global scale.

Through a common and evolving language and framework of collective leadership, working As One could create a significant difference in our world. This book is an initial contribution to an emerging body of thought. Real success over time depends on whether a growing group of collaborators will accompany us on this journey to advance our work.

Individual action. Collective power. Join us to help more people discover the power of working – As One.

Chapter 1

Landlord
& Tenants

"I like thinking big. If you're
going to be thinking anything,
you might as well think big"
—*Donald Trump*

" Translating retailers' ambitions into reality while capitalizing on opportunities to benefit his company "

Frank Lowy and the Westfield phenomenon

Born in 1930 into a working-class Jewish family and brought up in a small industrial town, Filakovo, in southern Czechoslovakia, Frank Lowy was the youngest of five children. For Frank's parents, life was tough. The effects of the Great Depression were still being felt around the world, and feeding and clothing their family took all the money the Lowys had. But after Frank was born, with help from family, they decided to buy a small house with a shop attached, and started selling sugar, bread, flour, and other staples.

World War II forced the Lowys to sell their house and move to Budapest. There, the entire family, including the young children, worked hard to make enough money to pay for their apartment. Though only about 12-years-old, Frank would help his older brother to sell metal pots and kitchenware, highly prized during the austere years of the war. Frank fondly recalls this period of his life in Budapest; his parents and family were happy and safe.

The idyll, however, was doomed. In 1944, the Nazis invaded Hungary, and Frank's father was killed. In an attempt to escape persecution, the remaining members of the family split up; Frank

lived with his mother, only occasionally visited by his siblings. He spent much of his time foraging on the streets, keeping his eyes open for food and his ears open for information.

After the Russians entered Budapest in 1945, the Lowys moved back to Czechoslovakia. But Frank didn't remain there long. He decided to travel to Palestine, where he remained until he was 21 during which time the state of Israel was created. His experiences gave him a sense of personal freedom and strength.

Moving to Australia

While in Palestine, Frank's mother, brother, sister and her husband had moved to Australia. Frank wanted nothing more than to be reunited with his family; so he and his other remaining brother left Israel for Sydney.

Frank got a job in a sandwich shop. After hours, he partied, and in December 1952, met a girl, Shirley. Despite the disapproval of her mother, the couple married on March 7, 1954. She was just 19; Frank 23.

Soon afterward, Frank left the sandwich shop and got a job as a truck driver, delivering ham, bacon and salami to local delis. His interpersonal skills and enthusiasm meant he was able to find new customers and increase sales. Now with a newborn son, he worked hard to support his family, and his efforts soon paid off. John Saunders, a delicatessen owner from a similar background, recognized his potential and asked him to go into business with him.

Lowy and Saunders decided to open another delicatessen in Blacktown, in the western suburbs of Sydney, where a railway had just been electrified, and with the daily flow of passengers from the train, their little shop – stocked with its barrels of olives and herrings, rounds of cheese, meats and fresh rye bread – flourished.

The birth and development of Westfield

Within a few years, Frank and John had made smart investments in a variety of businesses – from a coffee lounge to residential homes. Taking the profits from their businesses and reinvesting them, Frank and John slowly began to branch out further, buying land and building an office as well as shops. Soon, Westfield Investments Pty Ltd was born – combining the idea of developing in the western suburbs with greenfield sites.

Their real estate success continued throughout the late 1950s and coincided with a new phenomenon spreading throughout the United States: the shopping center. Frank and John bought a plot of land, much larger than the typical strips used for rows of shops, and earmarked it for a retail conglomerate called Westfield Place.

Shaped around an open courtyard, Westfield Place would consist of a dozen shops, a small supermarket and two department stores. It officially opened in July 1959 and was hailed as a huge success – as both an innovation and a commercial enterprise.

From the opening of the 12-store Westfield shopping center in Blacktown, Frank and John seemed unstoppable, and, in the 1960s, went on to open up in Hornsby, Figtree, Burwood, Dee Why, Yagoona, Eastwood, and Toombul. There was no other property company in Australia quite like Westfield – one that managed the whole business of retail outlets.

In her biography of Frank Lowy, Jill Margo writes, "Much of the strength and development of Westfield's shopping centers derived from the power and growth of the retailers, which, not possessing the managerial or financial resources for building and development, were happy to have Westfield undertake these activities. Frank and John could translate retailers' ambitions into reality while capitalizing on the opportunities to Westfield's benefit."

Finding tenants wasn't always easy – the Westfield name wasn't well-known; shopping centers were just taking off – but, with utmost dedication, Frank walked door-to-door asking shopkeepers whether they would like to move into the new center.

As Frank and John consolidated the business, the company's profits soared, and retailers lined up at their doors wanting to work with them in their next location.

From the mid-1960s to the mid-1970s, Westfield opened a shopping center a year – increasing both its company holdings and value. And with this growth, Frank further enhanced his control over Westfield's operations, obsessively reading every document that passed through his office. Margo quotes him as saying, "I wanted to maintain control over what the company was doing and that meant knowing about everything that was going on."

An overseas expansion strategy began during the 1970s and continued through the 1980s, as the two partners "outgrew" Australia. Malls were opened in Connecticut and California and then in 10 other states. Today, Lowy owns 24 shopping centers in California, two of which are the most profitable malls in the United States, delivering $800 million a year in sales.

Relationship with tenants

Those renting the space appreciated the amount of care Westfield paid to their needs. Although the rules were strict, they realized that if they abided by them, everyone would benefit. One retailer from a California shopping center said, "They want everything clean. Security guards will tell you if your music is too loud, and they'll call you into the office if your store opens ten minutes late. It's a very good thing; you go by the rules and they keep the mall in great condition."

Lowy recognizes and rewards the best of his tenants, further gaining their trust and loyalty. The company hosts a huge celebratory event called the National Awards for Retail Excellence for tenants that have "demonstrated consistently high standards in retail merchandising, business practice, customer service and the environment."

He milks his tenants, but he also motivates them. "You have to do your best to get the best possible return for your shareholders," he says. "I had very good relations with most of the tenants, and if they deserved some concession, they would get it."

Careful attention is also paid to the shoppers' needs – for the benefit of both landlord and tenants. "Westfield perceives its centers as living, breathing assets, which need to adjust and adapt to new trends, conditions and market forces. Unlike an office block, which is locked into its configuration and has limited scope for innovation, shopping centers are dynamic and responsive, capable of accommodating radical change."

During the 1990s, the Australian portfolio grew from 21 shopping centers with more than 3,600 retailers to 30 shopping centers with about 6,350 retailers. And today, around the world, Westfield owns a remarkable 119 shopping centers in Australia, New Zealand, the United Kingdom and the United States valued in excess of A$59 billion.

An innovative restructuring in the late 1970s enabled Westfield to increase its portfolio value eightfold. Investors who put A$1,000 into the company when it first sold shares in 1960 would have had more than A$133 million at the end of 2000.

Today at the age of 80, Frank Lowy is officially one of the world's most powerful retail landlords, named a world pioneer by the International Council of Shopping Centers in 1990. The second richest man in Australia has, from humble beginnings, built an enormous power and wealth base that continues to defy expectations. He and his ever loyal business partner, John, helped develop "Westfield's Eight Rules of Shopping Centre Development" which, though established in 1968, continue to provide the balance for landlord, tenant, shopper, and shareholders' interests. Through that equilibrium, Westfield grew – retailer by retailer, property by property – to become the only shopping center with an established brand around the world.

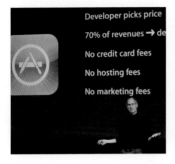

Apple App Store
Striking it rich from iPhone mania

For technology enthusiasts and gadget lovers, Friday June 29, 2007 was a memorable day. Many waited hours in line; some camped outside for two days. Even Apple CEO, Steve Jobs admitted he had butterflies in his stomach. Why? That Friday signaled the start of Apple's innovative foray into telecommunications: it was the day the iPhone was launched.

Soon, iPhone mania swept through the US. You simply needed to "tap," "flick" and "pinch." The hefty price tag of $599 didn't deter many. An estimated 270,000 handsets were sold in the first two days alone. One year later, Apple announced the launch of the second generation iPhone 3G. But this time, there were no flashy new features or cool hardware upgrades.

Apple needed a new "wow factor," and the Apple App Store was the perfect fix for iPhone neophiliacs.

The App Store, a virtual retail mall, opened on July 10, 2008 via an update to Apple's iTunes software. The appeal of the App Store was instantaneous; it generated $1 million a day in sales in its first month. As of the middle of 2010, more than 250,000 apps were available for download. The average price was only $2.70, and iPhone owners spent an average of $4.37 per month on new apps. That is the beauty of the App Store – it can transform your handset into a mobile computer. As Apple declares on its website, it has "Apps for Everything."

Behind the storefront are nearly 30,000 developers around the world plugging away at their computers with dreams of making their fortune, while tens of millions of iPhone devotees wait for the next cool app to download. Apple has developed an unrivalled virtual marketplace that brings together consumers and developers to conduct their trade. Its power has grown to rival and even surpass that of the seemingly omnipotent Google: Apple has begun to enter the mobile advertising market with its launch of iAds and is "[locking] the

search giant out of advertising on Apple's devices." Other competitors, such as Black-Berry, Microsoft, and Nokia have tried to emulate the App Store but with limited success. Why? Apple's App Store is more than just a temple for your fabulous phone: it's a tightly controlled ecosystem where Apple willingly shares pieces of its pie with Regular Joe developers and enables them to strike it rich.

Meet Joe Developer

Ethan Nicholas is a regular guy. He has a one-year-old son who keeps him busy in the evenings after work. He really enjoys working at Sun Microsystems as an engineer, and has made quite a name for himself there. In past lives, he's also worked at GeoCities and spent six years with Yahoo!. Lacking the money to buy books or take courses, he stays up late at night surfing the Internet and reading countless websites to hone his coding skills.

Over the past six weeks, Ethan thinks he's made a breakthrough in his programming. He's developed a little app called iShoot, an artillery combat game where you get to blow things up using a range of different high-powered weapons. Ethan decides to price it at $2.99, and, soon after, releases a free version. Ten days later, iShoot becomes the number one app on the Apple App Store with 17,000 downloads in one day and steals iFart's crown.

That was in January 2009. Now, Ethan Nicholas estimates he's made about $600,000 in one month on iShoot. He never intended to get rich from developing an iPhone app.

Share a piece of your Apple pie

Ethan's story isn't common, but more and more developers are achieving similar successes. Fantastical headlines such as "iPhone Developer Quits Day Job After 'iShoot' Hits No. 1" and "iPhone Developers Go from Rags to Riches" are further fueling developers' dreams. And with one app's success, other benefits follow. Some start their own game publishing firms, for instance. Thousands of programmers have turned the App Store into a living organism that's changing minute-by-minute based on consumers' love of iPhones.

Strangely, the App Store's primary aim was not to make money from selling apps. The original commercial goal was just to do slightly better than break even. Apple allows 70 percent of revenues from the store to go to the seller of the app, while 30 percent is retained by Apple for distribution, processing, supporting download capabilities, advertising, and overhead charges.

With the store's overwhelming popularity, estimates of Apple revenues in December 2009 exceeded $250 million per year. That may sound like a lot, but what's remarkable is that $175 million went directly to the developers. Moreover, a statistic from Steve Jobs' keynote in June 2010 stated that five billion apps had been downloaded and $1 billion in revenues shared with developers since the store's launch in 2008. This "fair split" has been extended to the publishing space with the iPad: Apple's deal has forced Amazon to rethink its 50–50 split with the Kindle.

The fact that Apple has been willing to share the success of its store with developers has created an environment that incentivizes them toward the same goal. Steve Jobs has declared, "The developers and us [sic] have the same exact interest, which is to get as many apps out in front of as many iPhone users as possible."

Developers are driven not only by the financial gain, but also the bragging rights that are associated with developing the number one iPhone app. One owner of a successful app development company stated, "Some kid in his bedroom can literally make a million bucks just by writing a little app." In the first month of the App Store opening, its top 10 sellers made $9 million between them. This wouldn't have been possible for independent developers without significant investment. Apple's virtual marketplace enables creativity to flow from developers and into the hands of iPhone enthusiasts.

Are the tides turning?

Like many things that have near-cult status, the App Store comes in for criticism. To some, Apple exploits and manipulates its followers through a cleverly constructed regime: it's both hero and villain. The rules of the game appear simple: access is easy and open. But this creative free-for-all comes at a price. While it's willing to hand out slices of its proverbial pie, Apple controls the rubric for the marketplace.

Developers have had to abide by the following rules to get their apps in the App Store:

1. You must only use the Apple platform and programming tools to create App Store apps.
2. You must not use outside services to measure how your applications are performing.

3. You must only use the Apple App Store to distribute your iPhone app. You must neither sell nor give away your iPhone app, except through Apple.
4. If your app is rejected, you must not publish the contents of your Apple rejection notice.
5. If your app is approved, you must not disclose the details of either the development of your app or its approval process.
6. You must remember that all apps are subject to approval or rejection by Apple; not every app that gets submitted gets sold.

There are also restrictions on what apps can and cannot do before they are listed. For apps to be approved, they are not allowed to:

- duplicate iPhone or iTune functionality;
- have limited utility (ie, basically do nothing);
- use offensive language;
- conflict with Apple branding;
- infringe on other third-party rights;
- contain objectionable or sexual content;
- ridicule public figures; or
- contain any combination of the above.

TechCrunch writer Jason Kincaid has raised "command-and-control" concerns: "Over the last few days we've been tracking Apple's recent decision to remove all sexual content from the App Store. It's an alarming move on Apple's part, if only because it shows that the company is willing to throw developers (and their livelihoods) under the bus without any notice at all. Now developers are left wondering: just what exactly *is* allowed on the App Store? As it turns out, the new policy may be even more restrictive than it first appeared." He goes on to say, "As far as we can tell, Apple hasn't spelled out its new policies anywhere (our request for more details has gone unanswered). Keep in mind that these rules may not be set in stone – Apple is purposely vague about its policies, and they're probably still changing."

With an ever-lengthening list of rules, Apple flexed its landlord muscles, emphasizing that it retained ultimate control over the look and feel, of every single iPhone. Restrictions were so tight that developers complained that "Apple's continuing ban on all discussion of the iPhone apps software development kit hinders the developers of games and programs tailored for the [iPhone] from collaborating with each other and sharing programming hints and tips. That's slowing development of iPhone programming expertise and might also be having a negative impact on the quality of iPhone applications."

Such stringent control means many developers and iPhone owners have been tested. Last year, software developer Molinker was expelled from the store along with its 1,000 apps. The problem was that Molinker's apps, though poor imitations of existing ones, were getting suspiciously high ratings. The company was essentially bribing individuals (with free copies of the apps) to provide top reviews. In response, Apple purged the store of all of Molinker's applications, saying it was "happy to do whatever it takes to keep its house clean." To some, the action (though justified) smacked of tyranny. It demonstrated "the power that Apple has over those that sell in its exclusive marketplace.

Sure, Molinker was caught cheating, and punished, but Apple could pull the same trick on any developer, for any reason."

Some rogue developers use unauthorized App Stores, such as Cyndia and Installer, to distribute their rejected or banned apps. And some iPhone owners also "jailbreak" their imprisoned handsets by overriding default Apple programming to install prohibited third-party applications. Jailbreaking your iPhone basically gives you full control over your iPhone but, of course, Apple is combating that by creating new operating system (OS) upgrades that will disable your jailbreak.

As the complaints pile up, has Apple's sheen begun to fade? If people want to strike it rich by developing iPhone apps, they really only have one choice, and that's to accept Apple's rules to sell approved apps. From a business perspective, Apple continues to increase its power – in May 2010, the company surpassed Microsoft in terms of market capitalization, with a value of roughly $222 billion – about $3 billion ahead of Microsoft. CNET writer Ina Fried states, "The fact that Apple, not Microsoft, is the more valuable franchise represents a remarkable turn of events in the history of computing."

And there doesn't appear to be a saturation point to the App Store. By 2011, it's expected to surpass 500,000 apps, with the add rate running at about 500 apps per day. Thus, one of the keys to Apple's App Store success is to keep the developer (tenant) community happy, successful and productive. Within Apple's internal marketplace, its tenants are able openly to compete with each other to develop the next big thing. However, what enables Apple to dominate the market is that it creates both the OS and the hardware, such as the iPhone, iPod, and iPad, and when you combine that with the proprietary app store and iTunes, it delivers the ultimate "Apple" customer experience from beginning to end.

Apple has engaged consumers in a way that no other competitor has. Although it's possible that other app stores like Google's may one day compete from a number-of-apps perspective, BlackBerry owners will probably never have the same adulation for their phones as iPhone owners have for theirs. Steve Jobs has stated – somewhat ironically given Apple's tight grip on the reins of power – that Apple is providing "freedom from programs that steal your private data. Freedom from programs that trash your battery. Freedom from porn. Yep, freedom."

And beyond the App Store, Apple's power continues to grow. In just 27 days, sales of the iPad, released in April 2010, hit one million. In addition, in July 2010, quarterly revenues reached record highs of $15.7 billion with profits of $3.25 billion. Good news for the tenant developers in the App Store, but not such good news for other companies. It's not just Amazon's Kindle that's under threat: the Flash platform, developed by Adobe for digital media, is banned from Apple's devices. The success of the iPad is forcing publishers to develop iPad-specific editions, putting Adobe under great pressure. It will be interesting to watch how Google, Microsoft and others respond.

Key characteristics of Landlord & Tenants

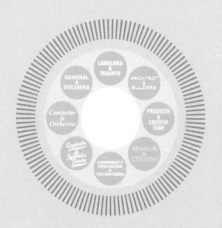

The Landlord & Tenants archetype sits firmly on the directive axis. Landlords alone hold the power and they alone set the top-down strategy. They control critical resources or access to a market and define the tenants' rules of participation. The tenants, who are clearly less powerful, voluntarily decide to join a landlord's domain, but, once they do, they have no choice but to agree to live by his or her rules. Landlords use their structural advantage and power – their control of scarce resources – to organize the behavior of tenants to their mutual advantage.

1 Landlords gain structural advantage through control of a power base.

2 Landlords articulate the overall direction and strategy.

3 Landlords clearly define and enforce the rules of the game.

4 The best-performing tenants are recognized and rewarded for their efforts.

5 Landlords have the power to set precedents and resolve conflicts.

6 As the number of tenants increases, the power of landlords grows.

1

Landlords gain structural advantage through control of a power base.

Landlords derive their power and influence through their control of highly valuable or scare resources – for example, funding, access, and relationships. Tenants voluntarily join them because of the benefits that can be secured. Knowing they are in a privileged economic or political position, landlords leverage their resources to maintain their power.

In the 1950s, America saw the beginning of an era of excess, in stark contrast to the austerity and frugality of the Great Depression and World War II. Gross national product rose from about $200 billion in 1940 to $300 billion in 1950 and to more than $500 billion in 1960. Communities expanded, and new homes were built. As city dwellers sprawled out to the suburbs, the 1950s became the age of the car.

American marques were bigger and more decadent than ever before – souped up with tail fins, bright paint work and shiny chrome. By 1950, the biggest car makers in America, General Motors, Ford and Chrysler, often known as the Detroit Three, offered their customers 243 different models, and a few years later, controlled 94 percent of the US market.

With consumerism and new prosperity came new power for the American worker. If the middle classes made statements about themselves by the goods they bought, the working classes made them by membership of trade unions. In the car industry, Walter Reuther, was the blue collar voice.

Reuther became president of the United Auto Workers (UAW) in 1946 and, six years later, president of the Congress of Industrial Organizations. He went, says author Nelson Lichtenstein, by the title "the most dangerous man in Detroit."

Named on *Time*'s list of the 100 most important people of the twentieth century, Reuther became known for his brilliant negotiation techniques. His key tactic was a concept called pattern bargaining. The UAW would target one of the Big Three and, if it did not offer concessions, withdraw labor from its plants, leaving its competitors to meet the gap in supply.

Desperate to limit the damage, the affected company would eventually give in to the union's demands, forcing the other two to fall into line. Put simply, Reuther made an example of one of the Big Three, using the "stick" of lost sales. Once the terms of the collective agreement were negotiated with one, they were then extended to the other two.

The concept of pattern bargaining was so powerful that it was adopted by other unions, for example, those in the steel, trucking, electrical and airline industries.

The UAW demanded higher wages, improved benefits and pensions, standard job classifications, sick leave, vacations, and improved working conditions. The work of Reuther, who died in a plane crash in 1970, outlasted him. Journalist Robert J. Samuelson wrote, "By the late 1970s, the union had won provisions that allowed retirement after 30 years with full benefits. Workers who were hired in their teens could theoretically look forward to retiring before they were 50... In total, fringe benefits represented roughly a third of the industry's total labor costs, up from a fifth in 1968."

Soon, the Big Three were unable to compete with each other on labor costs. Wages and working conditions were about the same across all the car makers in Detroit. The UAW created the most prosperous cohort of unskilled and semi-skilled laborers the world had seen. As

"

*The story of Reuther, the UAW and the
Detroit car industry highlights a key point about
Landlords & Tenants. When the former no longer
sets the rules, the archetype dissolves*

"

long as it represented all the workers in the car industry and there was enough work to go round, it was unassailable. It wasn't until the mid-1970s, when Japanese car makers arrived and the oil crisis plunged the world into recession, that its monopoly of labor came under threat and there was, once more, a rebalancing of landlord–tenant power.

In a classic reversal of the old boss-and-worker oligarchy, union man Walter Reuther became a landlord. He controlled what his tenants, the car makers, badly needed – labor – and he defined and enforced the rules of access.

In its glory years – the period between the late 1940s and the mid- to late 1970s – the UAW saw membership triple from approximately 500,000 to 1.5 million. Its power lay in its ability to control the means of production. In the end, though, it was, like its tenants, at the mercy of macro- and micro-economic change. In the recession of the 1970s, when Japanese companies such as Toyota rewrote the management rulebook, its proposition ceased to be compelling.

The story of Reuther, the UAW and the Detroit car industry highlights a key point about Landlords & Tenants. When the former no longer sets the rules, the archetype dissolves.

Landlords articulate the overall direction and strategy.

Landlords set a clear direction for tenants' behavior. They have the power to decide how to generate the most value for themselves, and they translate that power into terms of participation that are also beneficial for the tenants.

In 1975, Bill Gates and his friend Paul Allen, founders of a new software company called Microsoft, were on a mission. They wanted to put "a computer on every desk and in every home." Less than a generation later, their dream had come true, and Microsoft was one of the biggest names in the world. So when, in 1994, Gates announced a new mission, the world took notice.

Gates wanted to tackle the health problems of the world's poor, specifically HIV/AIDS, malaria, and tuberculosis. With an initial stock gift of US$94 million, he started his own charitable foundation, known today as the Bill and Melinda Gates Foundation (BMGF).

Inspired by the Gateses' commitment, Warren Buffett, one of the most successful investors in history, announced in 2006 that he would pool 85 percent of his total wealth with the BMGF. Buffett's gift of about $37 billion doubled the foundation's endowment to approximately $60 billion, making it by far the world's largest charitable foundation.

Dr Susan Okie, medical reporter for the *Washington Post*, described the "Gates–Buffett Effect" like this: "The example set by Bill and Melinda Gates has been as important as the money they've donated. By calling attention to global inequities, they have attracted funding from others and made it fashionable for the rich or famous to become involved in solving global problems. Buffett's move reflects that trend – and seems likely to intensify it."

The Gateses have created a virtuous circle of influence. At the end of 2009, BMGF had assets of $33.4 billion. It currently operates in more than 100 countries; its number of global partners is vast, and continuing to grow. According to *Time* magazine, the BMGF is one of the largest charitable foundations in the world. It paid out $3.0 billion in grants in 2009, and expected cash disbursements to be $3.5 billion in 2010.

One of Bill Gates's missions, essentially, is to bridge the yawning gap in healthcare research. Tuberculosis, malaria, and HIV/AIDS are the world's biggest killers, and yet some of the lowest-funded areas for research. Historically, aid workers, governments, and international agencies have only had the money to focus on specific areas of the problem. They could never dream of finding a cure for the diseases – until, that is, Bill Gates stepped in.

The Foundation has a magnetic pull, bringing the world's organizations, governments, philanthropists, and other agencies together to solve some of the world's biggest problems.

There is undeniable appeal in being associated with an organization to which "everyone who is anyone" is linked – and which attracts funding on a scale way beyond the dreams of other charities. The Foundation's plan to give away approximately $3 billion a year is unprecedented.

The Gateses are using their power, wealth and influence to shape the global agenda. Bill Gates says, "I believe that my own good fortune brings with it a responsibility to give back to the world."

The Gates Foundation is a landlord because it has a compelling proposition: money for "membership." Its tenants – thousands of researchers, educational institutions, and charitable organizations around the world – have adopted the Gateses' priorities simply because they have defined the agenda and they bring unprecedented clout to the table. "They have the potential to direct the overall pattern of what happens [in a field]," says Brian Greenwood, a professor at the London School of Hygiene and Tropical Medicine.

The best and brightest are drawn to the Foundation and its work. The passion that Bill Gates brought to Microsoft has convinced disparate groups to come together to solve problems. The Gateses' agenda has become their agenda. Their vision has created a focus for social innovation. Through his power, Gates has defined the agenda, attracting governments, private-sector partners, NGOs and NPOs and, crucially, vast sums of money, to the center of a cause.

Just as he popularized the personal computer, Bill Gates will popularize the idea of giving all of one's wealth in the pursuit of a personal dream. Says rock star philanthropist Bono, "He's changing the world twice. And the second act for Bill Gates may be the one that history regards more."

Landlords clearly define and enforce the rules of the game.

Tenants voluntarily decide to join landlords, believing that it's in their best interests to do so. There, however, is where their sovereignty ends. Landlords define the rules; and tenants must abide by them – tenancy violations are not favorably viewed. Tenants follow the landlords' strict rules because they derive value from the relationship.

An old stone building at 11 Wall Street in New York City belies the inspired history of the New York Stock Exchange (NYSE). Known as "the Big Board," the largest stock exchange in the world consists of approximately 2,800 leading blue chip, mid-size, and small capitalization companies; each of which must meet the NYSE's stringent listing requirements. In total, these companies are worth over $12 trillion in market capitalization – and account for approximately 25 percent of the $44 trillion represented by the top 20 largest global stock exchanges in December 2009.

Getting listed on the stock exchange is like belonging to an exclusive club. The companies listed on the NYSE are amongst the world's biggest and best. But to get on that list, companies must follow and maintain very specific financial rules and meet a list of stringent criteria before they are accepted into that club.

The NYSE started off simply enough. The genesis of the rules of the NYSE began in 1792, when 24 stockbrokers signed an agreement called the, "Buttonwood Agreement," underneath a Buttonwood, or American sycamore tree. The stockbrokers established regulations, fee limits and a set of general rules about how the stock market would operate, and then the official stock trading began. Today, the NYSE has more than 6,000 rules and regulations by which companies must abide.

Government rules and regulations weren't applied until 1934, after the market crash of 1929 that led to the Great Depression. The US economy is directly tied to the stock market, and with so much at stake, it's important that some degree of control is applied.

In the United States in 1934, the SEC (Securities and Exchange Commission) was created "to protect investors, maintain fair, orderly, and efficient markets, and facilitate capital formation."

The NYSE seeks only the cream of the crop companies. As the most powerful stock market in the world, rules and requirements are necessary because its reputation rests on the quality of the companies that trade on it. Thus the NYSE must ensure that each listed company has solid management, effective corporate governance, and an excellent track record.

Rules must be followed because the success of a stock exchange depends primarily on investors' confidence. Stock exchanges would not be "open and free markets" if investors were making decisions on inaccurate information. So, to maintain investors' confidence, only companies that meet the strict requirements are allowed to be listed on the exchange.

And clearly there are significant benefits for companies to get listed. Some companies will pay outrageously high fees to get listed. For one, companies receive an immediate increase of available capital, by basically selling a small piece of the business to anyone who is willing to buy. Along with the listing comes increased exposure as initial public offerings are advertised and investors may be interested in investing.

The full rules are codified in Section 303A of the NYSE's Listed Company Manual. But basically the initial listing requirements deal with aspects such as minimum thresholds for the number of publicly traded shares, distribution, total market value, size, stock price, number of shareholders and the reporting of company financial data. A few basic examples include:

- **Size.** To be listed, a company must have at least 1,100,000 shares in public hands. There must be at least 400 shareholders holding 100 shares or more each.
- **Price.** At the time of listing on the NYSE, a company's share price must be $4 or greater.
- **Finances.** The company must have earned at least $10 million in the last three years or have market capitalization of $500 million, revenues of $100 million and positive cash flow.

But a company's duties don't stop with the initial listing. They must also meet continuing standards. For example, if a company falls below the established threshold of number of outstanding shares, trades below a minimum share price, or if the market value of all outstanding shares fall below a certain total value, it could be delisted if it can't shape up within a 30-day grace period.

A recent example is Blockbuster. In July 2010, the company disclosed that it violated the NYSE listing requirement for market cap to exceed $75 million. The company had 45 calendar days to submit a plan to demonstrate its ability to achieve compliance within 18 months. However, its shares had also dropped to an average price of less than $1 over a consecutive 30-day period which was also a violation of the NYSE's rules.

Subsequent actions by the company weren't effective in saving its floundering stock price. The NYSE delisted Blockbuster the following week.

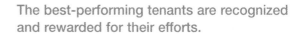

The best-performing tenants are recognized and rewarded for their efforts.

Incentives – typically market-based – are built into the land-lords' systems. Thus, tenants are constantly competing with each other and must give of their best to remain "preferred." The greater their value to the landlords, the more likely it is that opportunities will flow to them. Tenants who struggle with the system are easily replaced by others.

Topper the Trick Terrier is an extraordinary toy. Robotic, he can bark, spin around, and do eight tricks. He can also understand commands in both English and Spanish.

The most interesting thing about him, though, isn't what he can do, but how he came to be. Although he's assembled in China he, strictly speaking, isn't made there. He starts life as a series of bit parts scattered all over the world. His big eyes come from China, his little plastic legs from Taiwan, his plush coat from Korea, and the software that makes him respond to your voice from San Francisco.

Put together in China, he travels 6,200 miles to distrib-utors and sellers the Original San Francisco Toymakers in California. A few AA batteries, and he's ready for Young America. Although he travels half the world and back for an American child, ultimately, Topper is a present from the Hong Kong supply chain conglomerate, Li & Fung.

With more than 10,000 suppliers and offices in over 40 countries, Li & Fung works with companies such as Coca-Cola, Talbots, Timberland, Juicy Couture, Sanrio, and Marks & Spencer to put products on shelves. But it does not own a single factory or manufacturing facility, and it does not make a single thing itself.

Its goal is simple – source the highest quality, lowest price goods for customers around the world, and deliver

them in the shortest time possible. Victor Fung, group chairman (pictured below left), has said, "We're not asking which country can do the best job overall. Instead, we're pulling apart the value chain and optimizing each step – and we're doing it globally."

Suppliers are compelled to take part in the Li & Fung arena because the company has a dominant position. Its supplier network leaves little room for competitors. Each supplier is highly specialized, so Li & Fung knows just where to go for what it wants – eg, Topper's big eyes, little plastic legs, voice recognition software.

Li & Fung has the power to pick and choose the world's best suppliers to meet its customers' requirements. The more that suppliers want to fulfill Li & Fung's goal of better quality at a cheaper cost, the more likely it is Li & Fung will call on them to help build, say, its next robotic toy. Follow Li & Fung's rules and you're rewarded by more business.

Since Li & Fung is able to replace any given company for another in its network, suppliers make sure they present their best offer. If the price of Topper's little plastic legs had been too high, Li & Fung would have searched its global network for a cheaper solution. In Li & Fung world, the cream naturally rises to the top.

As part of the Li & Fung network, suppliers can access customers on the other side of the world. It's an irresistible proposition. You don't mind making two cents less on your product if you're going to be able to sell 50,000 more units.

The Li & Fung power base shows few signs of strain. In 2008, it earned revenues of US$14.2 billion, and is set to reach its target of $20 billion for 2010. Li & Fung is quietly but relentlessly ambitious, keen to create more connections to expand its global reach.

Landlords tend to use both authoritarian means and competitive market forces to align their tenants' behavior with their own interests. Nonetheless, the advantages of the relationship outweigh the disadvantages for tenants, who work hard for landlords in the knowledge there'll be a reward.

Landlords' power is often such that the option to leave the arrangement exists on paper and in theory only. When a company – Walmart, for example – dominates a market, it's an irresistible force for suppliers.

Tenants must adhere to the landlord's strict rules and often have to compete against each other to survive. Tenants' capabilities often overlap. Unlike the teams of specialists under the Architect & Builders model in chapter 6, they're dispensable. It's through this self-regulating internal market system that the best tenants rise to the top.

Landlords have the power to set precedents and resolve conflicts.

Tenants look to landlords to resolve conflicts or to set precedents. They have minimal decision-making power compared with landlords, who, as the "ruling class," make and break the rules.

Amazon, "the world's biggest bookstore," went live on July 16, 1995. There was no publicity, no press and no fanfare. Yet within two months, $20,000 of books a week were flying off Amazon's virtual shelves. CEO and founder, Jeff Bezos, and his team developed simple customer-centric online tools such as one-click buying, customer reviews and order verification by email. They made armchair shopping easy.

While many doubted its long-term chances, Amazon continued to grow. Even after the dotcom bubble burst in the late 1990s, it defied the skeptics, turning its first profit in the fourth quarter of 2002. It's become a primary distribution channel for books and US published ebooks. In 2009, it reported $24.5 billion in net sales.

One of its greatest achievements has been to overturn the traditional supply chain for books, and allow publishers to sell directly to customers. The company buys directly from publishers at a discount and passes some of the savings on to the consumer.

Why are publishers willing to cut their prices so much? Because as the world's biggest bookstore Amazon has access to billions of potential customers. Its global reach makes it the most effective and successful distribution channel for books. It's a simple Landlord & Tenants paradigm: Amazon has bargaining power because it can provide benefits others can't.

Though Amazon set the precedent early, recently, there have been signs that a sense of balance is being restored with a new landlord stepping in. In the ebook market, Amazon has a new and aggressive competitor: Apple. With the launch of its iPad, which rivals Amazon's Kindle, Apple's been doing deals with publishers, which is a potentially fatal flaw for a landlord.

At the beginning of 2010, a clash of the landlord titans began between Apple, Amazon, and one of the largest American publishing houses, Macmillan. All were trying to stake their claim in the nascent ebook industry and create the model for how the business will work.

The burgeoning ebook industry is huge. For the first time, in December 2009, there were more ebooks sold on Amazon than traditional ones. On January 29, 2010, though, all of the books published by Macmillan disappeared from Amazon's website.

The reason? A dispute between Macmillan and Amazon over the price of ebooks. Macmillan had pleaded with Amazon to raise the price of ebooks. Why did they think they deserved more? Because Apple had told them they did. Using the same structure as its App Store, Apple was taking just 30 percent commission, leaving publishers of downloaded ebooks with a very healthy 70 percent. Ultimately Amazon decided to remove all Macmillan books from its virtual shelves.

Apple is using what John Sargent, CEO of Macmillan, describes as an "agency" model in its deals with publishers. It enables publishers to set the selling price and then, as a distributor,

The key observation is that landlords need to find the right balance between setting the rules and disaffecting their tenants

takes a slice of the profit. Apple's ebook prices were 50 percent higher than Amazon's, significantly benefiting publishers who'd negotiated the 70–30 split.

With its early move into this space, Amazon experienced several years of virtual domination, but they may have pushed the limits of tenancy compliance. Five of America's six largest book publishers have signed up for Apple's agency deal.

In February 2010, an agreement was reached between Amazon and Macmillan, and the publisher's books reappeared on the Amazon website at the higher price. The outcome symbolized a shift in the economics of book selling, and was hailed as a "potentially golden opportunity for publishers to counter Amazon's control over the ebook market and regain some leverage over sensitive matters like pricing."

For now, Amazon is repositioning while continuing to defend its position as the world's largest online retailer – awaiting the next opportunity to extend its dominance. The key observation is that landlords need to find the right balance between setting the rules and disaffecting their tenants. The most successful landlords are able to find that equilibrium while continuing to attract, retain, and expand their tenant base.

As the number of tenants increases, the power of landlords grows.

Landlords act as gatekeepers to scarce resources. The more tenants who want access to these resources, the greater their power to dictate the terms. However, there may be natural limits to growth – a point where tenants begin to question the benefits gained from their participation in the landlord's system.

When Australian journalist Keith Murdoch died in 1952 he left his 22-year-old son, Keith Rupert, commonly known by his middle name, an Adelaide newspaper, *The News*. The somewhat modest paper wasn't doing well, but the young Murdoch, who'd studied politics, philosophy and economics at Oxford University, returned home to run it.

Carrying on where his father left off, Rupert has become not only one of the most powerful media magnates in the world, but also an influential figure in politics, with the political stance of his best-selling British tabloid the *Sun* said to influence millions of people at the ballot box.

Today, Rupert Murdoch is chairman and chief executive of a media empire that spans television, feature films, online services, newspapers and books in Australia, Europe, the Middle East, the US and Asia. His parent company News Corporation controls vast tracts of the media value chain.

He juggles over $60-billion worth of TV studios, printing presses, and broadcast satellites, owns 175 newspapers including *The Times* of London and the *New York Post*, 100 cable TV channels including Fox and 19 sports channels, nine satellite and 40 regular TV networks, 40 publishing houses, and a movie studio. His company is the world's leading publisher of English-

language newspapers, with more than 175 titles in the UK, Australia, Fiji, Papua New Guinea and the US.

Much of what Murdoch's achieved can be attributed to a shameless policy of sensationalism and "dumbing down". Buying the mid-market broadsheet the *Sun* from the Mirror Group in 1969, he took it down-market and tabloid and, over the coming years, turned it into Britain's biggest seller through "shock horror" news stories, celebrity gossip and sex. Right-wing and reactionary at heart, the paper is politically incorrect and proud of it.

Writer William Shawcross states, "Murdoch's achievement is that he is the only media mogul to have created and to control a truly global media empire. He understood sooner than anyone else the opportunities offered by new technology – computers, satellites, wireless communications – to create first an international press and then a television domain."

Murdoch provides access to what matters most in the media: a mass market. His media empire stretches across "five continents, reaching a TV audience of 280 million in America and 300 million in Asia. His magazines reach 28 million. With all outlets combined together, Murdoch's media empire reaches 4.7 billion people" – that is 75 percent of the world's population.

If controlling access to such a huge audience makes Murdoch a landlord, who, then, are his tenants? The answer is advertisers who specifically target an affluent, ultra-conservative audience. His seemingly limitless portfolio of newspapers, magazines, and TV networks around the world, means Murdoch has not only a global audience, but also the good will of global advertisers. In 2007, advertising comprised 45 percent of News Corp's fiscal revenues.

The scale of Murdoch's empire and the extent of his control inevitably raises concerns. Is it healthy for so much of the media to be monopolized by one man?

Celebrity British businessman and serial entrepreneur Sir Richard Branson, founder of the Virgin Group, thinks not, "If the government is so scared of upsetting him perhaps his empire should be looked at. It is not good for the democracy of Britain that one person should have so much influence."

Branson's fears won't be allayed by the fact that Murdoch has been quoted as saying, "My ventures in media are not as important to me as spreading my personal political beliefs."

Now nearly 80, Murdoch is still making waves. In the UK, his flagship News International hit the headlines in 2009 by announcing audacious plans to charge for online access to its titles. If it makes a profit, it will doubtless be followed by other British publishers.

Like his father before him, Murdoch has secured immortality for himself by grooming his children as his successors. Elisabeth, Lachlan and James Murdoch have all been in the "family business." The last is now head of News Corp Europe and Asia, overseeing News International and therefore the scorching, sizzling, high-circulation *Sun*.

Like history's earliest landlords, he's passing his wealth, power and influence on.

News Corp's power over its advertisers derives from its access to its specific audience. Because its media have mass-market appeal, they mean mass-market exposure for companies.

The ultimate demonstration of the Landlord & Tenants model in the media industry occurs every year during the Super Bowl, as companies pay ever-increasing amounts to showcase their advertisements.

In 2010, CBS sold out of its Super Bowl advertisement spots, even though at prices exceeding $3 million, they were the most expensive spots in Super Bowl history. In 2009, NBC sold a record $213 million in advertising for the showdown between the Pittsburgh Steelers and the Arizona Cardinals. In 2011, Murdoch's Fox, under the rotating Super Bowl broadcast agreement, is scheduled to cash in on that opportunity with Super Bowl XLV.

Advertisers will continue to agree to the terms of the networks to access their target audiences. The price, it seems, is never wrong. In 1967, the cost of a 30-second Super Bowl ad was the equivalent of approximately $245K. Today, it's over 12 times that amount.

Murdoch, has the ultimate landlord power, and he's convinced he can increase it. "We have no intention of failing," he declares. "The only question is how great a success we'll have."

Is Landlord *&* Tenants the right model for you?

Is this archetype right for your current situation? And, if it is, how can you be the best landlord you can be? The following sections will help you answer these questions.

Great if:

- You own or control assets whose value increases with demand.

- You dominate the market and/or your competitors are weak.

- Your business model is all about aggregation of users and increased scale.

Think twice if:

- You have yet to reach critical mass, your position in the market is precarious and you are under serious threat from competitors.

- You are not comfortable setting the agenda and direction for others.

- You do not have a grand ambition to define or redefine the market.

- New disruptive technologies or regulations are emerging that can undermine the value of your assets.

How can you be a better landlord?

1. How clear and compelling is your proposition to tenants?

Tenants voluntarily decide whether the benefits of joining a landlord outweigh the costs.

- Have you fully communicated the value of the relationship to potential and existing tenants?
- Is your proposition closely tailored to tenants' wants and needs?
- Which tactics – for example, pricing plans – are you using to make propositions more persuasive?

2. How quickly are you expanding your power base?

The most successful landlords focus not only on maintaining control of their scarce resources, but also on accelerating the rate of growth in "new membership."

- Is your ability to attract new tenants increasing over time?
- Have you set specific targets for the growth in tenant numbers?
- Is there a limit to growth, based on your ability to integrate new tenants? If not, should there be?

3. How effective are you at capturing information?

Successful landlords use all means, including centralized information, to maintain control. Data on tenants can be a management tool. Properly collected and properly stored, it can help landlords take advantage of and anticipate new opportunities to strengthen their power and re-assert their control.

- Are you capturing data frequently enough to chart changes over time?
- How effective are you at getting tenants to provide information in a standardized, like-for-like, format?
- Are you successfully analyzing data to make better decisions?

4. Are you setting rigid but reasonable rules and enforcing them effectively?

Landlords who rule too strictly or too subjectively risk losing the loyalty of their tenants. People are more likely to live by rules they see as just and fair.

- How do you ensure your tenants follow your rules?
- Are there clear consequences for breaches?
- How do you test whether rules are reasonable and fair?

5. Are you exploiting your tenants?

Ask too much of your tenants, get too greedy, and your power base will start to crack. If you're not providing a reasonably fair economic return for your tenants they will start to leave. Always avoid "slumlord" behaviors.

- How do you test the fairness of your formula for sharing profits with tenants?
- How do you monitor tenant satisfaction?
- What limits are there on the long-term sustainability of your relationship with tenants? Do you know your tenants' breaking points?

6. How effective is your "strategic radar" at scanning the environment?

Market shifts, changes in the external environment, could oust you from your privileged position. Successful landlords must be aware of changing conditions to stay ahead of future competition.

- How do you conduct periodic market "scans"?
- Do you have access to different external perspectives in order to cover your "blind spots"?
- What tactics are you using to spot future competitors and prevent them from affecting your power base?

7. Are you taking advantage of the opportunities your power brings?

A strong position in the marketplace and a strong and wide power base mean access to new capital and new markets. Successful landlords use their strengths to take advantage of opportunities as they arise.

- What are the best opportunities for "lateral development" of your organization?
- Do you have the ability to leverage your power to enter and compete in those related markets?
- Have you identified ways to shield your existing power base from any risks that a new market might create?

Chapter 2

Community Organizer & Volunteers

"A small body of determined spirits
fired by an unquenchable faith in their
mission can alter the course of history"
—*Mohandas Gandhi*

" Gandhi was fascinated by the meaning of truth. And he used truth as a powerful weapon against tyranny "

Gandhi: Uniting a nation through peaceful resistance

In 1915, the barrister Mohandas Gandhi, famous for leading a long, non-violent campaign against racial prejudice in South Africa, answered the call to return home to India to help in the struggle against British rule.

His was the homecoming of a hero. Crowds thronged the Bombay dock waiting for the crusading English-educated lawyer, who in Africa had dressed in a tailored suit and carried a tightly furled umbrella – the uniform of the British professional. Finally, the last passengers walked down the third-class gangplank. Among them was Gandhi – a small man wearing a traditional turban and dhoti, a long white piece of unstitched cloth knotted at his waist.

Jawaharlal Nehru and Sardar Vallabhbhai Patel, then leaders of the Congress Party, were shocked. "My God," said one British observer, "he's dressed as a coolie." But to the Indians

gathered at the docks his rejection of the tailored suit spoke volumes: he was one of them; he had shed the outer skin of British domination.

The man known as the mahatma or the "great soul" was no ordinary politician.

South Africa and truth and peace

Gandhi had first traveled to South Africa in 1893, to work as a barrister in an Indian law firm. Within days of his arrival, he was thrown off a train, barred from hotel rooms, and pushed off a sidewalk – just because of the color of his skin. Believing it would be "cowardice" to run back home, he decided to stay to help Indians fight for their civil rights.

His first concern was to unite the small Indian communities, which consisted of 60,000 people living in Natal and the Transvaal. The communities were dispersed, and divided by class, religion and language. But within a year of his arrival, Gandhi had made significant strides and helped establish the Natal Indian Congress in 1894 and then the Transvaal British Indian Association.

Gandhi realized that something powerful would be needed to create change. He identified three possible responses to oppression and injustice: to accept it or run away from it; to stand and fight by force of arms; to courageously stand and fight solely by non-violent means. For Gandhi, the only option was the third. He understood that passive or non-violent resistance, or what he named *satyagraha*, meaning "truth force," could be a powerful tool, leaving opponents with no choice but to face up to and deal with injustice.

The first time Gandhi used *satyagraha* was in March 1907, when the Black Act was passed, requiring all Indians to have their fingerprints taken and to carry registration documents. Mass protests were organized, and throngs of Indians traveled to the Transvaal to oppose the Act. When only about 500 of the 13,000 Indians in the Transvaal registered, the authorities began to beat and arrest the non-violent protestors, including Gandhi. When jailed, Gandhi pleaded for the maximum sentence, and others followed by example.

To quell the growing numbers of protestors, the authorities decided to make registration voluntary for local Indians. Gandhi agreed to the compromise, and those arrested were set free. But it took eight years of continued protest and imprisonment, before, finally in June 1914, the Black Act was repealed. Gandhi had at last proved that *satyagraha* was an effective way to create change.

India and symbolism and sacrifice

When Gandhi returned home in 1915, the Indian leaders assumed he would quickly activate the independence campaign. India had been under British rule since the 18th century, and the colonial administrators had never accepted the Indians as equals: the nation's wealth remained concentrated in the hands of the British – and a few favored Indians.

Hopeful upon Gandhi's return, one of the Congress leaders, Gopal Gokhale, a wise elder of the independence movement, advised him first to travel, to see India, and to devote himself entirely to preparing for the struggle ahead. "When I saw you in that costume," he said, referring to the moment Gandhi stepped off the Bombay dock, "I knew I could die in peace." The mantle had been passed.

Gandhi followed Gokhale's advice, but how could he level the Indian playing field? A vast bureaucracy of 100,000 British military and Indian civil servants governed 350 million people, consisting of Hindus, Muslims, Buddhists, Sikhs, Jains, and Christians, speaking hundreds of dialects and languages, primarily in 700,000 rural villages. Although the British had telegraphic communication and a railroad system for civil and military administration, ordinary Indians seldom traveled or communicated beyond their villages.

Although the self-effacing Gandhi seemed an unlikely leader for a movement, he had assets that proved invaluable. In the first place, he knew the British: he had studied in their universities, knew their laws, and as a student of human nature, understood the character and disposition of his adversaries. He was patient, awaiting opportunities to achieve maximum effect.

It was the people's courage, their strength in numbers, and discipline to withstand the anger and brutality of their adversaries that turned the tide. As Gandhi pointed out to the British Viceroy late in the process, 100,000 Brits could not hope to control 350 million Indians who refused to cooperate.

Gandhi seized every opportunity to dramatize the power of non-violent non-cooperation through symbolic public events. When the British killed hundreds of men, women and children during a non-violent protest in Amritsar, the slaughter shocked the world. On its anniversary, Gandhi called for a day of prayer and fasting that brought the country to a standstill, demonstrating the British could not control the country without Indian cooperation.

When the British imposed a tax on salt, Gandhi led a parade of thousands on a 241-mile march from Ahmedabad to Dandi on the Indian Ocean, where he made his own salt, an act of defiance broadcast to the world by reporters and cameramen from Europe, Britain and America. It was a simple but open rebellion against the British Salt Law. And within a month, this seemingly insignificant act inspired hundreds of thousands from across India to do the same. Though thousands were jailed and beaten by police, none used violence in their fight for freedom.

In an outcry over importation of British manufactured cotton in place of Indian homespun, Gandhi staged an incendiary event – a giant bonfire of British cloth, "large enough to be seen in England." Indeed, one colonial officer complained, "Back home, the children are writing essays about him." Although Winston Churchill referred to Gandhi as "that half-naked Indian fakir," British public opinion was moving steadily in his favor.

Leadership and legacy

Gandhi was one of history's most inspiring and powerful organizers for many reasons. His optimism, moral conviction, sacrifice, discipline, and ascetic lifestyle inspired those around him. As more heard of his dedication and pursuit of the truth, he persuaded millions of followers from around the world to join his cause.

India was a country plagued by religious differences. But Gandhi was able to ignite the rallying cry – the pursuit of independence from Britain – among the immensely segregated groups. He dedicated himself to the freedom of a nation and risked his own life for that of the poorest class in India, the untouchables, so that they could vote together with the Hindus and have opportunities for equal representation. He said, "Untouchability is a crime against God and men."

Even at the age of 77, his health declining, he walked barefoot for miles each day through 49 villages to the remote areas of east Bengal to help moderate rising tensions between Hindus and Muslims; his goal: "Come what may, there will be complete friendship between the Hindus, Muslims, Sikhs, Christians, and Jews…"

After a long and protracted struggle, India finally gained independence in 1947. Tragically, just one year later, on January 30, 1948, Gandhi was assassinated by a Hindu fanatic. Indian Prime Minister Jawaharlal Nehru told the world, "The light has gone out of our lives and there is darkness everywhere… The light has gone out, I said, and yet I was wrong. For the light that shone in this country was no ordinary light … A thousand years later, that light will still be seen… for that light represented… the living truth."

Linux
A powerful [open] source for change

Linux is a family of computer operating systems based on a core component, the "Linux kernel," developed by Finnish software engineer Linus Torvalds in 1991. (The name Linux is a conflation of Linus and Unix, the seminal 1970s operating system.)

Microsoft Windows' operating system dominates the market with an approximately 90 percent share; Apple has approximately 8 percent; Linux less than 1 percent. But don't be fooled into thinking small is insignificant.

Linux is the leading force in the super computer market. In fact, it runs more of the world's top super computers than any other operating system. The Linux ecosystem (its community of developers) is estimated to be worth $40 billion. And, as the leading proponent of free, open source software, Linux is an influential voice in the world computing industry, revered and (by proprietary software companies at least) feared.

The open source story begins with cult hero Richard Stallman and his passionate belief that access to free software is a fundamental right for society. Since the 1980s, Stallman has argued that it's wrong to give developers and mega-corporations such as Microsoft uncontrollable power over our computers, and that people should have access to the source codes of programs so they can develop them in the way they (rather than propriety software companies) want.

In 1983, he launched the GNU Project to create a free Unix-like operating system, later developing the GNU General Public License for free, open source software.

Stallman's concept of free software is not really about price. It includes:

- the freedom to run the program for any purpose;
- the freedom to modify the program to suit your needs;

- the freedom to redistribute copies, either gratis or for a fee;
- the freedom to distribute modified versions of the program so that the community can benefit from your improvements.

Because it's free or open source, Linux software is continuously being developed and improved by an informal network of thousands of developers from around the world.

From kernel to community

Linux didn't start off as a project of altruism. Nor did Linus Torvalds ever expect that one day he'd become the "godfather of the open source movement." He readily admits that, "[The vision] never was, take this and let us together build a better world."

He developed the kernel, posted it on the Internet, and invited anyone interested to help improve it. "My reasons for putting Linux out there were pretty selfish. I didn't want the headache of trying to deal with parts of the operating system that I saw as the crap work. I wanted help." Because it was "unfinished work" that would need the contributions of others, he never thought about charging money for it.

Torvalds' breakthrough came with the addition of a feature that enabled Linux to run on systems with limited memory. This meant that developers didn't need a super computer, or a lot of memory, to start adding to the code. Gradually, they began to create bug fixes and new and improved features.

Torvalds licensed Linux under the GNU agreement and allowed people to make money

> ❝
>
> *It's the power and robustness of the Linux software that compels partner companies to improve the kernel to benefit their businesses*
>
> ❞

from it – as long as the free, open source code remained at the heart of their products. That was the turning point, persuading many large corporations to come on board. Dell, IBM, HP, Oracle, Sun Microsystems, Novell and Nokia are among those that have sold, supported and contributed to the development of the Linux system. A Sony TV and a Nokia and Samsung cellphone are likely to have Linux components. Even Volkswagen has got in on the act, contributing a networking protocol to the kernel.

None of these companies is supporting Linux as an act of charity: it's the power and robustness of the software that compels them to improve the kernel to benefit their businesses. The estimated joint value of Linux supporters and distributors Canonical and Red Hat is close to $1 billion; German distributor SUSE Linux has annual revenue in excess of $100 million.

New model of motivation

In an article entitled, "Why Linux is Wealthier than Microsoft," *Business Week* argued that "Torvalds can muster more creativity from his far-flung [volunteers] than Bill Gates can from his corporate monolith." Russ Roberts wrote:

Microsoft uses money to motivate. And no doubt about it, that's a powerful incentive. But others exist. The community of Linux users and developers is held together by pride and the thrill of working toward a common goal of a universal, free, elegant, bug-free or bug-resistant alternative to Windows... Does Torvalds or Gates have more resources at his disposal? Gates, right? But that answer assumes that money is the most important asset. Even if money trumps idealism as a motivator, Torvalds has a bigger team – the millions who use Linux and continue to tinker with it. Potentially, he has more brainpower on his team.

Torvalds has another advantage. His organization is less organized than Microsoft. It's really disorganization.

Torvalds is just Linux's gatekeeper. He's not really in control – he's called the project leader... Being disorganized can actually leverage that knowledge more effectively than a command-and-control hierarchy. Innovation must rely on creativity generated by the mass of folks underneath. In a dynamic system, trial and error is a powerful force for change. A bottom-up system with a gatekeeper can be more innovative than the hierarchical system over which Gates reigns.

Since the kernel's initial posting, the Linux effect has snowballed. Over time, more people have joined the community – first students and programmers, Linux hobbyists, then commercial vendors and paid professionals.

Amazingly, more than 300 Linux "distributions," variants of the kernel, have emerged, each developed by a different person, each for a different purpose. Despite having only an informal figurehead to guide it, the community is remarkably structured. It delivers new releases of the kernel on average every two to three months, and each release involves some 10,000 patches from 1,000 developers representing some 100 corporations. Programmers are all connected through online forums and various services to share and improve versions of the Linux kernel. Linux is never static; it is constantly changing and evolving based on contributions across the global community.

Linux and its informal figureheads, Torvalds and Stallman, represent the metaphorical community organizer who has persuaded a large and growing number of developers and corporations to stand against the software behemoths and do things differently. They have united them for a single noble vision: to give all people the right to participate in the development of software and in the benefits it creates.

Since 2005, more than 3,700 developers from across 200 different companies have contributed to the kernel and shaped it in new ways. And Linux's reluctant leader, Linus Torvalds, is remarkable not only for the technical wizardry of the kernel, but also for inspiring and guiding an enormous collective to dedicate themselves to bringing the operating system to maturity.

Torvalds may not hold any direct power over his "loosely connected but increasingly powerful" throngs of volunteers, but he is the organizer who has ignited the passion to create an alternative to Windows, and forged a David "hero figure" to counteract the Goliath of the mega-corporations.

The community of Linux users and developers is held together by pride and the thrill of working toward a common goal

Key characteristics of Community Organizer & Volunteers

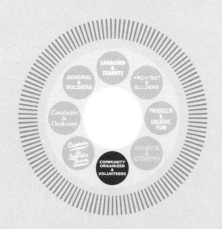

The Community Organizer & Volunteers archetype sits on the emergent axis, meaning that the power for setting direction emerges bottom-up from the volunteers and not top-down from the community organizer. A community organizer is the glue that binds the activities of the volunteers together: his or her narrative attracts others to the cause.

Volunteers cannot be told what to do; instead, they must be given the choice to join on their own terms. The persuasive message of the community organizer motivates them to join in the cause; and it's that common purpose that inspires volunteers to make a difference.

Volunteers view themselves as highly independent decision makers.

 Volunteers want frequent opportunities to express their opinions.

 Volunteers choose to opt into campaigns case by case.

 Community organizers often use narratives to motivate the volunteers.

 Volunteers are usually treated the same and have equal rights.

 Community organizers' power increases as the number of volunteers grows.

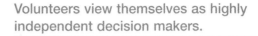

Volunteers view themselves as highly independent decision makers.

Volunteers are sovereign participants who choose to join with others – for reasons of enlightened self-interest or for the greater good of the group. Community organizers inspire volunteers to join by creating a framework for campaigns. The decision to participate, however, is taken by the individual.

On August 29, 2005, the eye of Hurricane Katrina passed over New Orleans. It had formed over the Bahamas, crossed southern Florida, and strengthened in the Gulf of New Mexico before heading toward Louisiana. Americans would remember it as one of the deadliest hurricanes in history. Damage estimates exceeded $100 million, nearly 2,000 people died, and nearly 90 percent of southeast Louisiana residents were evacuated to nearby cities and states. New Orleans was without power and clean water. Bodies floated on the water throughout the streets, looting and violence were rampant. People who remained in the city were stranded on rooftops or trapped in attics.

Though communication infrastructure had failed and local television services were disrupted, news spread via the Internet and radio that New Orleans was in desperate need of help. The moving stories of hurricane survivors were told around the world.

The Red Cross set up a number of relief centers throughout the city that provided food, water, and other sundry, necessary supplies. The Salvation Army provided free clinics and medical aid. Support also flooded in from other charitable organizations. Even though there was no specific, centralized governing body that coordinated these relief efforts, volunteers and aid miraculously appeared from all corners of the world.

The story of New Orleans shows a collective response to a human tragedy. It reveals what community organizers most rely on: the power of the cause or campaign.

Martin Luther King said, "An individual has not begun to live until he can rise above the narrow horizons of his particular individualistic concerns to the broader concerns of all humanity. Every person must decide, at some point, whether they will walk in the light of creative altruism or in the darkness of destructive selfishness. This is the judgment. Life's most persistent and urgent question is, 'What are you doing for others?'"

This is the mantra instilled in volunteers. They *independently* choose to follow the path of altruism or enlightened self-interest. Community organizers and volunteers may be passionate, selfless and dedicated, but, above all else, they are independent thinkers who, of their own volition, decide whether to get involved in a cause and for how long.

"A community organizer is someone who uncovers [volunteers'] self-interest," says Jana Adams, the National Training Coordinator at the Direct Action Training Research Center. "They give [volunteers] an opportunity to work in their own self-interest and address problems in the community that they could not address by themselves."

Volunteers don't join organizations or follow community organizers; they sign up for campaigns, and as autonomous individuals, they

alone choose which ones are aligned with their personal values.

Thus one of the biggest challenges for community organizers is getting a large group of independent thinkers on the same page. As *Business Week* said of Linus Torvalds, they need the ability to "herd cats" or "[be] an effective shepherd to a vast flock of very creative, un-sheeplike sheep."

The story of Visa, commonly regarded as one of the most successful business ventures in history, illustrates this point. Since 1970, the organization has grown by a phenomenal 10,000 percent (in round figures) and it continues to expand at an approximate rate of 20 percent per year, with operations in more than 200 countries. You can trace its roots to the BankAmericard, the first ever credit card, introduced in 1958 by the San Francisco-based Bank of America.

By the 1960s, the BankAmericard was faced with stiff competition from the California-based MasterCharge, and other burgeoning credit cards from large US banks. Credit cards were ubiquitous; thousands of banks had sent pre-approved credit cards to anyone and everyone they could find – including convicted felons, children, and pets.

By 1968, the unrestricted credit card industry was riddled with fraud and on the "brink of disaster." So when Dee Hock founded Visa in 1970, he sought to design an organization that would retain sufficient flexibility and decision-making control as well as manage the tensions between Visa's independent members – the various financial institutions that issued the cards.

Hock's new model of doing business emerged, what he called the "chaordic" organization (a combination of chaos and order). It was based on a balance between decentralization and collaboration, combined with authority, initiative, decision making and wealth; a model where "everything possible is pushed out to the periphery of the organization, to the members."

Members were given significant decision-making freedom to compete and innovate across the Visa products. They could independently "create, price, market, and service their own products under the Visa name," while "at the same time, in a narrow band of activity essential to the success of the whole, engage in the most intense cooperation."

This harmonious blend of competition and cooperation, supported by organizational processes, enabled Visa to expand and rise above different "currencies, languages, legal codes, customs, cultures, and political philosophies."

Visa now uses a different organization model to manage its independent global members, but for years the chaordic model allowed a vast and potentially divergent group of organizations to come together and create a very powerful global brand.

———————

Community organizers harness the enthusiasm and commitment of volunteers toward a shared goal. The more passionate and ardent their campaigns, the more likely they are to draw volunteers in. They use powers of persuasion to connect personally with volunteers and often appeal to emotions.

But that is about as far as their direct power takes them. They cannot force volunteers to join in their agendas, so, as you will see, they use multiple tools to help them build a power base.

As strong-willed opinionated and independent thinkers, volunteers must decide on their own if their views, opinions, and passions are aligned with that of the devoted community organizer. As Matt Sura, a community organizer for the 1,400-member Western Colorado Congress, says, "We show [people] that they already have [the] power... We [inform] people of [their] rights and responsibilities and [allow] them to decide."

Volunteers want frequent opportunities to express their opinions.

Because the will of the volunteers shapes the direction of campaigns, they must have the ability to voice their opinions. A networked, group-wide communications channel will enable them to contribute their ideas. As the number of volunteers increases, horizontal communication is crucial for information sharing and decision making.

In August 2000, Vesa-Matti "Vesku" Paananen was chatting with various local mobile technology enthusiasts at a party during the Night of Arts in Helsinki, Finland. They were all very keen to share ideas on innovation and were looking for the right forum in which to meet. As it happened, the only day that worked for everyone was Monday.

So a month later, on Monday September 4, in a little Irish pub called Molly Malone's in Helsinki, they held their first meeting.

Peter Vesterbacka, a serial entrepreneur came up with the name MobileMonday (MoMo) as well as the structure of the organization. Vesterbacka and Paananen decided on an open and relaxed presentation format. Once finalized, Paananen sent an invitation to over a hundred of his contacts and waited for the response.

Surprisingly, more than 60 people showed up, though not quite knowing what to expect. The meeting provided the opportunity to discuss the latest trends and exchange ideas. The group quickly grew in popularity and size. Word continued to spread, interest rose, and by 2004, new MoMo chapters had formed in places such as Tokyo, Silicon Valley, and Rome.

More than a decade later, MoMo is a global network: 90,000 people have joined chapters in over 60 cities across

the globe. From Austin to St Petersburg to Kuala Lumpur, local communities of mobile professionals gather together on the first Monday (or first available Monday) of every month to "share ideas, best practices and trends from global markets."

MoMo chapters operate under the umbrella of a global community and act as forums that connect "mobile industry visionaries, developers, and influential individuals." Although every local chapter operates with a single goal in mind, they cater in large part for local communities. Each chapter sets it own objectives and plans activities and events that are tailored to specific interests.

Mobile Monday members are passionate about their phones and the industry. These vol-unteers have a clear need for discourse, and a clear desire to exchange ideas and learn from others. They form a virtuous circle, helping each other and local companies connect with global ideas, concepts, and technologies.

Their story demonstrates the power of technology to connect like-minded people in distant countries and cities. Communities are no longer about proximity (geography and physical closeness); they are more about propinquity (affinity and kinship).

Regardless of how they are connected, volunteers need to express what's on their minds – particularly, if they're unhappy with their situations.

In 1970, Albert O. Hirschman published his ideas on individuals' reactions to deteriorating circumstances in his book titled *Exit, Voice, and Loyalty*. An example might sum them up best. Say, for the past few years, you've headed down to your favorite restaurant at least twice a month. You know the owner and you get great service. However, in the past month, a new chef and manager joined, and the experience just isn't the same. The service is slower and your steak's always overcooked. Your circumstances have deteriorated, so what do you do? According to Hirschman, you have two choices:

1. Exit – you can say to yourself, "I think I'll find a new favorite place" and never go back.
2. Voice – you can tell the owner what you think, and stick it out for a few more months hoping that the service and food will improve.

Similar decisions face people every day. Loyalty comes in when you are weighing your options between exiting and using your voice and, of course, consequences are usually one of the keys to the decision-making process. What will happen if I do *x*; and what will happen if I do *y*?

The balance of advantages between voice and exit can be delicate. Community organizers must recognize that volunteers are often passionate about the cause and want their opinions to be heard. Deny them a voice, deny them a feeling of direct involvement and you'll lose their good will – and eventually, their help.

Remember they are volunteers: they can choose to go, just as easily as they chose to join.

To maintain the energy of their volunteers, community organizers must not only provide them with opportunities to express themselves but also open communications channels across the volunteer group. Volunteers will want to know that, despite their differences, they are united by a common cause.

Volunteers choose to opt into campaigns case by case.

Volunteers can be passionate about a cause, but they don't always join the organization for the long run or participate in every campaign. They only support campaigns that are closely aligned to their personal values or interests. To secure their loyalty, organizers must make them active participants.

Between December 7 and 18, the 2009 United Nations Climate Change Conference was held in Copenhagen, Denmark. Over those 11 days, heads of state and government from 175 countries participated in discussions about climate change and its impact on our world.

The goal of the conference was for all of the heads of state to unanimously agree to a concrete plan to reduce greenhouse gas emissions and to commit their country to firm reduction targets. But by the morning of Friday December 18 it was clear that progress had been disappointing. After nearly two weeks of intensive, round-the-clock negotiations, few decisions had been made.

The acrimony that followed, with rich and poor nations blaming each other for the failure of the talks, exposed the fatal flaw: a palpable lack of trust. Wen Jiabao, the prime minister of China, himself accused by some commentators of sabotaging the conference, summed it up like this: "To meet the climate change challenge, the international community must strengthen confidence, build consensus, make vigorous efforts and enhance cooperation."

The efforts toward collective action were unsuccessful as many country leaders were unable or unwilling to opt in to the global climate change campaign and commit to making the necessary concessions.

COP15
COPENHAGEN

Game theorists call this scenario the "multiparty prisoner's dilemma (MPD)," a more complex version of the more commonly known "prisoner's dilemma." The MPD concept is readily evident in situations where resources are scarce and conservation is required. The trouble is, conservation is in no-one's short-term interests. Although committed to the principles of the cause, they remain unwilling volunteers.

The challenge for community organizers trying to get volunteers to opt in to various campaigns has been captured by Cesar Chavez, the famous American community organizer

who founded the first successful farm workers union. He said, "You have to convert people one person at a time; time after time. Progress only comes when people plow ahead and do it. It takes a lot of patience."

Similarly, in her book *Progressive Community Organizing*, Loretta Pyles describes a volunteer's choice to opt in as one of the first steps toward empowerment. "Empowerment is ultimately... a belief that people are capable of making their own choices and have much to offer in shaping society."

One of the key roles of community organizers is to move people from a passive and uninformed state to an active and empowered state. Gradually, as individuals opt in one by one, critical mass is reached. The pattern of involvement is commonly known as Arnstein's Ladder of Participation, where the lowest rungs are labeled manipulation (an illusory form of "participation" where people are not active), and the highest is control (where individuals are in full charge.) Thus as one ascends the ladder, one is more involved and participates to greater degrees in significant and influential decisions.

Arnstein's Ladder demonstrates the key point that there are stages of engagement for volunteers. The challenge for many community organizers is to move them up the ladder, one rung at a time.

But how do community organizers get volunteers to join in the first place?

Community organizers often use narratives to motivate the volunteers.

The persuasive message of the organizers provides the impetus for volunteers to join the group. Community organizers have little direct power over the volunteers, but they can tap into their interests by gaining their trust, promoting a strong brand, and understanding the volunteers' motivations. Community organizers use compelling narratives to unite the volunteers around a cause.

She sat amidst a group of young girls in a hot, crowded and dirty room in Thailand – none likely older than 13, each with their own numbers, all in red dresses. Her number was 146 and her identification tag was pinned to the front of her red dress. It was 2002 and a team of undercover investigators was exploring various brothels across the area trying desperately to crack down on the child trafficking industry. But for now, they couldn't do anything – only collect evidence to build a case, the first step in the process to save these girls.

The girls were sitting around a TV. They stared blankly at the cartoons that, in stark contrast, colorfully danced across the screen. But #146 was different. She stared beyond the glass at the strangers, her defiant eyes longing for freedom. She was a fighter.

A short time later, the house was raided, and the little girls were saved. Sadly, though, #146 was not among them. The investigators never found out what became of her. But they never forgot her and made it their mission to tell the world about girls like her. They founded the campaigning organization Love146, in homage to her.

Knowing he had a compelling story to tell, co-founder of Love146, Rob Morris approached the marketing and brand development agency Brains on Fire, which aims to

end child sex slavery & exploitation

"help organizations build movements," and, after a successful advertising campaign, support and funds started to flood in.

Human trafficking is estimated to generate over $32 billion annually, making it the second most lucrative crime in the world. But Rob wanted people to see more than just the faceless figures and staggering statistics: he wanted people to see the innocent children behind the numbers and to identify with the organization.

The storytelling aspect of the role of the community organizer is critical to the success of their campaign. People respond to imagery and stories in a way that is more emotional than intellectual. Stories provide the opportunity for aligning and connecting people. Community organizers need to develop and tell stories that invite their audience to share the mission and leave them with a clear motivation to act.

Kimble Forrester, state coordinator for Alabama Arise, an organization that attempts to improve the lives of low-income people, says, "An effective organizer is part empowerer and part storyteller, telling the stories that persuade people that they can make a difference…"

In December 2007, *Harvard Business Review* published an article by Peter Guber, chairman of Mandalay Entertainment, on the importance of storytelling. Guber argues that creating stories that resonate with audiences is dependent on four key factors:

1. The story must ring true for the teller. The storyteller must be genuine; they must *feel* the story they are telling.
2. The story must be true to the audience. If people are to listen, they must believe they will be rewarded by entertainment or enlightenment and a new understanding.
3. The story must be true to the moment. And it must resonate each time it is told.
4. The story must be true to the mission. It must reveal the storyteller's values and provide the opportunity for the audience to invest in the mission and make it their own.

In building a narrative that incorporates these four factors, a community organizer is more likely to be able to engage volunteers and turn organizational dreams into goals.

Barack Obama won his historic election victory in 2008 partly by telling his own story: his autobiography *Dreams from My Father: A Story of Race and Inheritance*. First published in 1995, it has become a bestseller. A political unknown until 2004, with barely one term in the US Senate, Obama achieved the impossible by connecting with people. His campaign slogan, "Change We Can Believe In," was fuelled by a strategy and story that were so stunningly imagined and so effectively implemented that they have changed forever the way political campaigns are fought. Every politician says they are running for the people. What Obama said was the same – and very different. He said: "This is not my campaign; it's your campaign." He meant it.

When Obama said you and we, he was tapping into a resonating narrative that personal responsibility, connected to a common goal and aspirations, leads to action. And so, millions of Americans spread Obama's story – an epidemic of change – around the country; a change that took Obama to the White House to become the first black president of the United States. It's no coincidence that as a young man in Chicago he spent several years working as a community organizer.

———————

Perhaps more than the leader in any other archetype, the community organizer must be able to reach the hearts and minds of volunteers and inspire them to act and get others involved. Storytelling, running campaigns and marketing one's causes bring the much-needed volunteers to create critical mass. And since volunteers don't join organizations, they join campaigns, they must first buy into the narrative that the community organizer is promoting.

Volunteers are usually treated the same and have equal rights.

Community organizers and volunteers tend to have equal say in the decisions of the group. No individual volunteer has more power than another, and decisions are reached unanimously. However, imbalance in the system can occur if "guerilla" volunteers dominate discussions.

Volunteers want change. They join the group because – for reasons of enlightened self-interest or social conscience – they want to make a difference. It follows that they will want to have their say in the decision-making process.

The democratic decision-making nature of the volunteers – often through consensus building and unanimous voting – can be an onerous and time-consuming method of gaining agreement. Formal conflict resolution procedures are extremely important; there has to be a structure that helps balance the power dynamic.

The Community Organizer & Volunteers archetype is typically characterized by equal rights to all members where possible, but is this mode of decision making really viable in the business world? Let's take a look at Star Alliance, the largest airline consortium in the world. Started in 1997, Star Alliance was the first of its kind. Large network carriers such as Air Canada, Lufthansa, SAS, Thai Airways International and United realized that if they cooperated instead of directly competed, they could jointly reduce their overall costs and improve customer service. What came about was a new kind of corporation: a company based on both cooperation and competition.

Membership grew quickly. There were ten members by 2000, 15 by 2003 and 20 by 2008. In mid-2010, there were

27 airlines in the alliance. And growth isn't expected to slow anytime soon, with numbers projected to rise to 50.

The benefits of belonging to the collective outweigh the $150,000 membership fee. But, as its numbers grow, how will the consortium preserve equality in decision making?

Because Star Alliance was founded on the premise of a consensus-driven business model, all member airlines had equal say. With only five original partners, gaining agreement on strategic decisions was relatively easy.

During the first several years of growth, Star Alliance was run virtually – with no physical corporate location – by member representations based around the world. However, it quickly outgrew this structure. Reaching consensus was time-consuming and inefficient; new members meant new layers of complexity. Doreen Riley, a marketing coordinator for Air Canada, remarked, "It felt like [the movie] *Groundhog Day*. For the launch, we wanted an ad that would be simple, easy but with strong impact. We'd get everyone's approval one day, but it would all change the next. And then we'd start from scratch."

The members decided to set up a management company – Star Alliance Services GmbH in Frankfurt – to help resolve member conflicts. Decision-making powers were given to the CEO and directors, relying on the input and experience of members. Member airlines, which each own an equal share in the management company, now rely on this centralized organization for conflict resolution.

Today, airlines have the option to choose their type of membership packages, which balance members' rights, responsibilities and costs while considering their individual capabilities.

Smaller regional companies such as Croatia Airlines, Adria Airlines, and Blue1 will now be absorbed under the one Star Alliance brand as full partners, instead of being branded under a Regional Carrier designation. Star Alliance will only use the principle of unanimous voting for areas that affect the group as a whole.

Martin Mueller, Director, Alliance Development, explained: "After 12 years of growth, it is healthy for any organization to review its processes, set-up and governance. In the case of Star Alliance, it is not only the foreseeable addition of members, but also their increasing diversity that required a review of membership structures and governance."

While Star Alliance GmbH protects the unique brand and the interests of its members, the individual airlines continue to reap the benefits of their cooperation and remain dedicated to what they do best – meeting customers' needs while delivering competitive flights for their regions. "We have made great strides," United Airlines' former president Rono Dutta, said "but alliances are committed to the end game, and we are committed to working as a single airline."

———————

Because volunteers are independent decision makers who want to express their opinions, it's critical that they have balanced opportunities

to contribute to the direction and progress of the organization.

Thus, across members, access to transparent information and communication is important. Formal decision-making and conflict resolution processes are especially useful in this archetype to maintain a balance of power across members. The integrity of the connected structure is more difficult to maintain if some individual volunteers hold disproportionately more power than others.

The Community Organizer & Volunteers structure is set up such that individuals have equal opportunity to voice their opinions, and in turn, to reap equal rewards.

In this archetype, power comes from the strength and numbers of the volunteers; thus, processes must be sufficiently robust to support unanimous outcomes. Loretta Pyles, in *Progressive Community Organizing*, says, "Coalitions should be attuned to the ways in which power within the group is distributed. Transparency in decision making is probably one of the best ways to avoid negative power dynamics. Paying attention to power issues is an ongoing part of coalition work."

Community organizers' power increases as the number of volunteers grows.

As the message of the community organizer spreads, the number of volunteers grows. Once a tipping point is reached, the volunteers find strength in numbers – and generating support for campaigns becomes easier for the community organizer.

During World War II, in a program led by Adolf Eichmann, infamous architect of the holocaust, Nazi-occupied countries came under pressure to hand over Jews to their German masters. In Vienna, Prague and Amsterdam Eichmann's Central Office for Jewish Emigration systematically forced the expulsion of Austrian, Czech and Dutch Jews.

Although most countries balked at the idea of deporting their own Jewish citizens, most, out of fear, acquiesced. Only the Danes stood firm.

Led by the estimable King Christian X, the first Scandinavian monarch to enter a synagogue, the Danes formed an inclusive and tolerant society. They saw an attack on their Jewish citizens as an attack on themselves. Following the example of their king and government, they rallied behind the Jews.

Their moment in history, their chance to make a difference, came in August 1943. After Danish shipyard workers refused to repair German ships, the Nazis attempted to round up all Jews. But the Danes resisted. Everyone from the King to simple citizens took the Jews in and hid them. Only 477 out of a total of 7,800 were found. They remained in hiding until the Danes smuggled them across the water to Sweden on Danish fishing vessels.

The cost of transportation for people without means was paid for by wealthy Danes and the rescue operation took about a month to complete.

Around 50 percent of Jewish Danes stayed in their country and survived the war in hiding. When they returned to their Danish homes, they found their gardens blooming and their homes cared for by their neighbors.

———————

What lessons can we learn from King Christian X? Through his own strength and courage he was able to inspire the same in others. One by one, his people put themselves at risk in order to help others. Put very simply, he led by example.

The ability to persuade people to act is key to the Community Organizer & Volunteers archetype. Without it, critical mass, strength in numbers, is impossible. A group gathers momentum as more people join. Once a tipping point is reached, individual volunteers have sufficient collective numbers to make a real impact.

As Malcolm Gladwell, author of the bestselling book *The Tipping Point*, explains, "The phrase 'tipping point' comes from the world of epidemiology. It's the name given to that moment in an epidemic when a virus reaches critical mass. It's the boiling point. It's the moment on the graph when the line starts to shoot straight upwards."

Through strength in numbers, the Danes proved unstoppable. The Germans could do nothing to thwart them. Examples such as the Danes defying the Nazis, Star Alliance and its growing member base and Linux and its 3,700 developers from around the world, demonstrate that significant change is possible when there is strength-in-numbers power behind volunteers. The success of this archetype is never based solely on the efforts of one person.

Is Community Organizer & Volunteers the right model for you?

Is this archetype right for your current situation? And, if it is, how can you be the best community organizer you can be? The following sections will help you answer these questions.

Great if:

- You want to realize economies of scale across a large group of like-minded people or across entities that don't traditionally work together.

- You have a noble purpose or cause that others can be persuaded to embrace.

- You have an anti-establishment agenda and need to unify a group to fight the status quo.

- There are low levels of trust among independent-minded people or among entities focused on their own interests.

Think twice if:

- You do not have much time (or there's a great sense of urgency) and the task coordination challenge is very complex.

- One or a small group of volunteers is disproportionately influential and actively opposes your collective agenda.

- Your noble purpose or cause does not connect logically with the idea of volunteers' enlightened self-interest.

How can you be a better community organizer?

1. How easy is it for you to sign up new volunteers?

To increase your power base quickly, you must ensure it's easy for new members to join.

- What have you done to make the sign-up process as simple as possible?
- How successful have you been at getting an initial coalition of volunteers?
- Is your first call to action a reasonable request for volunteers?

COMMUNITY ORGANIZER

VOLUNTEERS

2. How quickly has your volunteer community been expanding?

Since volunteers join case by case, you continuously need to build your power base and engage people's interest across multiple campaigns. The more volunteers who join the cause, the greater the shift of power to the community organizer.

- Have you set targets for yourself for membership growth?
- Do you have specific expansion events where new volunteers can opt in and join existing coalitions?
- Do you know when you will reach the tipping point for your volunteer base?

3. How effective are you at getting volunteers to do more over time?

To build a power base, community organizers must not only continue to increase volunteer numbers, but also get each individual to commit to participating in more campaigns.

- What tactics are you using to increase volunteers' participation?
- How rigorously are you assessing the success of different types of campaigns and different types of volunteers?
- What systems are there to measure volunteers' participation over time?

4. How strong is your brand?

For community organizers, branding is a very critical element. If people can identify with your brand, your message, you will be much more likely to attract loyal volunteers. A strong brand means a strong organization over the long term.

- How effectively have you created a sense of shared identity among volunteers?
- Do volunteers publicly connect themselves with the brand; do they market on your behalf?
- Are you using social networks to engage volunteers in brand development work?

5. How effectively have you shifted the conversation from what people won't do to what they are willing to do?

Dissent can be handled by positive thinking. Focus, at first at least, on the small things that volunteers are more likely to agree to do.

- How successful are you at removing roadblocks from discussions?
- What tactics are you using to get dissenters to agree to do something (even if fairly small)?
- How do you draw attention to what is actually being accomplished?

6. How easily can you distinguish "passengers" from those who are actually making a contribution?

In a large group of autonomous volunteers there will usually be a cohort of free-riders. Community organizers need to have transparent systems for measuring and monitoring volunteers' contributions.

- Do you have effective systems to gather information to identify free-riders?
- Is your information sufficiently transparent and granular?
- Do you publish or otherwise draw attention to those with the highest participation rates?

7. How effective are you at building trust with your volunteers?

As the community organizer, you are the motivator, the spokesperson, the glue that holds the group together. Your volunteers need to be sure you will represent the group's interests.

- Do your volunteers trust you to make decisions on behalf of the group?
- Are you using external standards (instead of your own subjective judgment) to justify your strategies and to build volunteers' confidence in you?
- What systems (for example, elections) do you use to build legitimacy and credibility?

Chapter 3

Conductor
& Orchestr

"Technique is communication:
the two words are synonymous
in conductors"
—*Leonard Bernstein*

" A small gesture from his little finger, and the orchestra was transformed into a velvet carpet "

Herbert von Karajan and his pursuit of perfection

Herbert von Karajan was a formidable man, whose small stature – just five feet 8 inches – belied both a towering intellect and a towering ego. In many ways, you could read his character on his face: patrician, chiseled cheekbones; arched and rather too "obvious" eyebrows; a straight, bird-like nose; piercing eyes. There was no mistaking the man who today, more than two decades since his death in 1989, continues to be one of the best-known conductors in the world.

Karajan is, for many, *the* kapellmeister, *the* maestro: a charismatic figure in classical music who, 30 years ago, helped shaped the music industry, pioneering digital sound. Even today, he remains the most recorded conductor in history, with more than 900 albums to his name.

His success brought him a high-octane lifestyle – fast cars, Learjets, beautiful women, homes in the Austrian Alps, St Tropez, and St Moritz. And some journalists liked to mythologize him as an

egoist of Machiavellian proportions, reporting that he considered "having himself cryogenically frozen so that he could later be thawed and re-record pieces from the standard classical repertory." Like many high-profile people, he was loved and loathed, praised and criticized, lauded and feared.

Few, however, could doubt his musical genius, which became apparent at a young age. Born in Salzburg, Austria, in 1908, he was a prodigiously talented pianist as a child.

The turning point came, however, when he was 20 and heard an opera performance conducted by Arturo Toscanini. "From the first bar, it was as if I had been struck a blow," Karajan later wrote. "I was completely disconcerted by the perfection which had been achieved." From then on, he vowed to follow where Toscanini had led.

Early success

Success came quickly in his early career, and, shortly after his 1937 debut with the Berlin State Opera, he was hailed by a German critic as "Das Wunder Karajan" (the Karajan miracle) for his performance of *Tristan und Isolde*.

During World War II, he earned the admiration of Hitler, but his star was tarnished at a gala performance for the King and Queen of Yugoslavia of Die Meistersinger when, without his score, he lost his way. Furious, Hitler announced, "Herr von Karajan will never conduct at Bayreuth in my lifetime!" And so, in February 1945, he conducted his final concert during wartime there before fleeing to Milan.

He resumed his career after the war, having been cleared by the denazification examination board, set up to rid Germany and Austria of Nazi influence in public life, in March 1946.

In the post-war period, he spent a lot of his time in the studio, working with the newly-formed Philharmonia Orchestra in London. It was this that laid the foundation for his enduring legacy: many rival conductors at the time were not interested in recording.

Leading the Berlin Philharmonic Orchestra

In 1955, he became the chief-conductor of the Berlin Philharmonic Orchestra, taking over from his biggest rival and one-time idol, Wilhelm Furtwängler, and demanded that he be made the orchestra's conductor for life. In return, he made the Berlin Phil "the best orchestra in the world" in the eyes of the critics.

Behind his achievements lay a relentless pursuit of perfection and an ability, despite his ferocity and egomania (or maybe because of them), to get the very best out of each orchestra member.

Karajan devoted more than six months of study to Honegger's *Symphonie Liturgique* before he felt sufficiently prepared to conduct it. It's reported that he would rehearse the orchestra for hours on end with tireless dedication and exacting detail. The only visual record of the maestro rehearsing an entire

Despite his controlling hand,
there's no doubt that Karajan inspired his musicians
to produce the most beautiful music

work, "Herbert von Karajan in Rehearsal and Performance," shows him as an autocrat who'd never accept second best. Within the first few minutes of Schumann's Symphony No. 4, he restarts the Vienna Symphony Orchestra at least seven times, each time outlining the minute details of his desired sound in specific and clear instructions. Not until the orchestra has produced the sound to his liking does Karajan move on to the next phrase. This is a man who puts no-one's interpretation above his own.

During his long tenure at the Berlin Philharmonic – from 1955 until just before his death in 1989 – Karajan courted controversy by maintaining the outdated tradition of dictatorial conductor and compliant orchestra. And of course, over time, the orchestra resisted his tyrannical efforts, causing much conflict and resentment between the two parties.

The Karajan Sound

Despite his controlling hand, there's no doubt that Karajan inspired his musicians to produce the most beautiful music. The characteristic lush "Karajan Sound" is compared with having the luxury, elegance and restraint of a Rolls-Royce supported by the power of a Ferrari engine underneath. James Galway, the principal flautist for the Berlin Philharmonic in 1969, said, "I always played better for him than anybody else. He brought out the best in you all the time. The orchestra sat on the front of their chairs. If you watch any movie of the Berlin Philharmonic, nobody sits back."

Karajan's skill was his ability to translate each nuance of musical phrasing from the heart of the composer (typically Strauss, Wagner or Beethoven) through the fingers of the orchestra to produce emotional and lyrical vitality. Michel Glotz, Karajan's executive producer from 1968 onward, said if Karajan wanted "a real *crescendo*, you must go from the most *pianissimi* to the loudest *fortississimo*." One of his most famous protégées, Anne-Sophie Mutter, whose career he launched at the tender age of 13, recalled, "A small gesture from his little finger, and the orchestra was transformed into a velvet carpet." He was the binding focus of the score, the orchestra and the audience.

But his influence extended far beyond the concert hall. He will also be remembered for the mass marketing of classical music. In the recording studio, he made a fortune estimated at more than $500 million. Some of his recordings from the 1950s and 1960s are so polished, so unparalleled in their musical opulence and so characteristic of the Karajan sound that they continue to sell well even today.

Remarkably, Karajan was a pioneer in the development of the compact disc in the early 1980s, and even conducted the first recording ever to be commercially released on CD, Richard Strauss's *Eine Alpensinfonie*. He championed the new format, and is said to have forced a change in the maximum playing time of early prototypes – from 60 to 74 minutes – in order to be able to record Beethoven's Ninth Symphony and put his existing library of recordings on to CD.

In search of perfection

In his last years, Karajan limited his repertoire to Strauss, Wagner, Mozart, Beethoven, Schumann, Tchaikovsky, Brahms, Mendelssohn, Schubert, and a small group of others. While he has been called "the greatest innovator in the classical music business," he was so obsessed with precision and the flawlessness of sound that he focused on conducting and re-recording the same works over and over again – attempting to perfect the already near-perfect.

Faced with criticism, he stood firm. Accused of creating an overly refined and overly produced sound, he replied that "if the details are right, the performance will work."

For conductors and orchestras around the world, driven by efficiency and cost management, precision and attention to detail are what makes the difference between mediocre and flawless performance.

Medco
Smart medicine

In 1946 Chemie Grünenthal felt they were on the verge of producing a revolutionary mass market tranquilizer that would provide relief from nausea, insomnia and morning sickness called phthalimido-glutarimide or thalidomide. Testers for the drug stated that they felt calm after taking the dosage and it appeared to have no toxic effects, so the company decided to market it as a cheap and safe alternative to barbiturates.

With no testing or systematic follow up, in 1955 Grünenthal distributed free samples of the new drug to doctors in West Germany and Switzerland. The drug's popularity grew and it quickly became the third-largest selling drug in Europe, and in some countries second only to aspirin.

Tragedy would strike though, before the drug was even formally placed on the market. On Christmas Day in 1956, in the town of Stolberg, Germany, a baby girl was born without ears. The father was an employee of Chemie Grünenthal who had received free samples of the drug and had given them to his pregnant wife. Soon after more cases appeared and in the end, it's estimated that over 10,000 children were born with severe congenital deformities.

In the 1950s, there were few stringent drug approval processes and regulations. In fact, in the United States, drugs only had to be proven safe, not effective. Richardson-Merrell, an American pharmaceutical applied to market the drug but because preapproval of clinical trials was not required by the Food and Drug Administration (FDA), the company had already begun distribution.

In total, Richardson-Merrell "distributed more than two-and-a-half million tablets to 20,000 patients handed out by 1,267 physicians" within the US. In December 1960, British medical journals had published articles on the potential side-effects of the drug. Yet in April 1961, thalidomide prescription sale began in Canada. In fact, Canada was one of the latest countries to remove thalidomide from its shelves – nearly four months after West Germany. Though word began to leak out that there were potentially harmful side effects from the drug, why did it take some countries, physicians and pharmacists months longer than others to put a halt on its distribution?

To this day, the case of thalidomide is remembered as "one of the biggest medical tragedies of modern times" due to inadequate testing, poor information sharing within the medical industry and slow reaction of governments, physicians, pharmaceuticals, and medical institutions to take the drug off the market.

While medical tragedies may not likely recur at this same scale, thousands of medical errors still happen virtually every day. The statistics are shocking:

- The average American is ten times more likely to be hospitalized from an adverse drug reaction than from a motor vehicle accident
- Nearly 784,000 people in the United States die every year from conventional medicine mistakes
- A recent review involving the medical records of 41 million Medicare patients identified $8.8 billion in error-associated costs and 238,837 preventable deaths. Moreover, a large subset of these errors is medication errors. An estimated 1.5 million preventable serious medication errors occur each year, with $217 billion (2006 dollars) in associated costs.

The need for precision is, perhaps, even more obvious in the pharmaceuticals and medical sector – where the business is, quite literally, human life. Medco Health Solutions Inc., named one of the most innovative companies of 2008 shows how the strict rules and scripted processes of the Conductor & Orchestra archetype can be applied to the world's most forward-thinking companies. They are in fact so bold as to say they are contributing to the reinvention of American healthcare.

Spun off from Merck & Co. in 2003, Medco is a pharmacy services and healthcare company operating in the Pharmacy Benefit Management (PBM) industry. PBMs administer prescription drug benefit programs on behalf of health plans, employers, government agencies and unions. They are basically middlemen who aggregate the buying power of their clients to negotiate discounts on prescription drugs. They also provide other clinically-based and administrative services such as mail-order fulfillment.

Since the 1990s, mail-order pharmacies have become increasingly popular. Their rise, however, has its detractors. They may be convenient, but are they safe? How can you be sure that you're receiving the exact medication your doctor prescribed? How does Medco ensure that its 3,000 pharmacists are providing the best and most accurate care to deliver more than 100 million prescriptions per year?

There are many points in the prescription process where errors can be introduced such as when a drug is prescribed (eg, wrong drug, wrong dose, allergy), dispensed (eg, wrong drug, wrong dose, interactions, allergic reactions), or administered (eg, wrong time, wrong patient). David Snow, Jr., chairman and CEO of Medco states, "In an era when preschoolers use the Internet to chat with friends half a world away, it is inexcusable that doctors write paper prescriptions – in Latin – which patients need to take to another professional in a process fraught with countless opportunities for error."

Medco's protocol-driven pharmacy processes and use of innovative technologies attempt to address these concerns by automating many of these points in patient care. Initially, pharmacists ran the mail-order center, which primarily involved the back administration and prescription fulfillment. Now, increased use of automation and more sophisticated robotics have freed pharmacists for more personalized and specialized care. Patients suffering from complex and chronic diseases are helped in the Medco Therapeutic Resource Centers® (TRCs), organized across 15 different specialties, such as diabetes, cardiovascular disease, cancer and respiratory/pulmonary conditions.

Today, Medco has more than 1,000 specialist pharmacists across the TRCs, who are specifically categorized by drug and disease specialties. If a patient needs to discuss diabetes-related issues, they are directed to a specific group of diabetes specialist pharmacists. If a patient was prescribed the beta blocker, Corgard, they can discuss the side-effects with a specialist pharmacist from the cardiovascular TRC. The multiple specializations across the

"

When individuals' lives are on the line,
there isn't any room for error

"

pharmacists can be likened to various specialized areas within an orchestra. They each are selected for the deep knowledge, precision and attention to detail with which they masterfully wield their instrument.

When individuals' lives are on the line, there isn't any room for error. Both patients and their medical practitioners need to have access to their medication information to reduce, if not eliminate the likelihood of mistreatment which will then significantly lower related costs. Medco is attempting to embed a degree of standardization into its pharmacy processes by implementing strict protocols for patient interactions.

Few patients would feel safe relying solely on the memory of their pharmacist to recall all of their medical history and the potential drug combinations (and their side-effects, etc). Thus, to ensure the utmost safety and stringent attention to detail, scripts – similar to an orchestra's score – are automated into the system, which then applied over 8,000 rules that help guide pharmacists to provide the best advice to their patients. By reviewing a patient's record, the Medco system helps their pharmacists determine which medications should be prioritized over others, which shouldn't be combined, and which need adjustment.

Additionally, because Medco's specialist pharmacists deal only with specific drugs or diseases, they are better able to recognize new patterns in patient symptoms and medical recommendations. Medco's automated dispensing pharmacies use the Six Sigma management controls in their dispensing and operating processes to ensure patient safety and quality of care as well as lower medication errors and costs.

Without this degree of precision and clarity, the largest mail-order pharmacy in the world (dispensing drugs to more than 60 million Americans) would not be able to function effectively. Scripting is built into the pharmacists' roles and daily working lives. Medco's platform removes pharmacists from the standardized, behind-the-scenes, mail-order administration and enables them to coordinate care with physicians, monitor the patient's treatment progression, and ensure that relevant protocols have been followed for dispensing medication and administering various diagnostics and exams.

But the pharmacists' development doesn't stop there. They must continue to learn and practice their knowledge. Each pharmacist must pass a 90–120 day probation period where 100 percent of their phone calls and every single word they say is recorded and monitored to ensure they are adhering to the required protocols. Training is of the utmost importance where this level of detail is required; and each phone call with a patient or physician is seen as another intense rehearsal.

Coaches are also used to follow up and support individuals, and if they can't maintain Medco's standards, they are moved out of the TRC. While this process may seem somewhat ruthless, Medco prioritizes their recruiting to ensure that only those individuals which have a natural inclination towards this type of environment are offered permanent roles. There is a

people component that allows pharmacists to support patients, but there is also a very rigid and rules-driven component to ensure a reduction in errors.

While many healthcare providers are reluctant to embrace protocol-driven care largely over the perceived interference with professional medical judgment, Medco states these rules aren't intended to eliminate the need for an experienced physician or a pharmacist but instead complements those roles and enables them to discover improved and more expeditious treatments for their patients. Some claim there is a 17-year gap between the time that a medical breakthrough is approved and the time that the breakthrough is applied by doctors. As a successful conductor with their finely-tuned orchestra, Medco's goal is to reinvent healthcare to combine speed with life-saving precision through the application of strict protocols and innovative technology in the pharmacy care they provide.

Key characteristics of Conductor & Orchestra

The Conductor & Orchestra archetype sits directly on the scripted axis, meaning that there is little room for improvisation or creative interpretation of the musical score. The orchestra's ultimate goal is to play exactly the notes that are on the sheet and follow the precise directions of the conductor.

The archetype shares characteristics with both the General & Soldiers as well as the Captain & Sports Team archetypes – specifically, the clear communication of the general and the uniformity of the sports team. The primary purpose of using this archetype is to focus on activities that demand efficiency, standardization and repeatability, characteristics typically found in an assembly-line setting, or where low cost and high quality matter, or in zero tolerance environments, where lives are at risk and safety is paramount.

 Orchestra members have clearly defined
roles and tasks.

 Orchestra members are given detailed and scripted
processes to carry out with utmost precision.

 Uniformity of orchestra members is critical
to reinforce standardization and efficiency.

 Extensive training and orientation ensure
the orchestra's tasks are precisely performed.

 People primarily join the orchestra to pursue
their own personal interests.

 There's a close relationship between compliance
and incentives.

Orchestra members have clearly defined roles and tasks.

Just as an assembly line depends on division of labor principles, an orchestra depends on clear definition of its members' roles. Everyone must know what they're expected to do and must complete specific tasks. Standardized roles and defined behaviors are specifically designed to increase efficiency.

In management and labor studies, there's a theory called Taylorism, which focuses on the study of efficiency. It's based on the work of Frederick Winslow Taylor, an American mechanical engineer who wrote a ground-breaking book in 1911, *The Principles of Scientific Management*.

Taylor argued that even the performance of the most talented, most hard-working, most conscientious individuals could be improved. He believed that if you could apply true science to the "simplest individual acts to the work of our great corporations," the results could be "truly astounding."

So what was the basis of Taylor's research? Essentially, he was saying that decision making and actions should be based on scientifically calculated methods, which, when followed, would benefit both employers and workers by maximizing output and decreasing waste. He is best known for breaking down tasks into individual elements, a technique used by Henry Ford to increase efficiency in his assembly-line car manufacturing plants.

Taylor's principles of scientific management focus on removing the subjective judgment of the worker and replacing it with standardized, scientifically-defined ways of working. In addition, employees would be given narrowly defined and discrete tasks, and be told exactly how to perform them. They would be selected and trained using very deliberate and detailed methods; learning would not be left up to them.

Scientific management was a breakthrough in increasing worker productivity. After Ford's adoption of the practice in 1913, its benefits became clear. By 1914, the entire assembly process – from the raw materials entering the plant to the finished automobiles coming out – took 93 minutes: a reduction from 12.5 hours. Between 1908 and 1927, Ford was able to drop the cost of the car from $850 to $300.

The principles of scientific management demonstrate what lies at the core of the Conductor & Orchestra archetype, where individuals are required to perform clearly defined roles and tasks according to detailed instructions. Each individual has a very specific role associated with their specific task, and each task has to be conducted according to specific standards to maintain consistency, maximize productivity, and minimize cost.

———

In 2003, Amazon teamed up with FedEx Ground and thousands of its drivers to deliver the biggest one-day shipment in e-commerce history – the newly released *Harry Potter and the Order of the Phoenix*. FedEx Ground handled 400,000 copies on the first day of the book's release and delivered 99.8 percent of them on time. Most reached customers over the weekend, when other competitors weren't fully operating.

Every day, FedEx Ground, a division of FedEx, delivers more than 3.5 million packages to business addresses across the United States and Canada. Fifteen thousand men and women get dressed in their black and purple

uniforms to set off on their defined delivery routes. And with near-perfect reliability, packages reach recipients in good time. The perception that FedEx Ground is fast, safe and reliable, which underpins the brand, ultimately rests on the pride and dedication of the driver.

One of the company's greatest strengths is that it achieves consistency and quality across a huge workforce that's not only geographically dispersed but also made up entirely of independent contractors: FedEx Ground drivers are self-employed, paid, not by salary, but by the volume of packages they deliver. The company says that this model has proved an effective motivation tool.

Each contractor is self-sufficient and manages their own business and their own time – there are no fixed start or finish times, and they can decide whether they want to deliver on weekends, evenings or by appointment. They buy the rights to (licenses for) FedEx Ground routes, own and maintain their own trucks and uniforms and are responsible for all related costs.

Given the fact that drivers are essentially their own bosses, how does FedEx Ground make sure they conform to the standards it wants? The answer is through role and task clarity, which help to improve overall efficiency and thus reduce the drivers' time and the costs of delivery.

FedEx Ground also influences the way drivers look and behave in order to ensure the consistency and quality of the FedEx brand.

Many drivers accept these consistency and brand guidelines because they are motivated by stories of drivers who've made it "big" by using the company as the route to running their own businesses.

One such is Travis Boardman. He enjoys working for FedEx Ground and feels that it perfectly suits anyone with an entrepreneurial drive. Boardman has been a contract driver since 1993, covering areas of Maryland's eastern shore. With six drivers working under him, he personally nets a six-figure salary and grosses anything from $250,000 to $500,000 a year. Travis argues that task clarity is needed to increase drivers' efficiency and reinforce quality standards across the thousands of drivers nationwide.

———————

For conductors and orchestras, clearly defined roles and tasks are an effective mechanism for optimizing efficiency. When strict deadlines need to be met, clear division of labor ensures that orchestra members understand their roles and the tasks they need to accomplish. Clarity, however, does not just mean greater efficiency. Without it, brand standards will slip and, for some organizations, such as Medco, safety will be put at risk.

The conductor who makes clarity a priority is taking care of far more than the smooth operation of their orchestra.

Orchestra members are given detailed and scripted processes to carry out with utmost precision.

Members of the orchestra must be comfortable with a rigid and structured approach to performing their tasks. They must complete them with precision and pay attention to detail as well as conform to the required behaviors.

Igor Stravinsky, the Russian composer, once said that conductors should have "flawless" technical facility to realize what a composer wants: "The first condition that must be fulfilled by anyone who aspires to the imposing title of interpreter is that he be first of all a flawless executant." While a clear division of roles and a common understanding are key components of a successful orchestra, precision and detail are also crucial. It's the combination of these characteristics that makes the Conductor & Orchestra archetype so efficient and effective.

Standardization and attention to detail are important in industries that are focused on cost savings, efficiency, safety, and the integrity of a brand.

It's important to remember that details and scripted processes must be aligned to the business and its strategy. Sometimes, rules are imposed for reasons of lack of trust or the pursuit of personal power. In his 1993 book *The Trust Factor*, John O. Whitney, reminded us of two precepts: "First, man can defeat any system man can devise. Second, the more controls you have, the less control you have." He showed there was a "darker side of control," that, when taken too far, control has a subtractive force that can cause working relationships to deteriorate.

As Whitney argues, controls only work when those controlled believe they're necessary. If employees mis-

understand the rules or believe they hinder them rather than make them more efficient, they will think up ways to circumvent the rules – or just make trouble. They might, for example, manipulate expense accounts, doctor timesheets, or get round recruitment freezes by bringing in part-timers or contractors.

What does this mean for the Conductor & Orchestra archetype? There are times when strict controls are required and are effective. The role of the conductor is to understand the score inside out in order to provide the right instruction for the orchestra and to ensure individual members follow their direction.

Employees' expectations need to be managed; they need to understand the realities of such a strict working environment or be specifically selected for their ability to work well under those conditions.

Conductors need to be aware not only of the degree of control they are exerting over the orchestra but also what motivates the members. The clear lesson is that there are aspects of the archetype that can be taken to the extreme: overly scripting tasks can be counterproductive and lead to behaviors that threaten the unity – and the efficiency and effectiveness – of the orchestra.

Uniformity of orchestra members is critical to reinforce standardization and efficiency.

Although orchestra members play different instruments, they all essentially share the same deep training in music. They typically follow a formal dress code, and speak a common language. To work efficiently, they must perform their tasks and behaviors to specific standards.

1957 was a big year for Toyota. That year represented its first foray into the American automobile market, with the Toyopet Crown. Less than $2,500, the Crown was touted as "the world's greatest automobile value" and "the kind of car that Americans had been asking for."

Indeed, the model had a few remarkable features, such as its fuel-efficient engine which achieved 33 miles per gallon and its interior and high-quality chrome fixtures. But as "the first car of the Orient to be introduced in the United States," the Toyopet failed miserably in comparison to other American cars. The driving experience was likened more to that of a tank than an automobile, and it was significantly more expensive than other foreign cars. After one year in the US, only 287 Toyopets had been sold, and in 1961, Toyota withdrew the car from the US market altogether. The failure was seen as a big blow to Toyota.

Since then, the company has tried to learn from its mistakes. It became the world's largest automaker in 2007, surpassing General Motors, but over the past few years, it's been experiencing significant quality issues. While some believe Toyota's aggressive global expansion strategy has diluted its ability to transfer its famed Toyota Production System (TPS) to its factories around the world, new research indicates that Toyota's mass recalls from 2009 were in fact overwhelmingly due to driver error instead of Toyota's manufacturing defects. In February

2010, Michael A. Cusumano, professor at the MIT Sloan School of Management, stated, "As far as we know, Toyota is still the best manufacturing company in the world when it comes to production management."

———————

Automobiles are made of thousands of mechanical parts. Yet with all the complexity, Toyota was consistently able to produce higher-quality cars with fewer worker hours, lower inventory levels and fewer defects, than its competitors. The famous "Toyota Way" not only means following lean production and management techniques but also engraining in all line workers and managers a culture of continuous improvement.

The Toyota Way is based on systems and tools for people to continually improve their performance, particularly where the tasks are standardized or regimented. Although much of today's car manufacturing is automated by robotics, it's still based largely on the principles handed down by Henry Ford. The difference with Toyota is that, as employees repeat their tasks, they are trying to make miniscule process improvements to reduce the opportunities for error.

It's a culture that Toyota managers admit is getting more difficult to replicate. Recent production problems show that something has impeded the concerted actions and precision in execution that all workers were at one point following. Can the company turn things around? "Toyota has been exemplary at surfacing problems in the factory and stopping production before a crisis was reached," says Jeffrey Liker,

who has written books on the Toyota Way. He adds, "Failure to follow all the principles of the Toyota Way led to this crisis. Now the Toyota Way is the only way out of it."

———————

Balancing the needs of the individual with the greater good of the team, is one of the aspects that signifies a good Conductor & Orchestra model. Things will go wrong if uniformity is taken to extremes and becomes a byword for elitism and exclusivity. Voltaire, the French writer, once wrote *"le mieux est l'ennemi du bien"* – the best is the enemy of the good. There's a point at which striving for perfection becomes counter-productive. And the best conductors and orchestras know when it's been reached.

What does it really mean to be a Conductor & Orchestra? Conductors are often the strict task masters who ensure the orchestra plays in unison and according to the score. Members of the orchestra must, literally, play by the rules, if they're to form a cohesive group.

For large groups whose members perform individual tasks and who may not always see the big picture, getting everyone on the same page is a challenge. However, as characteristic number 6 makes clear, conductors can be helped by remembering that sharing a common bond and a sense of belonging motivates many people to succeed. The orchestra is not for someone who likes to operate in a vacuum. Conductors must also only select individuals who want continuously to strive for perfection, often through constant repetition of precise and detailed tasks.

Extensive training and orientation ensure the orchestra's tasks are precisely performed.

If they're to fit the culture of the orchestra, new members need not only to be carefully selected but also carefully trained. The conductor's role is to ensure synchronization across the group.

Frederick Winslow Taylor developed the core ideas for *The Principles of Scientific Management* over a period of 20 or 30 years. And by 1911, when the book was published, he had a catalogue of examples that, when adapted for specific audiences, would prove the virtues of his theories.

On October 12, 1911, when he was the keynote speaker at the Conference of Scientific Management in Hanover, New Hampshire, he illustrated one of his key points with one of his favorite metaphors: the surgeon and the apprentice.

The finest mechanic in the world had developed scientific management long before we touched it or ever dreamed of it. You all know him, every one of you; he is the modern surgeon.

How does that finest mechanic teach his apprentices? Do you suppose that when the young surgeons come to their teachers, the skilled surgeons, they are told first of all: "Now, boys, what we want first is your initiative; we want you to use your brains and originality to develop the best methods of doing surgical work. Of course, you know, for example, when we are amputating a leg and come to the bone, we take a saw and cut the bone off... If you like it better, take an axe, take a hatchet, anything you please; what we want is originality. What we want of all things is originality on your part.

Now that surgeon says to his apprentices, "Not on your life. We do not want any of your originality until you know the best method of doing work that we know, the best method that is now known to modern surgery. So you just get busy and learn the best method that is known to date under modern surgery; then, when you have got to the top by the present method, invent upward; then use your originality."

Taylor's central point, of course, is that proper training, based on a rigorous foundation in best practice, is required before apprentices can make their own decisions. Put another way, there can be no freedom without discipline.

Effective training is a critical aspect of the Conductor & Orchestra archetype. It is necessary not only to transfer knowledge and understanding of these highly detailed tasks and precision in the work but also to identify people who will find it difficult (perhaps even impossible) to adjust to the culture of the unit. As the previous section made clear, the scripted tasks, and attention to detail of the orchestra mean membership is not for everyone. Proper orientation and training of each individual – including honesty and clear communication – will help build and maintain an orchestra that's a coherent whole.

———

Belief in training was one of the highest priorities for one of the founding fathers of the Toyota Production System, Taiichi Ohno.

In his book, *The Total Production System: Beyond Large-Scale Production*, he stated, "In this age, I am painfully aware of the fact that people tend to forget the need for training. Of course, if the skills to be learned are not creative or stimulating and if they do not require the best people, training may not seem worthwhile. But let's take a hard look at the world. No goal regardless of how small can be achieved without adequate training."

For Toyota, training doesn't simply happen through one, two or even three different channels. It's a hands-on, continuous experience, passed down from managers to workers every day by an osmosis-like process. This is reflected in the company's motto, "We don't just build cars, we build people." The intangible aspects of the training help to explain why the knowledge hasn't traveled all that well.

Harvard Business School professor, Steven Spear, encapsulated the problem in 1991 when he paraphrased a contact who said, "It's not that we don't want to tell you what TPS is, it's that we can't... But we can show you what TPS is." Toyota managers aren't just people who oversee employees; they are teachers who pass on knowledge and experience daily.

Spear explains how the continuous improvement philosophy runs through training and orientation, and is engrained in every aspect of workers' tasks. He states, "The team members, when they were first hired, were inex-

"

*The Conductor & Orchestra archetype
is built on attention to detail and consistent use
of standard processes*

"

perienced with, at best, an average high school education. The [first] hurdle was merely learning how to do the routine work for which they were responsible. Soon thereafter though, they learned how to immediately identify problems that occurred as they did their work. Then they learned how to do sophisticated root-cause analysis to find the underlying conditions that created the symptoms that they had experienced. Then they regularly practiced developing counter-measures – changes in work, tool, product, or process design – that would remove the underlying root causes."

What's interesting is that Spear is emphasizing the same progressive key themes as Taylor, only 90 years later. The Conductor & Orchestra archetype is built on attention to detail and consistent use of standard processes.

To achieve a state of real efficiency, fulfillment and/or productivity, orchestra members must first become experts in the basics. They must develop a solid foundation, reinforced by specific training that supports their daily tasks.

Before they play professionally, musicians, typically at a young age, must learn how to master their instruments. They must spend countless hours practicing – learning keys, scales, and then basic pieces. As they progress, they build on this foundation, honing their musicality, interpretation, and tone, as well as learning to play more complex pieces. Only then, once the basics and intermediate levels are mastered, can they use their own originality and inventiveness to become true virtuosi of their instruments.

People primarily join the orchestra to pursue their own personal interests.

Orchestra members like the rhythm of repetition; and they like knowing they can complete a narrow range of tasks to a high standard – possibly a higher standard than most other people. Their job, and the environment in which they work, enable them to achieve what they want in life; they enable them to make a living by doing what they do best.

Jose Antonio Abreu is in his early 70s. He is a stern-looking man, balding with a prominent forehead and bushy dark eyebrows. Thick square glasses perch on his rounded nose. He speaks commandingly and articulately, with gravitas and passion, and gesticulates for emphasis. There's something about him that you immediately respect just by hearing him speak – a certain depth, spirituality and wisdom.

Ever since he was child, Abreu wanted to be a musician. He dreamed of more than just his own personal musical fulfillment; he wanted to bring the "magic" of music to Venezuela, his homeland, believing that he could help alleviate the social problems that dogged the country.

In 1975, Abreu founded a national program, the Foundation for the National Network of Youth and Children Orchestras of Venezuela (Fesnojiv) or El Sistema (the System, as it's popularly known). Over the past 35 years, he has built a pathway for children from across Venezuela to grow up as part of an orchestra, contributing to their own personal development as well as the cultural growth of a nation.

Today, El Sistema is a national organization of 102 youth orchestras, 55 children's orchestras, and 270 music centers with more than 250,000 young musicians. But it's not its scale that's remarkable so much as the caliber and dedication of its members and the role it plays in their lives. The Simón Bolivar Youth Orchestra was recently recognized by *The Times* of London as one of the most dynamic and brilliant orchestras in the world. Its members are aged between 16 and 22, and all come from some of the poorest cities in Venezuela. Yet from the age of about four, these children commit themselves to a grueling rehearsal schedule of four-hour practices, six days a week.

The goal of the program is not to create an army of musical prodigies, but to enable generations of children to achieve their personal dreams through a disciplined and structured environment. Igor Lanz, the executive director

of the foundation behind the System, explains, "In an orchestra, everybody respects meritocracy, everybody respects tempo, everybody knows he has to support everyone else, whether he is a soloist or not. They learn that the most important thing is to work together in one common aim."

Under 7 percent of members leave the program – not bad for a country where the average school's drop-out rate for those aged 14 and over is 26.4 percent. Each member is there for a very specific reason: their own personal growth and fulfillment and the realization of an innate and special talent. In one of South America's most violent countries, where kidnappings and car-jackings are not uncommon, these teenagers are shown another way: discipline and structure to achieve their own personal dreams.

In his acceptance speech for a US Technology Entertainment Design (TED) award in 2009, Abreu said:

> In its essence, the orchestra and choir are much more than artistic structures, they are examples of schools of social life because to sing and to play together means to intimately coexist toward perfection and excellence, following a strict discipline of organization and coordination in order to seek harmonic interdependence of voices and instruments. That's how they build a spirit of solidarity and fraternity among them.

Conductors have the opportunity to develop individuals' talents and interests into something much bigger and more fulfilling by creating the right environment.

Research on child prodigies suggests exceptional musical abilities are a question of nurture as well as nature. Supporters of the Suzuki method, for example, believe that immersing children in a musical environment from a very early age will help develop advanced musical ability – in much the same way as growing up in a bilingual household will help them speak foreign languages. Creator of the Suzuki method, Shinichi Suzuki, stated, "More important than whether one is talented or not is a good environment in which a child will become talented…"

How is this relevant to the Conductor & Orchestra archetype? Conductors have the opportunity to develop individuals' talents and interests into something much bigger and more fulfilling by creating the right environment. (It may be helpful to think of the word "conducive" as well as the word "conductor" here.)

The Conductor & Orchestra model may often work toward goals such as efficiency and cost savings, but it's about matching the right conductor with the right orchestra. In the best pairings, the conductor sets the rules, and the members of the orchestra fully understand them, and are able, within that strict environment, to flourish.

Though not for everyone, the Conductor & Orchestra archetype supports its members and enables them to focus on achieving what they want in life – as long as their goals are aligned with those of the conductor.

There's a close relationship between compliance and incentives.

Orchestra members are rewarded for their ability to complete the specific tasks of their roles to the required standards. They must stick to the rules, and they must pay close attention to detail. In a culture that depends on precision, tools – such as incentives and penalties – are used to reinforce conformity.

Who likes Ryanair? Not many people. According to Trip Advisor, customers voted it the "world's least liked airline" in 2006. Passengers have complained about everything from cramped seating, unfriendly staff, delays, hidden fees, limited customer services and misleading advertising. *The Economist* states, "Ryanair has become a byword for appalling customer service… and jeering rudeness toward anyone or anything that gets in its way."

The company's obsession with the bottom line has raised eyebrows – and customers' blood pressure. Its idiosyncratic and "colorful" CEO, Michael O'Leary, seems to like nothing more than to be provocative. Speaking in 2009 about charging for use of the in-flight toilet, he said, "If someone wanted to pay £5 to go to the toilet I would carry them myself. I would wipe their bum for a fiver." He's already designed the stand-up "vertical seat" available on short-haul flights which will only cost about £5.

Despite this, Ryanair is Europe's biggest low-cost airline and continues to grow at more than 20 percent a year. In just over two decades, it's transformed itself into the third-largest airline in Europe in terms of passengers, carrying over 58 million people in 2008 alone. How has it done this? By giving customers what they most want: low prices.

In many ways, Ryanair takes the same approach as Southwest Airlines: frequent point-to-point flights on short-haul routes; one standard aircraft model; quick turnarounds to keep planes in operation. But it goes further. It's become so good at cutting out extraneous costs, the "frills", that people are – perhaps in spite of themselves – choosing it first. Think your boarding pass is a necessity? Think again: at Ryanair, it's a luxury.

Ryanair makes customers do what it wants them to do by offering them the incentive of ever lower fares.

Essentially, the Ryanair customer agrees to a trade-off: low-cost flight; no free service. This is not a company that aims to "surprise and delight" or offer people "experiences". The only "product differentiation" is the low fare.

Travel writer Damian Corrigan created a list of possible Ryanair "extras" that includes:

1. Boarding pass reprint fee: $60 per person.
2. Name change fee: $225 per person if paying at the airport.
3. Excess luggage fee: $30 per kilo.
4. Unusual hand luggage allowance: if you've already reached your checked-baggage allowance of 15kg and are forced to check in your 10kg hand luggage, you'll have to pay $300 to do so (€20 per kg).
5. Credit/debit card fee: $7.50 per person per flight.
6. Priority boarding fee: just $4.50 per person.
7. Flight change fee: if you can't board, you'll pay a $82.50 flight change fee and price difference.
8. Food and drink: a bottle of water costs $4.05.

Passengers could be charged up to an additional US$781.08. Ryanair uses the tactic of strong financial disincentives (penalties, in effect) to force employees and customers to stick to the rules. The last thing it wants to do is to encourage customers to follow practices that would slow down operations.

The fees are designed to change customer behavior: purchase tickets online, travel with carry-on luggage only, check in online and print boarding passes before you arrive and you'll be rewarded for being a "good" passenger. Do the opposite and you'll have to be punished.

Ryanair effectively controls customers through a disincentive system. But, despite the poor treatment and high fees, they keep coming back for more. No other airline beats it in terms of both passenger number and profitability. One passenger laments that, "Your only choice with Ryanair, really, is not to fly Ryanair. Your dignity goes out the window." But, if you can get a one-way flight from London to Dublin for $4.50, how can you complain?

––––––––––

Ryanair is defying all the marketing trends that say that customer service should be the number one priority. It also seems to contradict the received wisdom on "reputational damage." When the millionth Ryanair passenger, Jane O'Keeffe from Dublin, did not receive the free flights for life that she was promised, she took Ryanair to court. But O'Leary was typically cavalier, "For three days, we got the worst

publicity any company has ever had in its life. Our bookings soared by 30 percent, day by day, by day. The more we were in court, the bigger the bookings were."

The company has succeeded because it's been able to open up a new market for people who could not typically afford to pay for a flight in Europe. Thanks to the individuals who end up paying those exorbitant fees, it can even offer some tickets for free.

Ryanair pulls passengers' strings. Like a conductor, it creates a system of rules on which its model depends. Customers enjoy the reward of low fares if they comply; face the "punishment" of fees if they fail to toe the line. By encouraging the behaviors it wants through financial incentives, it makes sure its customers (orchestra members) understand and share its goals.

———

Thus, both personal and financial incentives can reinforce the orchestra's integrity – as well as its precision-driven culture. Members are rewarded for their ability to complete the specific tasks required of their role as well as their compliance with the rules and their attention to detail.

The most successful conductors, however, are those who understand their members' reasons for joining – and devise incentive programs and rewards accordingly.

Is Conductor & Orchestra the right model for you?

Is this archetype right for your current situation? And, if it is, how can you be the best conductor you can be? The following sections will help you answer these questions.

Great if:

- You require and value work of absolute precision and consistency.

- You believe that the division of labor and standardization of processes will lead to the lowest possible costs.

- The work of the people you manage only needs to be coordinated at a local level.

- Lives are at stake and safety procedures are the top priority.

- You have the time for extensive training and re-training and rehearsal (or the structure and culture of the organization mean knowledge is constantly being transferred to perfect performance).

Think twice if:

- Your organization is turning into a bureaucracy and its members are becoming bored or growing stale.

- Your operating model is being challenged by new, disruptive alternatives.

- You have set expectations that are different from the reality of what's on offer.

- Your training/support programs can't sustain the level of precision and consistency necessary.

How can you be a better conductor?

1. How detailed are your instructions to the orchestra?

It's important for conductors to identify the behaviors they expect of the orchestra. Orchestra members are typically focused on the completion of the tasks; while conductors provide the details on how tasks should be performed.

- How easy have you made it for members to understand the specific tasks and behaviors expected of them?
- How do you know whether or not they have learned the required tasks and behaviors; what's the evaluation method?
- How effective are you at communicating any required changes in behavior?

2. How clearly and consistently are you communicating with the orchestra, so that new members understand the detail of what's required?

Members need to be aware of the "script" when they begin their jobs; they need to understand and accept the strict environment in which they'll work. Failure to communicate clearly and consistently during recruitment and induction stages wastes time and money. Members will leave if the culture of the orchestra comes as a surprise and they're asked to work in an entirely alien environment.

- How effective is your recruiting program in identifying those who fit your culture – and those who don't?
- What tactics are you using to ensure new recruits are comfortable with the rigidity of the rules?
- Are you sending messages that set the wrong expectations – or contradict your standards for tasks and behaviors?

3. How effective are your induction programs at helping people to learn at initiation?

The orchestra must perform repetitive and detailed tasks to perfection. Extensive training and "onboarding" are needed to lay a strong cultural foundation. Members must be helped to make the transition into the structured environment.

- Are you evaluating members' behavior before and after induction to test the program?
- Do you use a "buddying" scheme to help new members integrate and become part of the culture?
- Is there a planned response to members who are not adapting well?

4. How tightly linked are incentives to objectives?

Incentives and rewards must be aligned to the desired behaviors. Individuals who thrive in these rigid environments need absolute clarity on how the incentive system will work.

- How effective is your incentive program across different roles?
- Have you successfully created a culture that rewards specific behaviors and adherence to defined tasks?
- How are you evaluating your incentive programs?

5. How well-defined are career paths and opportunities for promotion?

The "boredom factor" that comes with repetitive work and the performance of specific tasks needs to be countered by the knowledge that there's a chance to progress. Upward career paths motivate members by giving them the hope of more challenging and rewarding roles.

- Are your career paths broad and deep enough to make members feel their ambitions will be fulfilled?
- Are there enough steps on the paths or levels in the hierarchy?
- Do you have a plan to accommodate individuals who do not wish to follow the standard career path?

6. How quickly can you disseminate important "news" to members?

Any changes to the script and the detailed processes must be efficiently and clearly broadcast to all members so that they can start performing the new tasks immediately.

- How efficient and effective are your channels of communication?
- Are you able to broadcast messages to the whole orchestra at the same time?
- Do you spend enough time "face to face" with frontline staff?

7. Is the environment you've created so rigid that it prevents you from adapting to environmental changes?

The structure of the organization must be robust enough to work effectively but flexible enough to move with the times. The members of the orchestra have very specialized skills, and it can be difficult to re-train them quickly.

- Do you think your organization has become too rigid?
- What's the mechanism for ensuring the orchestra can adapt to environmental changes?
- What's the plan for responding to changes that force a review of your current operating model?

Chapter 4

Producer & Creative Team

"It's a creative process and everybody contributes ... that's what filmmaking is, collaboration"

—*Jerry Bruckheimer on producing a movie*

" He's always trying to capture lightning in a bottle. He gets you in a state where everyone's charging and electric together "

Jerry Bruckheimer: The Man with the Golden Gut

Jerome Leon Bruckheimer was born on September 21, 1945, and grew up in Detroit, Michigan, the only child of lower-middle class German Jewish immigrants. Quiet and conservative as a child, he dreamed of becoming a photographer, and developed a love of cameras and film through hand-me-downs from his uncle.

Mild dyslexia made school life difficult at first; photography awards from Kodak and National Scholastics at high school compensated. In the early 1960s, he moved to Arizona to go to college and, in 1965, graduated with a degree in psychology. There was no doubt, however, where his métier lay. In an interview with Michael Shelden in London's *Daily Telegraph*, he's quoted as saying, "I knew I had to get into the movie business. I loved it. I wasn't going to be an actor or director. That didn't matter. Somehow, I had to be a part of the thing I loved."

He returned to Detroit to start a career in advertising and ended up working on an award-winning Pontiac commercial. He caught the attention of executives at a high-profile agency, and they lured him to New York, where he slowly worked his way up to producing commercials.

From advertising into film

In New York, Bruckheimer met aspiring film-maker, Dick Richards, and, after four years with the agency, decided to move to Los Angeles to work with him on the Western *The Culpepper Cattle Co.* After a couple more films, he began working with director Paul Schrader, making the commercially successful *American Gigolo* and *Cat People* in the early 1980s.

By this stage, however, he'd already formed the association that would change his professional life. In 1973, aged 28, he had met Don Simpson, then a publicist for Warner Brothers, at a screening of *The Harder They Come.* Things were going well for him in his career – he had just wrapped up *The Culpepper Cattle Co.* – but his personal life was in trouble. Going through a divorce and needing a place to stay, he moved into Simpson's large house in Laurel Canyon. It was the start of a friendship that, ten years later, would turn into a formidable professional partnership.

Founded in 1982, Don Simpson/Jerry Bruckheimer Productions was one of the first production companies to aggressively develop a recognizable brand. It took more control over its films and built a reputation for guaranteed –

somewhat formulaic – hits. *Flashdance, Top Gun, Beverly Hills Cop, Days of Thunder,* and *Crimson Tide* were all from the Simpson/Bruckheimer stable.

As their string of successes lengthened, Paramount gave them "several hundred million dollars in financing, a large cut of the box office" and more or less the freedom to make whatever films they wanted.

Bruckheimer's and Simpson's personalities complemented each other. The larger-than-life, fast-talking Simpson had the creative ideas; the more understated, serious Bruckheimer was the businessman who made them happen. It was a partnership that seemed perfect. So perfect in fact that when Simpson died of a drug overdose in 1996 some predicted the end of Brukheimer's career.

The Bruckheimer brand

But Bruckheimer bounced back. Taking even greater control of his production company, he honed his brand. Some describe his "signature" style as "a mixture of explosive action, heartfelt sentiment, dazzling techno-magic and an uncanny sense of anticipating the zeitgeist of American culture." Bruckheimer seems to prefer a more prosaic description. "It is," he says, "about good entertainment… whether it's a car chase or whether it's a hard-hitting story about a true individual… we're gonna tell you stories that are impactful and moving and grab your attention."

Today, Bruckheimer is one of the most powerful men in the entertainment industry. His nicknames include Mr Hollywood, the Megaproducer, and the Man with Golden Gut. As the head of Jerry Bruckheimer Films, he's worked with directors such as Michael Bay and Ridley Scott and actors such as Nicholas Cage and Johnny Depp. *Armageddon, Pearl Harbor, Black Hawk Down, The Prince of Persia, The Sorcerer's Apprentice,* the *Pirates of the Caribbean* and the *National Treasure* series are all his work.

Bruckheimer's logo shows lightning striking a tree with the background of a cloudy gray sky. It is, according to Cage, a fitting image. "He's always trying to capture lightning in a bottle ... He gets [people] together whom he trusts and keeps you in a state ... where everyone's charging and electric together. Then he captures it."

In 2000, Bruckheimer did what few could have predicted. He crossed over into television, producing a record ten shows in 2005, including *CSI* and its spinoffs, *CSI:NY* and *CSI: Miami, Cold Case,* and the reality hit, *Amazing Race.* "Jerry Bruckheimer," said CBS chairman and CEO Leslie Moonves in 2003, "has gone from being a man who had no presence in television to being the No. 1 supplier of network programming ... It really is quite remarkable."

Bruckheimer is widely considered the most commercially successful producer ever, with revenues from his films topping $14 billion.

Working for Mr Blockbuster

Known for his work ethic, Bruckheimer rolls up his sleeves to support his team. At the same time, though, he places absolute trust in his directors. One of the writers on the *Pirates of the Caribbean* saga, Terry Rossio, says, "Jerry gave [director] Gore such freedom, and Gore was confident enough with his ideas that he had no problem being collaborative."

The technicalities of film making are not Bruckheimer's thing. But he does get involved in the details. Everything, he says, crosses his desk. It's a balance of trust and control. Of TV production, he says, "Even though I read every episode and watch every episode, they run their own businesses." He adds, "I don't get involved in the technical aspects, but I get involved in the other creative areas."

Despite the frenetic pace of his business – his team juggles between 35 and 45 projects at one time – and the colossal scale of his productions,

Bruckheimer always seems to stay calm. Some describe him as having a Zen-like quality: quiet confidence and patience. Jordan Mechner, creator of *Prince of Persia*, says, "I can see why the studios feel confident entrusting him with hundreds of millions of dollars. If he's making the movie, everything's gonna be OK."

Excellence begets excellence

Producers are big-picture thinkers who provide the freedom for their teams to be creative, while exerting enough control to get the project done. They are the invisible hands back stage. From finding a good script to securing financing to casting the right actors and working with distributors, the film and TV producer co-ordinates every step, brings together hundreds of individuals and, literally and metaphorically, sets the stage. Bruckheimer can feel confident because he surrounds himself with the best talent possible.

He says, "We always try to populate our movies with great talent. Excellence begets excellence, and with every additional actor we signed, the bar just moved higher and higher ... I don't insist on things. You stand on your work and ... they might listen to you a little more, but it's a creative process ... It's like a piece of clay and everybody gets their hands on and molds it. That's what film-making is."

Cirque du Soleil
Nothing short of magic

Cirque du Soleil calls auditions treasure hunting because you never know what kind of talent you'll find. Performers come in many shapes and sizes: tall, thin, and wiry; short, stocky, and muscular. The mix is always eclectic, always multinational.

Throughout the year, auditions are held for musicians, singers, clowns, athletes, circus performers, and other artists. This time, the "hopefuls" are dancers. Once the judges have approved the performers' résumés, photos, and 15-minute videos, they've passed the preliminary screening. They are then called for the all-day audition. You don't need specific circus experience to make it as a Cirque performer – but technical precision, stage presence, and versatility are high on the list. Dancers must perform first in a group and then in pairs.

The judges know what they're looking for, and eliminations begin. During the second and third parts of the audition, dancers are required to perform a solo to show off their personal strengths as well as learn and perform choreography from one of the Cirque shows. But this isn't your traditional ballroom dancing class. There are hip hop street dancers, belly dancers, Brazilian capoeira artists, trained Russian ballet dancers, break dancers, even jugglers-cum-acrobats.

By the end of the day, all are required to break out of their "dancer" mold to demonstrate their range across acting, improvisation, and singing. The day is grueling. And even if you have the talent to be one of the last dancers standing, you're not guaranteed a spot in a Cirque show. Your name is added to a databank and, if there are openings for specific roles that match your talent, you may be lucky enough to get cast in a future production.

For the few really talented ones, the Cirque du Soleil initiation has just begun. Several months can pass before a dancer ever gets to don the amazing costumes and see the audiences and the bright lights. That's because the induction process is one of the most important aspects of the Cirque du Soleil magic,

where regular people are transformed into fantastical artists of almost superhuman strength and grace.

A very different vision

The magic and creativity that happens every night on a Cirque stage has been more than 25 years in the making. After years of dazzling crowds on the streets of Europe and Quebec as a teenager, Cirque founder Guy Laliberté approached the Quebec government to help sponsor a show called Cirque du Soleil (Circus of the Sun) in 1984. But Laliberté's vision of the circus was going to be very different. He would mix street entertainment with circus arts, acts of athleticism, costume, and music.

After a series of ups and downs, Laliberté took a major gamble by booking an act for the opening of the Los Angeles Arts Festival. He says, "I bet everything on that one night... If we failed, there was no cash for gas to come home." Fortunately, the show was a huge hit. The risk paid off and paved Cirque's path to success.

In 1984, Cirque had 73 employees and a single show. Today, over two decades later, it has 20 shows around the world across five continents, such as *Mystère*, *Dralion*, *KOOZA*, *"O,"* *OVO*, *Saltimbanco*, *Allegria*, *Love* (based on the music of The Beatles), *Corteo*, *Quidam*, and a new vaudeville act, *Banana Shpeel*. A team of 4,000 employees represents 40 nationalities, speaking 25 different languages. Each person brings something new from their own culture to the creative process. Lyn Heward, former president, creative content division, states, "Brazilian percussion and capoeira, Australian didgeridoo, Ukrainian and Africa dancing, Wushu, Peking Opera and Kung Fu have all found their way into our multidisciplinary shows."

There is no "cookie cutter" approach to Cirque – the combined work of the performers, directors, and backstage crew add up to a show that's never been seen before. Multiculturalism, peace, mythology, joy or isolation, power, water, color, burlesque, martial arts, and vaudeville – the endless list of Cirque's themes toys with the imagination.

From concept to stage

The success of Cirque du Soleil, however, is not based on unbridled creativity. The diverse team brings a wealth of creative ideas to the initial development phase, but thereafter it's about discipline and hard work. Taking a production from concept to stage takes years. *Kà* – showing at the MGM Grand in Las Vegas – took four years and cost $165 million to conceive, cast, design, train, and produce.

First, the theme is created. Sometimes it emerges from the staff themselves; sometimes it's suggested by Laliberté himself. For *Kà*, Laliberté instructed creator Robert Lepage to craft an epic tale that included martial arts – a form no other Cirque show had yet explored.

When working with artists to develop a concept, the frame of reference can be broad. Acrobat "mentor" André Simard says: "I try to use a personal approach with every artist to bring out his or her own energy ... We can't close any doors. Instead, we let ourselves go and join in the adventure." Once there, though, personal energy is harnessed, used to transform performers into characters on stage. The creativity, theme, music, and costumes provide the context for the visual adventure; the performers provide the "life."

Cirque has more than 20,000 artists in its databank who wish to be performers, and over half of the recruits are gymnasts. But Cirque scouts don't just go after dancers, gymnasts or athletes. Their huge list is said to include "24 giants, 23 whistlers, 466 contortionists, 14 pickpockets, 35 skateboarders, 1,278 clowns, eight dislocation artists, and 73 people classified simply as small." They have even had a 7-foot tall, 400-pound Argentinian opera singer, a septuagenarian Danish husband-and-wife acrobatic team, and an acrobat from Brazil, who stands 3-feet-10 inches tall.

Recruitment

To achieve a combination of athletic and artistic perfection, they often recruit the near-great and accomplished athletes who have competed in the Olympics or World Championships teams. Twenty-one of the approximately 1,000 Cirque du Soleil performers are former Olympians; two won gold medals in synchronized swimming. From this basis, Cirque can transform both the athletes' exceptional technical skill and drive to succeed and create circus magic.

Gathered from around the world, these special performers are pushed to their limits, learning their craft for up to four months before a performance. Although auditions are demanding, people are not hired for who they are, but for what they may become. Transformation is the key. Heward states, "Creative transformation is the most important doorway for us. We're trying to find the 'pearl,' the hidden talent in that individual. What is the unique thing that person brings?"

At Cirque, it's all about spontaneity, creativity, imagination and risk taking – not always qualities associated with Olympic athletes. Many gymnasts, athletes, and dancers come from competitive environments where individual excellence, instead of team work, is reinforced. Boris Verkhovsky, Cirque head coach and trainer notes, "A lot of athletes come from an environment where they are literally told when to inhale and when to exhale."

Training

Before stepping on stage, performers must complete an intense multi-stage training and immersion program to hone their acrobatics, artistic performance, and, importantly, their team skills.

With new productions constantly being developed and a high annual attrition rate of 20 percent, a key to Cirque's success has been the ability to recruit, train, and replace injured or retiring performers. Scouts from Cirque's recruiting team are constantly on the lookout globally for talent – many of them dedicated to specific skills. Cirque has a trainer who scouts out talent in the Mongolian State Circus where they specialize in contortionists. Athletes who

"

People are not hired for who they are, but for what
they may become. Transformation is the key

"

haven't achieved the medal are good targets – the scouts are constantly at Olympic and World Championship competitions. Talented gymnasts and dancers are being sought from around the world to support the creative machine that is Cirque du Soleil.

At training "boot camps," new recruits are, over the course of many weeks, pushed to their limits. Cirque's mission: "Turn athletes into artists and form a cohesive team of brothers."

The immersion program not only hones performers' technical skills, but also develops their understanding of and connection with their roles. Cirque's long-time stage director, Franco Dragone, aims to get beneath the stereotypes and self-parodies that often dog young performers. It's a visceral exercise to bring forth the raw emotion and discovery of the character, and has been described as being "like peeling an onion to get to the sweet, intense core." Another Cirque analogy is that of Michelangelo's David: the sculptor simply revealed a figure who already existed within the stone.

More than 90 million spectators around the world have seen a Cirque show. In 2008, Cirque had sales of $733 million. In a poll of brands with the most global impact, Cirque ranked twenty-second – ahead of McDonald's, Microsoft, and Disney. Productions have captured the imaginations of children and adults in Japan, Brazil, Canada, China, the US, Barcelona, Russia, Mexico, and Dubai. Live music, costumes, mood, and stunning visuals are used to transcend global boundaries and language barriers to transport audiences to another world.

Through the creativity and vision of the production team, and the grace, strength and flexibility of the people on stage, Cirque continues to enthrall audiences each and every night. And whether the company is recruiting contortionists in Mongolia, martial arts experts in China, or fire jugglers from Brazil, one thing is clear: the way it transforms athletes into performers while continuously reinventing the medium of the circus is nothing short of magic.

Key characteristics of Producer & Creative Team

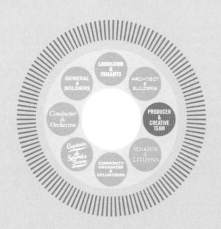

The Producer & Creative Team archetype sits firmly on the creative axis. An open culture of collaboration allows a team of independent-minded, highly skilled individuals to focus on free expression and come up with innovative concepts and solutions. The hands-off producer has the big idea and sees the big picture, and he or she help guide the team – but the product emerges through a natural creative process. The freedom to voice opinions and dissent is critical to developing the idea and finding the best solution.

Producers articulate an overall objective or idea; the creative team, made up of the right people with the right chemistry, brings it to life.

 Members are recruited not only because they excel at what they do but also because they complement the rest of the team.

 The creative team is given complete freedom to express ideas.

 Success is measured by the ability to innovate as well as by the ability to match the original objective.

 Dissent is used to push the creative boundaries of the team.

 The creative team collaborates closely: discussions will be intense; communications continuous.

Producers articulate an overall objective or idea; the creative team, made up of the right people with the right chemistry, brings it to life.

Producers ensure that the best people are involved with the project and they create the right conditions and creative environment. They allow something to happen, they are the agents of an idea, but they do not hold a tight rein over the creative team. In fact, the creative team often seeks a healthy separation or distance from the producer.

John Lasseter was just 25-years-old when he started at Walt Disney Studios. But his love for animated characters began when he was five years old. Of course, his mother, a high school art teacher, encouraged his artistic abilities and would bring home various art supplies to keep young John busy. When he was five-years-old, John won $15 in a grocery store contest for a crayon drawing of the Headless Horseman.

Interested in animation throughout high school, Lasseter enrolled at the California Institute of Arts and learned techniques from the Disney masters alongside classmates such as Brad Bird, Tim Burton and John Musker.

After graduation, in 1982, he began a job with Disney Studios as an animator and admits he wasn't the best pencil-and-paper draftsman. He found the overall experience, "a crushing disappointment."

Lasseter felt like the studios weren't taking advantage of the technology innovations and simply used technology to make processes more efficient. After seeing the computer-generated effects for the movie *Tron*, he created a short demo using similar innovative animation processes. Unfortunately, his ideas were shot down and ten minutes later he was fired.

He left Disney to work at Lucasfilm in 1986 and six months later, Steve Jobs purchased the department and renamed it Pixar.

Lasseter's first big break came with his involvement on a script about "a personality conflict between toys that come to life when neglected by their human master," which became the blockbuster hit *Toy Story*. It cost approximately $30 million to make and ended up bringing in over $360 million worldwide.

Lasseter has been the director on *A Bug's Life* and *Toy Story 2*, and the executive producer on *Monsters, Inc., Finding Nemo, Ratatouille* and *The Incredibles*. Though his title is Chief Creative Officer of both Disney and Pixar, he's been called the Man Who Could Save Animation, the Creative Engine behind the Pixar Hit Machine, the Animation Guru. Gaby Wood, former writer for the *Observer*, describes Lasseter as "almost single-handedly turning cartoons from Saturday morning TV fodder to one of the biggest money makers in the film industry." Not too shabby a feat considering "the world's most preposterously imaginative geek" was ahead of Oprah Winfrey and the Dalai Lama on *Newsweek's* 2008 year-end compilation of the "Global Elite."

—

Making a film is a long and tedious process filled with tens of thousands of ideas; not just how the characters look, what they say, and how they talk. But behind it all, the movie is created by a team that includes lighting experts, make-up artists, sound producers and script writers. Hundreds of technical experts are needed to create a movie, but they all need to be held together by the creative idea of the producer.

How many producers can you name? Chances are, not very many. Their names will sound familiar; take for example, Frank Marshall, David Selznick, George Lucas, and Harvey Weinstein. They are some of the most powerful people in Hollywood, but you can't quite pinpoint what they do. Movie producers aren't as well-known or visible as actors and directors, and that's because they are often working their magic behind the scenes. So while the film industry often plays up the director's role, it's really the producer that wields the ultimate creative control.

David Wolper, the American producer best known for *The Thorn Birds* and *LA Confidential* said:

> A producer is a man with a dream. I say, "I don't write, I don't direct, I don't act, I don't compose music, I don't design costumes. What do I do? I make things happen." A producer is like a chef. You get all the right ingredients together and make a tasty stew. You put the wrong ingredients together, it'll taste bad."

But what exactly is it about Pixar's DNA that has allowed it to become, movie for movie, the most successful studio in the history of cinema? Ed Catmull, president of Disney Studios and Pixar states, "Creativity involves a large number of people from different disciplines working

> "
>
> *It's not necessarily about getting the people that have*
> *the most impressive credentials, but more about getting*
> *the right people to create the best team possible*
>
> "

together to solve a great many problems... Every single member of the 200- to 250-person production group makes suggestions. Creativity must be present at every level of every artistic and technical part of the organization."

Another part of the magic of Producer & Creative Team is getting the chemistry of the team just right. It's not necessarily about getting the people that have the most impressive credentials, but more about getting the right people to create the best team possible. In his book, *So You Want to be a Producer*, Larry Thurman, producer of the award-winning movie *The Graduate* writes, "Hire the very best people. They will make your picture better, and they will make your life better."

Producers have an extremely important role not only in establishing the overall clear idea and objective for the direction of their movie but also in creating the right conditions and creative environment for the team to work success-

fully together. They also ensure that the best people are involved and must be very selective about who is on their creative team. The team needs to have the right skills across a broad range of specialties, but more important, they must have the right mix of personalities and characteristics to make the movie a success.

What makes Lasseter a producer? Since his time working at Disney, Lasseter had the creative genius and understanding of what makes a successful animated film. Both he and Catmull have been able to home in on the best talent and build the best team with the right skills to make Pixar the legendary animation studio it is today.

Pixar is a remarkable example of how creativity can drive amazing results, but it's not just that their people and ideas are better than its competitors, their unique chemistry, culture, and how they work together lays the foundation for creating real movie magic.

Members are recruited not only because they excel at what they do but also because they complement the rest of the team.

Each member brings a special or unique skill to achieve the objectives of the producer: they are experts in their fields. But there must be sufficient diversity and breadth of skills across the creative team.

In 1910, Dr William J. Mayo, one of the iconic founders of the Mayo Clinic told the graduating class of Rush Medical College:

> The sum total of medical knowledge is now so great ... that it would be futile for any one man ... to assume that he has even a working knowledge of any part of the whole ... The best interest of the patient is the only interest to be considered, and in order that the sick may have the benefit of advancing knowledge, union of forces is necessary... It has become necessary to develop medicine as a cooperative science; the clinician, the specialist, and the laboratory workers uniting for the good of the patient, each assisting in elucidation of the problem at hand, and each dependent upon the other for support."

A century later, ask any physician, nurse, or staff member at the Mayo Clinic what they are there to do and they will likely refer to this Mayo mantra, "the best interest of the patient is the only interest to be considered." Simple and to the point, this core principle drives every strategy, policy, process, and decision made by the hospital and its employees. When Drs Charles H. and William J. Mayo conceived the Mayo Clinic, they envisaged physicians of

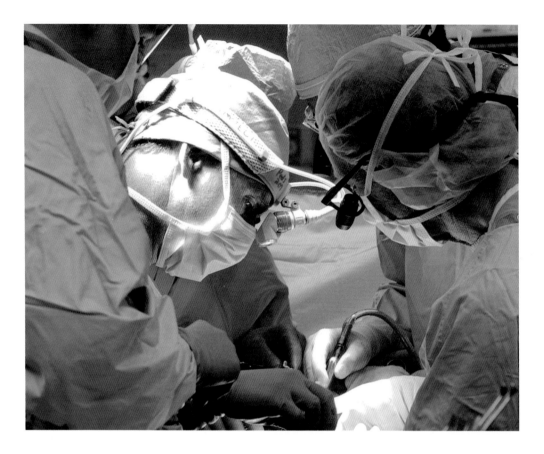

many specialties working collaboratively with only the interests of their patients to consider.

Today the Mayo Clinic is ranked as one of the best hospitals in the US with a staff of almost 55,000 representing nearly every medical discipline, and more than 520,000 people visiting annually from around the world.

Part of their success is due to the top talent they attract as it is one of the most coveted hospitals in the world at which to work. Mayo's physicians are predominately "home-grown," often coming up through the Mayo med school, indoctrinated in the patient-centric "Mayo way" right from the beginning. Since its inception, Mayo's model of integrated care is based on a multidisciplinary practice and supportive infrastructure.

Take for example the case of Martha, a woman in her late 30s who was diagnosed with breast cancer. Martha was referred by her primary physician to an oncologist at the Mayo Clinic. In turn, this oncologist assembled a team of specialists whom she selected based on the nature of the problem, their skills and experience, and the patient's preferences. It included a surgeon, a radiation oncologist, a radiologist, as well as the patient's primary care physician. They worked closely with Martha to ensure she understood the rationale behind their recommended decision.

As it turned out, Martha did not agree with their surgical decision, and wanted to explore other options. So they replaced the existing surgeon on the team with another who had a different skill set, and therefore might be able to contribute to an alternative recommendation.

This is the "Mayo way," and there are no hurt egos or potential losses of reward. It's all about doing what is best for the patient. Sometimes that means that a team must be expanded – or taken apart and reassembled. Each team member bringing a diverse and specialized skill set to diagnose the problem.

At Mayo, everything revolves around the doctor–patient relationship. By working directly with the patient to identify the issues, bringing in specialists to assess the holistic situation, and involving the patients' needs and interests in the process, the Mayo way helps improve both patient experience and recovery rates. And although new equipment, surgical techniques, and drugs are important, the real differentiator between success and quality of the treatment is that intangible aspect called the "Mayo experience."

Why is the Mayo Clinic part of the Producer & Creative Team archetype? Doctors at the clinic follow a clear overriding objective: the best interest of the patient is the only interest to be considered. And though other healthcare institutions may claim to follow a similar patient-centric model, few can replicate the essence behind the Mayo way. Chuck Salter from *Fast Company* writes, "Dr Charlie and Dr Will founded their rural group practice in the late 1800s around a new concept at the time: integrated medical care, which involved various specialists working together in the same building, performing comprehensive evaluations, and administering coordinated treatment."

As with the Mayo Clinic, each member of the creative team brings a special or unique skill to the table. They are experts within their domain; they know their trade and can apply their expertise to achieve the objectives of the producer. So while individual excellence of each team member is crucial, the most successful producers know that there must be sufficient diversity and breadth of skill across the team.

The creative team is given complete freedom to express ideas.

Creativity cannot be forced. Producers set guidelines, but allow team members sufficient freedom to apply their individual and collective skills.

One of Walt Disney's earliest memories was of moving to rural Marceline, Missouri from Chicago. It was 1908 and he was four-years-old. His father had bought "a very cute, sweet little farm with a beautiful front yard and lots of weeping willow trees."

Disney didn't start at school until he was almost eight-years-old. As a child, his neighbors and relatives would encourage him to draw. An older neighbor in his 70s, Doc Sherwood gave him a nickel to draw a picture of his horse. Disney often spoke fondly of his childhood in Marceline, but due to his father's illness, they sold the farm in 1910 and moved to Kansas City in 1911 where Disney entered second grade at the Benton School that fall.

To make extra money, Disney and his brother, Roy would wake up at 4:30am to deliver newspapers on their two neighborhood routes. His teachers often complained that Disney would fall asleep during class and that he spent too much time day dreaming and doodling rather than focusing on lessons. One day, Disney's fourth-grade teacher asked the class to draw a bowl of flowers. Disney's page had flowers with human faces, and waving arms instead of leaves. Frustrated by what she thought was poor listening skills, the teacher chastised Disney saying that flowers do not have faces and that the purpose of the assignment was to draw a still life. As you can guess, Disney didn't listen to her rules and continued to draw faces on his flowers well beyond his childhood years.

As children, we are constantly reminded of boundaries. Can you imagine if Disney had listened to his teacher? The world wouldn't have had the opportunity to experience what Disney called "one of the greatest mediums of fantasy and entertainment yet developed."

Similarly creativity cannot have rigid boundaries and it cannot be forced. This is one of the key attributes that producers use to empower their creative team. Instead of second guessing or micro managing the creative team's activities, producers present guidelines for working; they trust the creative team's judgment and allow them to do what they do best while providing feedback to hone their progress.

Take for example one of the most iconic producers in history, George Lucas. It was 1976.

Lucas was 32-years-old, and at the end of his rope. For the past five months, he had been trying to finish filming *Star Wars: Episode IV – A New Hope*. Twentieth Century Fox gave Lucas only three days to complete two weeks of work. To get the most out of his last three days, Lucas hired three film crews and created three sets to film continuously in parallel. And though he completed the remaining shoots within the allotted three days, Lucas was exhausted and was eventually hospitalized.

That was a pivotal moment for him and Lucas decided he was going to step back from directing. For *Episode IV*, he had conceived the plot, written, directed, and produced it, but knew that he had to relinquish directorial control. "That's when I really confirmed to myself that I was going to change," Lucas said. "I wasn't going to direct anymore. I was going to get my life a bit more under control."

So Lucas entrusted his vision to his one-time professor, Irvin Kershner, to direct the highly anticipated sequel, *Episode V: The Empire Strikes Back*. Kershner's direcorial style focused on character development, attention to detail, and his easy way with actors was a refreshing divergence from *Episode IV's* cinematic style.

From the beginning, *Empire* was fraught with numerous challenges including a fire at the studios in England and blizzards and avalanches in Norway which hampered filming of the opening Hoth scenes. The film even ran out of money just prior to the end of shooting and Lucas ended up borrowing an additional $3.5 million from Fox to complete filming.

Despite the complications, Lucas kept his promise to not get as involved in the day-to-day directorial details. Known for his controlling nature, Lucas had to trust Kershner to inject his own unique perspective into *Empire* yet remain true to his overall concept.

Throughout the filming, Lucas was heard promising Kershner, "It's going to be *your* picture." He kept to that promise and continued to support Kershner. And even when the film went over budget; Lucas would say, "Don't change a thing! Keep going as you're going."

As difficult as it may have been for Lucas to sit back and let go, it may have been one of the best decisions for Lucas, Kershner, and Twentieth Century Fox. He said, "I thought I'd stand back and see how everything falls apart because I'm not there. And it didn't." Many movie critics believe that *Empire* is the best in the *Star Wars* saga. It made over $10 million in its first weekend and went on to become the highest grossing film of the year.

Within three months, Lucas turned a profit and as a testament to the quality of the film, when the studio rereleased a special edition of the trilogy in 1997, *Empire* required the fewest alterations.

———————

Giving up creative control as a producer isn't always easy, but the most successful ones are able to create a supportive environment that enables their team to express their creativity. The producer has hired his or her technical teams for a reason: they have the skills needed to deliver on the producer's overall movie idea. And while the direction and process that the creative team takes may be different from what the producer had in mind, providing the creative team with the freedom to work can produce amazing results. And sometimes even the producer can be surprised by the outcomes that the creative team delivers.

4

Success is measured by the ability to innovate as well as by the ability to match the original objective.

The challenge for the creative team is to satisfy the objectives of the producer in an imaginative and original way. Derivative or copycat work seldom gets the producer and creative team noticed. To last in their industry, they must continuously come up with new and innovative ideas.

After the success of *Toy Story* in 1995 and Disney's acquisition of Pixar in 2006, Lasseter and Catmull had a brilliant idea. Their goal wasn't just to create one successful full-length computer-animated film, but to build a team that could continually produce a string of animated blockbusters long after they and Pixar's members of the "brain trust" (creative leaders, such as Andrew Stanton, Brad Bird, Pete Docter, Bob Peterson, Brenda Chapman, Lee Unkrich, Gary Rydstrom, and Brad Lewis) were gone.

Both Catmull and Lasseter wanted to change the structure of the film-making process at Pixar from "an executive-led studio" such as that at Disney to a "filmmaker-led studio." Lasseter explains, "[Previously] there were layers of executives – the development executive would come up with the idea for the film, a lot of it based on marketing and toys and all that stuff, then they would assign a director to each film." Catmull and Lasseter, both agreed they wanted to develop a culture where the filmmakers drive the vision and "really own the movie."

To do that, talent couldn't reside solely within the leadership team. Lasseter and Catmull's concept was based on bringing together the most talented group of directors who were brimming with creative ideas. They would then get them to commit to long-term success of their ideas by giving them the creative license to make their own unique visions come to life. In essence, the new idea allowed the directors to own their ideas and become vested in their realization – even though the concpt went against the grain of then-CEO Michael Eisner's strategy that no new films would be made using the classic Disney hand-drawn techniques.

But the two Pixar co-founders believed that the directors should have the creative control both over the type of animination used, as well as over the entire movie-making process. Claudia Eller from the *Los Angeles Times* wrote of Catmull, "He's empowered the production teams to set their own schedules, manage budgets and control all other aspects of the filmmaking process. Most important, he's entrusted them to solve their own problems."

To maintain, if not exceed this level of success, the Pixar leads made another rather controversial but brilliant hiring decision with reputed troublemaker Brad Bird. After three hits, *Toy Story*, *A Bug's Life*, and *Toy Story 2*, Lasseter and Catmull wanted to make sure they weren't getting too comfortable following a set "template." They wanted to shake things up and make sure that fresh ideas were being brought in to the mix. So they hired Bird who recalls, "I had been fired for rocking the boat, never hired for rocking the boat." Bird may have been an interesting choice at the time, but he added a whole new dimension to Pixar's computer-generated animation bringing never-seen-before details to the characters and the sets of *The Incredibles*.

When selecting his technical team Bird had only one request, he said, "Give us the 'black sheep.' I want artists who are frustrated. Give us all the guys who are probably headed out the door." It was the exact creative injection that Pixar needed. And in the end, despite the risky investment in the "black sheep," *The Incredibles* cost Pixar less per minute than any of its previous films while unbelievably having three times the number of sets.

In their book, *Innovate the Pixar Way*, Bill Capodagli and Lynn Jackson state, "Pixar is in perpetual motion, always exploring the world through a child's eyes of wonder. Creativity at its best means beginning each new project with a clean slate – not resting on one's laurels of past accomplishments. It's all about chasing a dream that is fresh and exciting – not driven by any formula – leading the company by those most important intangible measurements."

There is a timeless quality to Pixar's outputs that transcend age, language and culture. As a producer, Pixar's leadership is able to draw on their proven track record of success but continuously produce new and innovative ideas to ensure their longevity within their respective industries. For the archetype, the ability to bring new and fresh ideas to the world is paramount. These types of organizations' creativity appear infinite as new productions continue to exceed previous successes, raising the bar higher with each and every release. The most successful producers are able to channel their creative team's innovation and build on their successes while drawing on their diverse teams' expertise and staying true to their overall vision.

Dissent is used to push the creative boundaries of the team.

The creative team must be free-thinking. Challenge and dissent must be encouraged. Different perspectives and views can help generate bigger and better ideas. Stimulating discussion should always be preferred to simple agreement.

Working at Bridgewater Associates is not for the faint of heart. Ray Dalio (pictured below left), the global investment company's founder, will be the first to tell you. He's known for driving a hard culture; one that's open, honest, and fair, but demanding and confrontational. And Dalio isn't shy to tell the world, "If you are thin-skinned and don't like conflict or criticism, you should be somewhere else."

The controversial corporate culture is the ultimate meritocracy. The company's philosophy is rooted in "the pursuit of excellence at all costs" and provides employees with the opportunity to prove themselves. Founded in 1975 out of Dalio's spare bedroom, Bridgewater eliminates the hierarchy and stuffiness associated with traditional firms. And over the years, it has become one of the most successful hedge funds in the world, no doubt in part due to its unique and "debatable" corporate culture.

In 2008, 70 percent of hedge funds lost money, with the average fund falling 18 percent. Bridgewater's flagship hedge fund, Pure Alpha, was the exception and generated a return of 14 percent. In fact, Bridgewater has never suffered an annual loss greater than 2 percent. It even correctly predicted the meltdown of the American financial institutions in July 2008.

And while shrinking violets need not apply, there is merit in this meritocracy. Bridgewater focuses employees on using openness and understanding rationale to get at the truth, or otherwise to make improvements.

Challenging conversations are not just welcomed but required at Bridgewater in the pursuit of better decision making.

Dalio has openly stated that Bridgewater employees "challenge [his] views about just about everything just about all the time and they are rewarded for it... Besides believing in truth, I believe in radical transparency." He goes on to explain that "speaking totally honestly about what people think others' strengths and weaknesses are is healthy, not vicious."

Passing an interview with flying colors at Bridgewater Associates must be like trying to find a needle in a haystack, only harder. Bridgewater's recruitment and selection process is critical to assessing fit. And you either fit or you don't. There's no in-between and turnover is purported to be relatively high – around 30 percent in one's first year. Bridgewater's interview techniques reflect their open and brutally honest culture. Interviewers ask questions to challenge candidates' thinking and see how they react under pressure. They want to get to know you inside and out to see if you can hack it at the company.

The inculcation period is understandably lengthy, some say around 18 months. You have to live and breathe the philosophy to be successful at Bridgewater. If a culture of brutally honest feedback and a barrage of daily questioning aren't up your alley, it could be a tortuous experience. Some find Bridgewater's approach refreshing and empowering, others find it overly aggressive – and most experience an "initial adjustment period." Either way, cultural fit is critical. The culture forces employees to think more critically and logically then they ever have before.

Within Bridgewater, Dalio's principles are gospel. Only tough, bright, and thick-skinned individuals who are willing to challenge and question the norms can thrive on Bridgewater's confrontational culture. And as controversial as Dalio's principles are, Bridgewater's results are proof in part that conflict in the pursuit of excellence can be a terrific thing.

———————

Voicing dissent is particularly valuable in the Producer & Creative Team environment. Francis Ford Coppola once said that producers create a picture three times: first, you write it; second, you shoot it; and third, you edit it. That's a lot of feedback to collect. To do so, producers need to create a culture where team members feel comfortable enough to say what they think. Each member brings a different perspective to the table. Through stimulating and perhaps difficult conversations, not simple agreement; bigger and better ideas can be generated. Challenges to everyday, taken-for-granted ways of thinking are often encouraged and as with Bridgewater, dissent is viewed as an obligation.

The creative team collaborates closely: discussions will be intense; communications continuous.

Although specialized "splinter" groups might be necessary for the incubation of ideas and the constituent parts of the project, integration will ultimately be essential. No one member and no one group should work in a vacuum. Intense collaboration – through frequent interactions – will be critical. The sharing of ideas and opinions is the lifeblood of the creative process.

An Eli Lilly insulin pen, the U2 mobile experience and HackFwd, an early-stage investment company, may seem like they have little in common, but they were all designed by one of the most creative companies in the world, IDEO – a company that's small in size but big on innovation. IDEO employs about 500 people worldwide, but the team has designed some of the most remarkable products and experiences of the past 20 years such as the first mouse for Apple, Bank of America's Keep the Change service, the Palm V PDA and Steelcase's Leap chair. Over the years, the company has helped thousands of organizations in the business, government, education and social sectors innovate and grow.

At IDEO, interdisciplinary teams of design thinkers – a mix of psychologists and ethnographers, engineers and scientists, marketing and business experts, writers and film-makers – roll up their sleeves and become immersed not only in the product, service or strategy that they are creating, but its environment, and how it's being used. They follow a very human-centered process where they "observe human behavior and see where the opportunities are."

But what separates IDEO from other design firms is its unique design process, called the Deep Dive, which includes the following five steps:

1. **Observation:** IDEO's diverse teams work with clients to understand the customer experience through such practices as shadowing, behavioral mapping, interviews and customer storytelling.

2. **Brainstorming:** This intense, idea-generating session uses the data from the observation exercise. Brainstorming principles include: encourage wild ideas, go for quantity, don't dismiss but build on ideas, and stay focused.

3. **Rapid prototyping:** Mock-ups of working models are created, so that the group can quickly understand and visualize each solution. Team members then interact with prototypes to simulate consumer behavior and develop empathy with individuals for whom they are designing.

4. **Refining:** Teams narrow down prototypes and work with the client to make the best possible decisions.

5. **Implementation:** IDEO's diverse workforce, across disciplines and geographies, are involved to implement the agreed solution.

Throughout the process, ideas are free flowing to generate countless insights fueled by transparent exchange of rapid and open feedback. A key to IDEO's success is that their systematic approach includes fast turnaround times for prototypes. The designers observe the consumers to try to feel, touch, and interact with a product or service, and then redesign how it is used.

The philosophy on which the design process is based is similar to a creative and collaborative process in the film industry called "dailies," where ideas get refined to become bigger and better.

Dailies are basically a daily review of works-in-process that is often reserved for a small group. They are timed such that feedback can be gathered on a frequent basis so that regular improvements can be generated and implemented immediately producing a significantly better product.

During dailies at Pixar, the entire team shares its work with any employees who are interested in attending – and not just senior executives. Dailies ensure that there is minimal wasted effort and get everyone in the team on the same page.

According to Catmull, "First, once people get over the embarrassment of showing work still in progress, they become more creative. Second, the director guiding the review process can communicate important points to the entire crew at the same time. Third, people learn from and inspire each other; a highly creative piece of animation will spark others to raise their game. Finally, there are no surprises at the end: When you're done, you're done."

One of the keys to success of the Producer & Creative Team archetype is the intense collaboration and constant refinement of ideas. The entire creative team becomes immersed in solving a design challenge. However, as being able to work together is such an important aspect of what the creative team does, cultural fit and personalities are as important as technical design skills.

Producers must ensure that their creative teams not only have the depth and breadth of skills, but are kept relatively small, flat, and flexible. (Apple's design team has about a dozen people, while IDEO's teams also keep small.) The team size can help avoid bureaucracy and support quick decision making. And with the Producer & Creative Team, you'll never find a single individual toiling away at problem solving and coming up with the flash of brilliance – even Thomas Edison worked with a 14-man team; the same with Michelangelo on the Sistine Chapel.

The integration of the creative team's ideas will not happen properly without a structured process focused around intense collaboration through frequent interactions. It's this innovative yet ordered process that remains critical to the success of the Producer & Creative Team so that the clash of differing and diverse perspectives generates a flow of truly creative output.

Is Producer & Creative Team the right model for you?

Is this archetype right for your current situation? And, if it is, how can you be the best producer you can be? The following sections will help you answer these questions.

Great if:

- You value creativity and innovation above all else.

- Your people want creative independence and respond negatively to being told what to do.

- You have license to be creative (eg, funding, sponsors, a proven track record, trust and time).

- You have a very clear sense of what you want to achieve, but know you need the input of others.

Think twice if:

- You have a clear sense of what you want to achieve and would like people to arrive at the same idea.

- Your culture does not encourage open feedback and dissent and the sharing of ideas.

- You need to produce something quickly – or will feel pressure to deliver interim results.

- You do not have access to a pool of exceptional people who will help you achieve your objectives.

How can you be a better producer?

1. Have you got the right mix of talent?

Producers need to bring together a team that's not only capable and creative but that's also made up of complementary personalities, skills and experience.

- Is the balance of skills and the overall chemistry of your current team right?
- Do you have special access to a talent pool from which you can recruit the best candidates?
- How effective is your recruitment program at identifying candidates who fit well with the culture of the team – and those who don't?

2. How disciplined is your creative process?

Successful producers know the difference between "hot air" ideas and true creativity. The latter is about getting things done, making things happen; it's about a structured and disciplined approach that links ideas and objectives in an "end product."

- How do you test the balance between open creativity and process discipline in your organization?
- What are you doing to develop your own specific and systematic way for driving the creative process?
- How do you evaluate the output of the creative team and decide when ideas are good enough to develop and "produce"?

3. Does your culture effectively encourage openness and constructive criticism?

The most productive environments enable a disciplined creative process and encourage open feedback. Constructive criticism must never be taboo: it's vital for stress-testing ideas.

- What are you doing to create a culture that supports openness and encourages feedback?
- How good is your team at giving and receiving constructive criticism?
- How do you incorporate members' feedback in continuing "product design"?

4. How do you ensure new recruits know what's expected of them?

People joining the team must be made aware that, while their own working style will be respected, they will be discouraged from producing or "creating" in silos. The induction process needs to explain how the creative, yet disciplined, culture works.

- How effectively do you set expectations for recruits' contributions to the creative process?
- Are you ensuring that the messages you're communicating are consistent with the creative working environment and processes?
- Do you reserve the right to depart from the default creative process if you need to?

5. How regular are your scheduled checkpoints?

Because the skills of the creative team are diverse, regular checkpoints are needed to make sure that everyone remains on the same page.

- Do you have a review and reporting process that brings different groups together?
- Are reviews sufficiently frequent?
- Have you created a culture where commitment to excellence is stronger than the fear of failure or ridicule?

6. How prepared are you to close ranks and take the final decision?

No matter how disciplined and robust the overall structure and process, sometimes creativity is difficult to rein in. A producer needs to have the authority and vision to make a final decision when required. They need to use their experience and discretion to choose the best idea from the multitude of good ones.

- How do you decide when good enough is good enough? And how do you manage the creative team's disappointment when it's back to the drawing board?
- How high is your personal credibility; will your team trust your final decision?
- Are you prepared to intervene if your team comes to a creative standstill?

7. How strong is your brand?

Once your big idea becomes a reality, you'll need to protect it from imitators and "me-tooism." A strong brand identity will help you stay ahead of the competition. You need to provide something others won't or can't.

- Is your brand strong enough to withstand copycat strategies?
- Can you maintain the strength of your brand in your spin-off products and ideas?
- What's your long-term strategy for ensuring that your team stays fresh and continues to beat its rivals?

Chapter 5

General & Soldiers

"I am a soldier. I fight where I am told,
and I win where I fight"
—*General George S. Patton*

" He was never known to issue an order to anybody of any rank without saying 'please' first "

Omar Bradley: The last five-star general

In 1950, Omar Nelson Bradley received one of the highest honors in US military history: five-star rank. He was designated "General of the Army" in recognition of his extraordinary leadership and service. Reserved for those who distinguish themselves in war-time, five-star rank is extremely rare; no-one has achieved it since. Made Chairman of the Joint Chiefs of Staff the previous year, Bradley had already gone as far as any soldier in America could. But five-star rank conferred something else: it was for American heroes.

Bradley will for ever be remembered as the man who led the victorious US forces on D-Day and, in the months that followed, the largest body of US soldiers ever to serve under one field command. In Operation Overlord, he and British general, Bernard Montgomery, liberated France; and in following campaigns, they decided the war.

His achievements are all the more remarkable given his personality. Known as the GI's general, he was a quiet man, in some ways the opposite of the more colorful Eisenhower and Patton. "The thing I most admire about Omar Bradley is his gentleness," wrote journalist Will Lang, Jr in *Life* magazine. "He was never known to issue an order to anybody of any rank without saying 'please' first."

Early years

Born on February 12, 1893 in a log cabin near Clark, Missouri, Omar was the only child of schoolteacher John Smith Bradley and his wife Sarah. Highly intelligent, he did well at school and excelled at sports, captaining both the baseball and football teams.

The family was not well-off, and to pay for university, Omar took a clerical job with Wabash Railroad. He'd intended to study law at the University of Missouri, but was dissuaded by his Sunday school superintendent, who recommended West Point Military Academy. He took the entrance exams for the academy and was offered a place for the fall of 1911.

Bradley was quick to adapt to the strict discipline of military life at West Point, but failed to excel, achieving only the rank of cadet lieutenant in his final year. On June 12, 1915, he graduated from West Point and served on the US–Mexico border. When America declared war on Germany, he was promoted to captain, and sent to guard the copper mines in Butte, Montana. Between the wars he spent much of his time teaching and studying, returning to West Point to teach mathematics in the early 1920s and attending the Command and General Staff School at Fort Leavenworth at the turn of the decade. He was promoted to major in 1924.

Working at the War Department in the 1930s, Bradley, now a lieutenant colonel, came under the tutelage of Army Chief of Staff George C. Marshall. It proved a turning point. He deeply impressed Marshall, who rated him "quiet, unassuming, capable, [with] sound common sense ... absolute dependability." In February 1941, he was made a brigadier general and sent to command Fort Benning.

Bradley's war

It wasn't until December 8, 1941, however, when the United States joined World War II, that Bradley's planning, instruction and experience came to fruition. Now a major general, he took command of the 28th and 82nd Infantry Divisions.

Bradley knew that preparing civilians for battle meant combining discipline and care. He ensured that new drafts of soldiers were properly welcomed, that they had a hot meal and that their barracks were stocked with uniforms and the right equipment. Concerned about their poor physical shape, he instituted a rigorous physical training program. He balanced the need to indoctrinate with the need to treat soldiers as people. The morale of his divisions remained a primary concern.

In February 1943, Bradley was sent to North Africa. Initially acting as a trouble-shooter for Eisenhower, he rose to command the II Corps, the first American formation to see combat in Europe or Africa during World War II. To prepare for battle, the II Corps had to move more than 100,000 men, plus equipment, an average distance of 150 miles over difficult country. Accomplishing this was seen as fundamental to the success of the North African campaign. In May, the II Corps attacked northward toward Bizerte, dislodged the Germans from Hill 609 and captured it. In just a few days, more than 40,000 German troops surrendered.

Bradley then travelled to support the invasion of Sicily in the late summer of 1943. By now, he was becoming a household name, a symbol of hope for a nation at war. Pulitzer Prize-winning journalist, Ernie Pyle, who had dubbed him "the GI's or soldier's general" due to his "obvious care of and compassion

> "
> *Bradley balanced the need to indoctrinate with the need to treat soldiers as people. The morale of his divisions remained a primary concern*
> "

for those soldiers under his command," wrote a six-part series on him. Author Alan Axelrod writes that Pyle saw "Bradley as a 'regular guy' hero who just happened to be a general." He says that the "GI General" epithet "gave home front America a hook on which to hang a simple and appealing identity for Bradley."

There was little time to bask in the fame, however. Shortly after the invasion was over, Eisenhower informed Bradley that he would command an army in occupied France. "I've got good news for you, Brad," he said. "You've got a fancy new job."

Before the invasion of Normandy, Bradley spent months refining the assault plans and troop training. One by one, he called each general up to a map of France and asked each to describe in detail his outfit's plans. The lesson over, "Bradley folded his hands behind his back, his eyes got a little moist, and in lieu of a speech, he simply said, 'Good luck, men.'"

Finally, on the morning of June 6, 1944, as the Commander of the US 1st Army, Bradley boarded the cruiser USS Augusta, and at 06:30, landed on the beaches of Normandy. The 1st Army broke through German lines at Saint-Lô. In face of stiff German resistance in July, Bradley mounted Operation Cobra, calling in strategic air power.

The US air bombardment successfully spoiled the German communication system, leading to confusion and ineffectiveness, and opening the way for the ground offensive. Moving in after the bombers, Bradley sent three infantry divisions to crack the German defenses.

By August 1944, Bradley was in charge of some 900,000 men, the largest body of American soldiers ever to serve under a single commander. Comprised of four field armies, including General Patton's 3rd Army, his 12th Army Group numbered 1.3 million men at its peak. In September, they reached the Siegfried Line.

The 12th Army Group swept through France, Belgium, the Netherlands and Germany. Pursued by Bradley's forces in early 1945, disintegrating German troops left the bridge across the Rhine River at Remagen vulnerable. With this opening, American forces encircled the German soldiers, resulting in the capture of over 300,000 prisoners. Caught between US troops advancing from the West and Soviet troops advancing from the East, the Germans were finished.

World War II was finally over, in part, due to Bradley's tactical brilliance and persistent leadership.

Later years

As Chief of Staff of the United States Army, and later as the first Chairman of the United States Joint Chiefs of Staff and first Chairman of the Military Committee of the North Atlantic Treaty Organization, Bradley helped shaped the development of post-World War II military strategy.

Three years after being named a Five-Star General, he retired from active military service. Nearly 25 years later, in 1977, Gerald Ford gave him the Presidential Medal of Freedom. The highest civilian award in the United States, this recognizes individuals who have made "an especially meritorious contribution to the security or national interests of the United States, world peace, cultural or other significant public or private endeavors."

It was a fitting tribute. Bradley had commanded an army of a million with patience, dedication and common sense.

"He had none of what some might call the flash or arrogance of a Patton or MacArthur," said Brigadier General James Robinson, assistant adjutant general of the Missouri Army National Guard. "Soldiers always knew [Bradley] had their best interest at heart. They trusted his leadership, his character, and they followed him...."

Marriott
Leading a legacy of hope

In the mid-1980s, Sara Redwell, her mother, and her seven siblings left Mexico for the United States. Sara could speak very little English, but, as the eldest child, she needed to help with the family finances. So when she was 23 she started her first job – as a housekeeper at the Chicago downtown Marriott hotel. She would wake up early to start the 5:30am shift.

"

Every day, Sara worked hard to develop her staff in the hope that – like her – they, too, would be promoted and do well

"

Sara was one of many housekeepers who worked at the hotel, some of whom traveled almost an hour for their jobs. Her colleagues were a diverse group, ranging from young adults to mature workers, and including individuals from many countries and backgrounds.

Sara would complete the same specific housekeeping tasks every day: fill the cart with toiletries and supplies, replace amenities in the rooms, make the beds, clean the bathrooms, and straighten and dust the rooms.

It wasn't always easy but the job was important for her. It gave her financial stability and the chance to look after her family.

In addition to her housekeeping duties, she enrolled in Marriott's Work Specific English Program (WSEP), which was developed to teach English to entry-level workers.

After demonstrating her attention to detail, her initiative and her dedication to her work, she was promoted to more supervisory roles, to managerial roles with greater responsibilities, and then to assistant general manager, and eventually, after two decades, to general

manager of the 147-room Courtyard Marriott Arlington South before she retired in September 2009. Every day, she worked hard to develop her staff in the hope that – like her – they, too, would be promoted and do well.

Improving language skills

Both Sara and the WSEP have been success stories for Marriott. Championed by CEO Bill Marriott, the WSEP was developed in the 1990s and grew quickly: by the end of 2000, nearly 150 hotels had a certified trainer. In a hands-on, 10-week course, employees – or associates as they are called – are taught the basic words and phrases necessary to communicate with customers and co-workers, and then go on to learn more advanced, job-specific language.

Through its programs, Marriott has been able to help associates turn a potential "limitation" into an opportunity to feel part of the "Marriott family" and, most importantly, to excel at work. "Almost immediately, employees started feeling more confident about their language skills and, as a result, more confident in their jobs." The WSEP has been superseded with other language programs such as Sed de Saber.

For Marriott, the programs are key. Immigrants provide a critical labor supply for the hospitality industry. If this supply were to disappear, it would be "more than a tremendous challenge to try and continue with business as usual." And while new immigrants often bring with them a strong work ethic and a desire to rebuild their homes and families, without the ability to communicate in English they may feel isolated and be unable to function fully in their new environments. Marriott has helped thousands of entry-level employees to become dedicated and loyal Marriott ambassadors. The programs meet both the personal needs of employees and the needs of the business.

Building confidence

At its core, Marriott's philosophy is to support its staff and show them that they, too, can be successful. The company believes that if you build the confidence of people they will repay

"

*Bill Marriott continues to welcome members
into his "family" – a family where people take care
of people, where employees look out for one
another and help each other succeed*

"

you: productivity will increase; staff turn-over rates and operating costs will decrease; customer service will be exceptional.

Marriott provides new immigrants with opportunities. More than teaching them core skills, the programs give them the chance to be successful in their new country, providing them with a sense of belonging and a work "family."

Bill Marriott says, "It's common sense. It's very simple stuff... It's basic Christian principles: treating your people right, loving your people. And if you love them, they'll do anything for you, and your customers will get wonderful service..."

Since 1957 when J.W. Marriott opened his first hotel, his strong work ethic and hands-on management style have become integral to the company's culture. More importantly, his fun-damental philosophy – take care of the associ-ate, and they'll take care of the guest – lives on in the more than 3,400 Marriott International

properties. J.W. Marriott's son, current chair-man and CEO Bill Marriott, has also taken care of his family of associates.

In his book, *The Spirit to Serve: Marriott's Way*, he insists that employees are number one – ahead of property owners, shareholders, fran-chisees, competitors, and even customers. More than 60 years after J.W. Marriott entered the hotel industry, Bill Marriott continues to wel-come members into his "family" – a family where people take care of people, where employees look out for one another and help each other succeed.

As the story of Sara Redwell shows, employees who have been given a chance by Marriott are motivated to help others – fellow *family members* – succeed. Since the very early days of Marriott's food stand "Hot Shoppes," when experienced waitresses would mentor new employees, there's been a strong emphasis on a "buddy" culture.

Valuing employees

One of Marriott's greatest strengths, arguably, is that it's recognized the need to develop – and therefore to value – those doing entry-level work. Despite the routine work and lower salaries, Marriott's turnover rate is the lowest in the industry. (In 2006, the US accommodation and food services turnover rate was 56.4 percent.)

Clear policies and procedures ensure that entry-level employees know precisely how to deal with guests and conduct their activities. The company recognized that it needed to address the limited English-speaking skills of new hires and developed programs specifically to provide basic but valuable skills that can be applied outside the workplace long after the employee has left the company.

Although it's been nearly 25 years since J.W. Marriott's passing, his legacy lives on. Part of Bill Marriott's philosophy is about listening to his employees, and he continues to travel to nearly 200 hotels per year ensuring that employees realize the extent to which he values their work.

The company continues to promote leaders that have been "through the ranks" and who truly care about and appreciate their employees.

Natasha Rasheed, Director of Human Resources of the Sydney Marriott hotels, says: "We're selecting leaders that really do care about our associates, and they know that they're not going to be successful in their job unless they really want to make a difference in our associates' lives."

Key characteristics of General & Soldiers

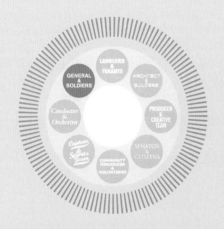

The General & Soldiers archetype is a hybrid between Conductor & Orchestra and Landlord & Tenants, meaning that the top-down direction of an authoritative general is translated into very specific and detailed tasks for soldiers to carry out. In addition, this archetype is extremely hierarchical and typical of a command-and-control culture. Although generals control in a dominant top-down manner, they also create paths with well-defined roles, levels and incentives for soldiers to progress up the hierarchy.

At each level, soldiers must complete strict training requirements before advancing. In this way, soldiers can continue to pass on their knowledge and experience to newer individuals advancing up the ladder. There is a high degree of shared identity and commitment of soldiers to the overall organization as well as to each other.

Generals take charge of a mission; they implement a strategy through detailed and clear instructions for soldiers.

 Roles, processes and tasks have to be clearly defined and rigidly followed.

 The organizational model relies on hierarchy and rank.

 Career paths are clear; soldiers' achievements are celebrated and recognized through regular promotion.

 Training is highly specialized; soldiers learn specific skills and are initiated into the culture.

 Uniforms and rituals reinforce the sense of common identity and common purpose.

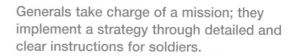

Generals take charge of a mission; they implement a strategy through detailed and clear instructions for soldiers.

This is the most common version of the command-and-control model of leadership. Generals give orders and expect full compliance from soldiers. They are able not only to see and understand the "big picture" but also to dictate the terms of specific missions and detailed tactics and maneuvers.

Li Ka-shing is one of the world's richest men. His primary company, managed through his holding in the listed Cheung Kong Group, Hutchison Whampoa Limited, has a hand in nearly every business in Hong Kong including retail, energy, real estate, telecommunications, and infrastructure; the company even operates the world's largest port. But Li wasn't born into a wealthy family. His father died of tuberculosis when he was a child, and to help support the family, he quit school before the age of 15 to work in a plastics company.

By the age of 22, he had borrowed enough money from his network of family and friends to start his own plastics manufacturing company. "The first year, as I didn't have much capital, I did everything myself," Li recalls, "which kept my overhead low." After a short period of time, he made a fortune by becoming the largest supplier of plastic flowers in Asia. From flowers to fortunes, his company grew and diversified into one of the largest developers of residential, office, retail, industrial and hotel properties in Hong Kong.

Although Li's' story is remarkable, it is not entirely unique. He belongs to a group of some of the most successful business families in Asia – a group of expatriate Chinese family-oriented enterprises that dominate the economics of Thailand, Malaysia, Indonesia, Singapore and Taiwan and account for 80 percent of "foreign" investment in China. The network is comprised of complex and highly intertwined connections in the form of large family conglomerates is referred to as the "Bamboo Network."

The Bamboo Network is made up of hundreds of overseas Chinese business families, all of whom left China at the dawn of the Communist Revolution in 1949. In 1978 when Deng Xiao Ping transformed the country to a market economy, a drastic shift was made across both agriculture and industry. With extremely high unemployment, poor production of goods, inconsistent shortages and gluts of products, the country looked to the Bamboo Network for massive external investment to support the development of its burgeoning industries. From this economic and social environment, the Network emerged.

The Network is based on mutual trust, kinship, education, and common experiences. They share the traditional Chinese culture and Confucian values defined by hard work, respect and loyalty for elders, frugality, and trust amongst family. This form of "social capital" becomes the family company's core competency and distinctive competitive advantage – it is the basis of facilitating business.

The head of the enterprise – the patriarch – is all powerful and often has a fascinating rags-to-riches story – similar to Li Ka-shing. He is the ultimate decision maker and few question his authority. He entrusts key business activities primarily to male family members, even son-in-laws and nephews as well as occasionally daughters. Impenetrable by outsiders, the family is the basic economic unit which enables loyalty, flexibility, quick decision making, and low overhead. The family unit alone underpins the key principle of the Bamboo Network and its success: trust.

The entire network and the nature of all interactions and dealings that take place within the network is completely dependent on the trust that each member has for one another.

Decision making is strictly centralized – strongly held by the family patriarch or his immediate family. And information is controlled tightly by this group and only disseminated on a verbal, informal, and need-to-know basis. "Our agenda arrives scribbled on the back of a Cathay Pacific in-flight menu," says a hired director of one large family-run group in Hong Kong. Also the ethnic Chinese billionaire Henry Sy of the Philippines typically coordinates social and business activities with his six children, all managers in the family enterprises, over a Sunday lunch that he cooks for their families.

The more trust the patriarch holds with an individual, the more information and company knowledge will be revealed. Considering the family orientation, virtually all of the top positions are held by direct family members, while more distant family members or individuals that have had long tenure with the company tend to fill secondary posts. The business dynamics of the typical Bamboo Network conglomerate tend to focus on financial efficiency and cost effectiveness within a paternalistic environment. Although trust is key within the family, this core value extends also to connections outside the organization including suppliers, customers, and even financial institutions – each who "understand" the Confucian mentality and closeness of the Bamboo Network.

And as the world is changing, the Bamboo Network is changing with it – reflecting increased openness toward Western business philosophy and learnings. Many of Asia's most famous tycoons are now aging and expecting their sons to take over the family business. As the enterprises get handed down from one generation to the next, the primary challenge for the Bamboo Network is continuity. A Chinese saying holds that wealth doesn't survive three generations. And while there are many examples of patriarchs' sons acquiring American engineering and business degrees, the fundamental values of family will not change. Integrating Western concepts does not mean being Western. "The techniques are modern," says Fung, "but the culture is still Confucian."

Why is the Bamboo Network considered a General & Soldiers archetype? The power and decision-making ability of the Network stems from one person: the patriarch of the family, each branch of the Network is headed by a dominant male figure that calls the shots for the entire business.

Carl von Clausewitz, a Prussian military thinker and one of the foremost strategic theorists once wrote, "War is the realm of uncertainty; three-quarters of the factors on which action in war is based are wrapped in a fog of greater or lesser uncertainty… The commander must work in a medium which his eyes cannot see; which his best deductive powers cannot always fathom; and with which, because of constant changes, he can rarely become familiar." These are the circumstances under which generals operate and a strong top-down type of control is required to maintain order, clear communications and direction in times of ambiguity. The concept of command-and-control is designed to reduce uncertainty to a manageable level. For generals, their combat circumstances may not always be well-defined, as such, it is critical that their soldiers clearly understand what needs to be done and what directions to follow.

The control held by the patriarch is the primary difference between typical Western firms and the Bamboo Network; he is the one that tightly controls the vast empire. And throughout his life, he passes that knowledge and innate decision-making ability down to a son who will carry his business legacy forward. He hones and guides his successor to ensure he will be prepared to take over the family reins. And if possible, Chinese patriarchs tend to assign different parts of the business to different sons; thus leading to large networked conglomerates that are still reliant on the family channels to consolidate control. And while the patriarch is not involved in the routine daily decisions, he is the only one that makes the big strategic decisions for the company.

The most successful generals are able to not only visualize strategic opportunities, but also to use their key soldiers to execute more tactical and detailed missions. Similarly, the Bamboo Network patriarchs don't run the daily business, nor are they involved with the everyday decisions.

However, they focus on the strategic relationship and business development with key contacts to maintain control of their markets while using the hierarchy and their power to cascade specific commands and actions to their business heads.

Confucianism – the key philosophy on which the Bamboo Network dynamic is based – reinforces the themes of hierarchy, authority and loyalty. Instead of turning to market research to base decisions, the patriarchs act with legendary speed based on gut instinct. In the heat of battle, generals don't always have the resources and time to plan out their next mission but must rely on their years of extensive experience, based on intuition, to make the best decision for their soldiers. They know that their trusting soldiers will readily comply and that they will do anything to defend the family business.

The most successful generals are able to not only visualize strategic opportunities, but also to use their key soldiers to execute more tactical and detailed missions

Roles, processes and tasks have to be clearly defined and rigidly followed.

Bypassing the chain of command is prohibited. Soldiers are dedicated to order and discipline. They are trained to perform very specific tasks and duties while following the rules and code of the army. The division of labor is the foundation on which effectiveness and camaraderie are built.

The story behind the Starbucks' barista came from Howard Schultz, chairman and CEO of Starbucks, while exploring the espresso bars of Italy in the early 1980s. In many parts of the world, a barista is a well-respected professional who is highly-skilled in coffee preparation. Schultz was amazed by the prominence of the Italian neighborhood coffee culture combined with the barista's technique and the experience they created for the customer. So when Schultz decided to recreate the "Italian espresso bar experience in the US," he knew the role of barista would be pivotal.

The art of making the perfect cappuccino lies in the science behind the detailed process required of each of these artists. There are multiple Starbucks drink variables that customers can alter such as category of drink (latte, espresso, Americano, etc), type (iced, warm), kind of espresso (decaf, regular, half-caff), amount of espresso, size, milk type, syrup type, amount of syrup, temperature, with/out whipped cream, and quite few others. For lattes alone, there are almost 200 million variations. Such precision requires extensive training and a great deal of practice.

Each barista undergoes an extensive and comprehensive training program to ensure that each action is perfectly timed (to the second) and executed. If takes less than 18 seconds or more than 23 seconds to pull a shot, they need

to "keep trying until the timing is right." Also milk must be steamed to at least 150 degrees Fahrenheit but never more than 170 degrees. One pound coffee bags must be exactly one pound (not 0.9995 or 1.2 pounds), then sealed with a sticker applied exactly one-half inch above the logo. All utensils must be cleaned in a specific manner, and baristas must know the differentiating characteristics of each coffee roast, how to explain the drink names, and how to sell the US$1,000 espresso machines.

As an employee on the frontline, the barista is closest to the customer. Aside from concocting the perfect cup of joe, he or she also educates customers on the various roasts of coffee, proper coffee making techniques, as well as explaining coffee-drink names. In fact, by the time a customer has ordered and received their beverage, the name of their customized drink has been repeated three times out loud (by the customer, by the cashier, and by the barista delivering the finished drink.) Through this practice, Starbucks has introduced a new vocabulary to the coffee consumer. Today, the Starbucks language is so common that most would understand it, even if they've never ordered one.

It's not easy becoming a Starbucks barista. Baristas must perfect the precise techniques required to make and customize a Starbucks beverage. Every barista must take courses on Coffee Knowledge, Brewing the Perfect Cup, Customer Service, and Retail Skills. They must read a 100-page booklet on the details of coffee growing regions, coffee tasting, farming and roasting techniques, and basically the fundamentals of brewing Starbucks coffee. Once they have passed a test on each booklet and gained hands-on experience, they can proceed to more advanced learning.

For more advanced skills, experience-based simulations are often used to emphasize the importance of great customer service and the Starbucks' Five Ways of Being: Be welcoming, Be genuine, Be considerate, Be knowledgeable, and Be involved. Practical tools such as role playing combined with training dice are typically used. An overwhelming part of the training process is learning by example. New baristas shadow experienced ones to learn how to make the drinks, how to talk with customers, how to interact – key behaviors that can't be learned from a book.

The sense of community and pride combined with the precision of the process demonstrates the importance of the barista as brand ambassador for Starbucks, and each barista has a role in determining how the brand is perceived by customers. The "secret power" of the Starbucks brand is "the personal attachment our partners feel and the connection they make with the customer." Whether it's brewing coffee, designing software, or mopping floors, a commitment to "Surprise and Delight" literally transforms the very nature of work.

The Starbucks brand, product, and experience has come a long way since the original vision to bring the "authentic Italian espresso bar experience to the United States." Customers have built a strong connection to

Starbucks – thanks in part to the ambassadors of the brand, your local Starbucks baristas.

———————

The clear definition of roles and responsibilities is critical for organizations that fall under the General & Soldiers archetype. Soldiers are often required to train intensely to learn very detailed tasks and processes and thus instantly execute them as if they were second nature. Soldiers are often put into situations where they are required to react based on their learned foundation of knowledge, and the role and task clarity ensures that they will know how to respond without second guessing.

The different roles across the organization are specifically planned such that there are few if no overlaps in responsibilities; thus every soldier works together to produce an effective combined response with minimal confusion. This balance and clear definition of the roles within the hierarchy is critical for organizations that operate under the General & Soldiers archetype as operations often tend to occur in high pressure situations or when quality or precision of response is critical.

Role designations are strictly aligned with the hierarchy therefore more senior roles take on more strategic responsibilities and those lower on the hierarchy conduct more operational roles. Thus, soldiers primarily focus on perfecting operational roles and know exactly the tasks that need to be completed. For example, a well-trained barista will be able to readi-

ly make any combination of drinks listed on the complex Starbucks beverage menu.

In addition, within the hierarchy of roles, it's not important for every soldier to receive every bit of information. Information needs to flow both up and down the hierarchy, so that generals know what the soldiers are doing and soldiers know what commands to follow. The key is that at each level in the hierarchy, the correct amount and type of information is available.

Imagine a troop of soldiers conducting their drills. Soldiers are somewhat homogeneous; they often look the same, act the same, and perform their tasks to perfection. Through discipline, practice, and training, once a drill is internalized, the soldier is accustomed to the discipline and intense rigor of the exercise. In ancient history, the most powerful, efficient and advanced empires developed ways of moving organized units of troops from one place to another on the battlefield, without confusion or their soldiers becoming mixed in with other units. They formed a single impenetrable troop in battle and their coordination meant their communications and role clarity were effective, disciplined, and well-organized.

However, due to this degree of organization and rigid coordination, sometimes it's difficult for soldiers to perform well in more autonomous environments. For this reason, soldiers are best prepared to react in situations or for specific missions where quick and orderly execution of previously planned tasks is required.

The organizational model relies on hierarchy and rank.

Soldiers depend on generals for direction setting, leadership, and judgment. Decisions are communicated through a clear reporting structure. The chain of command enables the generals to mobilize units from one mission to another effectively; without it, the organization crumbles.

Jay Van Andel and Richard DeVos had been friends for years when they decided to launch a variety of small-time business ventures together, such as a hamburger stand and an aviation business. So it was no surprise when in 1959 they launched yet another business selling dietary supplements door-to-door with stock stashed in their basements. Most people were familiar with and needed these types of products so they were relatively easy to sell. Jay and Richard were both patriotic ex-servicemen and believed that hard work led to success, the basis of the American way, which resulted in their company's name: Amway. Amway's basic premise was to encourage people to found their own businesses and become financially independent by selling Amway products.

Both Jay and Richard knew how to sell and develop key relationships. But in order to grow, they needed to find a way to efficiently expand and leverage the work of others to multiply their own efforts. They based the Amway marketing structure and business model on a multi-level hierarchy to use the power of many individuals to sell their products.

The overall business model for Amway is relatively straightforward and is sometimes referred to as network or multi-level marketing. Amway sells its products, which include lotions, cosmetics, soaps and toothpaste, as well as vitamins and weight management supplements, to

individuals, called independent business owners (IBOs). Each of the products has a specific point value assigned. IBOs can then 1) sell the products they bought to regular consumers, and 2) recruit more people to become IBOs to sell Amway products. If the IBO can successfully conduct both activities, he or she is able to move up the Amway hierarchy by accumulating and earning commissions based on their newly-recruited IBOs' sales.

To accomplish these acts of selling and recruiting, Amway's recognition levels are highly structured and this multi-level marketing system is core to how Amway makes money. Similar to a military hierarchy, there are many different levels within Amway – 22 in fact – which are known as pin levels. Each level is typically named after a precious metal or gemstone. As individuals progress up the hierarchy, they achieve a higher pin level which means that they will have more IBOs working under them.

The pin levels are an indication of the number of IBOs in that group, their income, and essentially their knowledge and expertise in the field. IBOs with top pin level may have hundreds, if not thousands, of people working under them. The first major level is **Platinum**. The Amway recruitment plan typically shows that such a group will have a total of approximately 100 people.

A next major level is **Diamond**. At this level, six people under the IBO need to have reached at least Platinum level. Nearly all IBOs aspire to achieve this level; at this point, the IBO is making approximately a six-figure income based on the sales of the people working under them. In Amway terms, it essentially represents "financial freedom."

The highest level is **Crown Ambassador**. There are two ways to achieve this level: 1) an IBO must either have 20 people under them with at least the Platinum level, or 2) they can have nine people under them but each must have a Diamond within that group. Very few people in the world have attained this pin level, and their annual remuneration is reported to run into the millions.

One of the key aspects to the General & Soldiers structure is the importance of hierarchy. Hierarchy distinguishes between levels and achievements. In addition, it recognizes the accumulated experience of individuals as they progress up the levels. Thus the hierarchy demarcates not only lines of communication but also connotes authority and respect between levels such that higher-level IBOs act as mentors to newer ones; they are also in demand for motivational speeches, recruitment and training seminars.

The Amway hierarchy is similar to modern military structures which have their roots in Ancient Rome. Military structures are built on extensive multi-leveled chain of command and were used to efficiently organize Roman soldiers.

The Roman army was broken down into different groups to have a clear chain of command during battle; from the smallest unit called a *conturbenium* or a group of eight soldiers to a *legion* which contained about 6,000 men. This enabled generals to effectively communicate and mobilize large numbers of soldiers.

The hierarchy helps maintain a manageable span of control or number of individuals assigned to each "commander." In a military setting, if the number of teams for which a specific commander is responsible exceeds a manageable limit, additional commanders are introduced into the hierarchy to reduce the demands on that individual.

This arrangement enables the organization to cover large global geographic areas so that IBOs can more efficiently map where other IBOs have been and in what areas they are selling. The hierarchy is so structured that it is forbidden for "downline" IBOs to cross or switch into each other's lines of sponsorship. In addition, it is the original sponsoring IBO's responsibility to guide and support new IBOs. Thus there is a higher status and type of seniority associated with being further up in the line of sponsorship.

So, the hierarchy is critical at Amway for more than just reasons of geographic efficiency and coordination. It represents an important system of recognition where high-standing IBOs can visually display their coveted achievements to which all IBOs aspire. It is in fact the only way a multi-level organization can survive as it needs to constantly bring in new people to make money.

The structure is important because it enables individuals that are further up the hierarchy to leverage the power of individuals that are lower down. There will always need to be far more IBOs in the network with only a few individuals at the top levels. For example, a 2007 British government investigation revealed "that just 10 percent of Amway's agents in Britain make any profit, with less than one in ten selling a single item of the group's products." But while the top performing IBOs, such as the Crown Ambassadors may be fewer in number, thousands of incoming IBOs remain driven to achieve the levels of freedom – motivated by stories of fortune – that are experienced by their more senior counterparts.

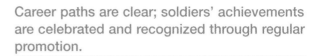

Career paths are clear; soldiers' achievements are celebrated and recognized through regular promotion.

Moving up the ranks is part of the reward for being a soldier. Internal promotions are always preferred. The soldier is motivated by a sense of possibility: the general instills the idea of progress and opportunity. As soldiers move up the ranks, they mentor new soldiers in a virtuous circle of knowledge and experience.

Cement may seem like nothing special. But for millions of low-income residents across Mexico, who can't afford even the basics, cement represents something much more than a simple building material; it symbolizes hope for the future.

With a population nearing 110 million, Mexico has one of the world's worst housing shortages. Over 1.5 million homes are required annually and 3.7 million existing homes are estimated to be inadequate. With little money, credit or skills to build homes, millions of families seem destined to a life of overcrowding with slim possibility for "building" a brighter future for their families.

Through Patrimonio Hoy – a division of CEMEX, Mexico's largest multinational corporation and cement manufacturer – 130,000 Mexican families are, for the first time, achieving their dream of building a home. Patrimonio Hoy, meaning "patrimony today," is enabling families to come together in small groups to save funds toward building their new home – one room at a time.

The company has achieved a unique ability to penetrate this market, while connecting to the foundation of Mexican society. In 1994, when the value of the Mexican peso crashed, revenues from CEMEX's large-scale customers dropped by 50 percent. However, its low income,

do-it-yourself (DIY) customer segment only dropped by 10–20 percent. While the value of the DIY segment represented total sales of US$500–600 million per year, these same customers also tend to live in shacks and earn less than $5 per day.

An opportunity lay before CEMEX, but the company didn't know how to reach the millions of low-income customers. CEMEX's director of development, Hector Ureta, came up with an interesting solution. A group of CEMEX professionals lived anonymously for a year in Guadalajara's low-income communities. What they discovered was striking:

- Low-income families view housing as patrimony or building an asset to pass down through their family.
- Due to their limited funds, families tend to build homes incrementally.
- Women in the community are more reliable borrowers who focus on saving and often belong to a *tanda* or savings club.
- Customers are DIY builders but they lack the required building techniques.

From these findings, CEMEX developed the following five-step structured process for the Patrimonio Hoy program which is based on the entrenched Mexican community values and is reinforced by public celebrations when customers are able to achieve their dreams:

1. Promoters – mainly women – don their bright blue T-shirts to "sell" the program through word of mouth to other women.

2. Sales and information sessions are held within the community to explain how the program works. The registration and payment rules that customers need to follow are simple and transparent, but strict.

3. Registration sessions for self-financing are held to initiate weekly payments covering the cost of materials and membership.

4. Free technical building and planning support is provided to assist customers with their customized projects.

5. Finally after about two weeks, each customer receives a delivery of their specific construction materials to their home.

Patrimonio Hoy works because it is directly aligned with the tight-knit culture of the Mexican communities. By immersing themselves in the community, CEMEX was able to understand low-income families' values and tap into a market segment that was initially both undesirable and difficult to penetrate.

One of the keys to the success of Patrimonio Hoy is the company's ability to celebrate customers' home building progression. At first, Patrimonio Hoy delivered smaller bags of cement at a higher frequency to the customer's homes – thinking that this was the best way to reward the customer and minimize waste. Instead, what they learned was that customers preferred larger bags to be placed in front of their homes. Customers valued the "public celebration" of having a large bag of cement propped up in front of their house for their neighbors to see.

In addition, the program celebrates the success of its customers by publishing their achievements in local newspapers, by sponsoring block parties and open houses, and by holding events to honor its top savers, builders and promoters. When a room is completed, the family receives a diploma and is given a "celebration kit" – a box of family-size soft drinks and a bowl with tacos for the party that they will throw with their neighbors. Customers become "living testimonials" to their success with the program.

These public celebrations not only encourage existing customers to continue their relationship with the program, they also drive new customers in the community to sign up.

And now, for some customers, their involvement in the program is potentially life changing. A "transaction of equals" occurs between customer and company to not only build community homes, but also respect. Patrimonio Hoy is achieving something much greater than simply building houses – the organization is collectively changing the buying patterns and behavior of low income homeowners. Communities have moved from a culture of resignation to one of hope in that achieving their "dreams" is indeed possible.

When we get promoted, there is an intrinsic sense of pride and accomplishment. Under the structured hierarchy within General & Soldiers' organizations, there is no better motivation than having the opportunity to progress up the career ladder and to be recognized for one's achievements. Soldiers can clearly see what they need to achieve to progress up the hierarchy. While rewards can be extrinsic and include financial gains or increases in rank, some of the best rewards are intrinsic and allow individuals to make a difference in their communities or with new generations of soldiers.

For example, one of the key reasons that the Patrimonio Hoy program is so successful is due to its close alignment with the cultural values of the Mexican communities. First, very specific rules and processes must be followed, but gradually as Patrimonio Hoy participants learn the proper procedures, they can continue to increase both their social and financial capital and progress up the CEMEX ladder. With each move up the hierarchy, participants can publicly celebrate within their communities their achievements as families move closer and closer to achieving the ultimate goal – a house that they can pass onto their children.

Marriott and the company's development programs give low-income employees hope for the future. The story of Sara Redwell demonstrates that hard work and dedication can result in steady moves up the company hierarchy to more challenging and rewarding roles.

The most successful generals are the ones that can instill a sense of achievement, motivation and purpose by passing on their knowledge and wisdom. In turn, this culture can become a positively reinforced environment where older generations are continuously mentoring newer ones.

Training is highly specialized; soldiers learn specific skills and are initiated into the culture.

Army training must transform average civilians into soldiers. For the generals, it's more important than any form of previous education: unless recruits learn the necessary skills and are integrated fully into the army, they will be unfit for command – and for mission. Continuous training and development helps soldiers learn more advanced skills and strategies as they move up the ranks.

The Society of Jesus is a Roman Catholic religious order of clerks whose members are called Jesuits, Soldiers of Christ, because the founder, Saint Ignatius of Loyola, was a knight before becoming a priest. Jesuits are the largest male religious order in the Catholic Church, with approximately 20,000 members: 13,305 priests, 2,295 scholastic students, 1,758 brothers and 827 novices. They are best known in the fields of education (schools, colleges, universities, seminaries, theological faculties), intellectual research, and cultural pursuits and are also known for their missionary work, social justice, and human rights activities.

Founded on August 15, 1534 by Ignatius Loyola and six other students from the University of Paris, this group called themselves the Company of Jesus, and also "Amigos en el Senior" or "Friends in the Lord," because they felt they were placed together by Christ. The name had echoes of the military (as in an infantry "company"), as well as of discipleship (the "companions" of Jesus). The word "company" comes ultimately from Latin, *cum + pane* = "with bread," or a group that shares meals.

Ignatius Loyola became the first *Praepositus Generalis*, or the Superior General of the Society of Jesus or simply "superior general" or even, "president general." Today, this title is commonly referred to as Father General. And while the term may appear to have military connotations, it is meant to imply the opposite of specific or particular, similar to today's commonly used terms Postmaster General, Attorney General and Receiver General.

Jesuits' activities concentrated on three things. First, they founded schools throughout Europe. Jesuit teachers were rigorously trained in both classical studies and theology. The Jesuits' second mission was to convert non-Christians to Catholicism, so they developed and sent out missionaries. Their third goal was to stop Protestantism from spreading. The zeal of the Jesuits overcame the drift toward Protestantism in Poland, Lithuania and southern Germany.

Ignatius and the Jesuits who followed him believed that the reform of the Church had to begin with the conversion of an individual's heart. One of the main tools they used to bring about this conversion was the Ignatian retreat, called the Spiritual Exercises.

Today, the training process, otherwise known as formation, to become a Jesuit priest is lengthy: the average length of Jesuit formation is about 10 years which makes becoming a Jesuit priest one of the longest of any religious order.

The first training stage of Jesuit formation is called the Novitiate, where the novice learns the traditions, rules and expectations of the Society. Think of this as the initial indoctrination process. During this time he conducts the Spiritual Exercises in a thirty-day retreat and engages in a variety of activities which involve service to the very poor and needy. At the end of this two-year period, he announces vows of poverty, chastity and obedience to prepare for priestly ordination. Following the Novitiate, a Jesuit begins a three-year period of graduate level studies in philosophy and theology, called First Studies.

The second formation stage is called Regency, where the Jesuit works for three years in a school or other approved apostolate and lives in an apostolic community. After Regency, Jesuit scholastics begin an advanced three-year study of theology which leads to a Masters of Divinity and in his last year of studies, ordination to the priesthood. This may be followed either by full-time apostolic work or specialized studies. After completing his theological studies and some further active ministry, the Jesuit completes his formal formation of prayer, guidance and studies with Tertianship. After which, the Jesuit is called to final vows in the Society of Jesus.

Leaving aside the numbers and external measures of achievement, the core of the order is to be found in the still-vivid tenets of Ignatian spirituality embodied in the Spiritual Exercises, whose purpose is "to conquer oneself and to regulate one's life in such a way that no decision is made under the influence of any inordinate attachment." In other words, after the intense training and self-discovery, Jesuit priests continue along dedicated paths free from likes or dislikes, comforts, wants, needs, drives,

appetites and passions so that they may choose based solely on what they discern is God's will for them.

___

With its hierarchical multi-leveled structure and extensive decade-long training process, the Jesuits, as an organization, have clear similarities to the General & Soldiers archetype. Training and indoctrination change individuals and shape them into part of a group with a strong collective and unique shared identity; the process produces individuals that have internalized the values of the organization.

Charles Jean Jacques Joseph Ardant du Picq, the nineteenth century French army officer and military theorist wrote, "Four brave men who do not know each other will not dare to attack a lion. Four less brave men, who know each other well, sure of their reliability and consequently of mutual aid, will attack resolutely."

Thus, to prepare for their missions through life that are focused on education and spirituality, the Jesuits take part in an extensive indoctrination program to ensure that at every step of the formation, they are of sound mind and pure heart to continue their lifelong dedication to their religion.

Similarly, military organizations are renowned for their intense training and preparation programs. By focusing on a clear set of tasks, conditions, and standards, they take thousands of recruits and train them both physically and psychologically to operate under challenging conditions. Essentially, the training programs are designed to dissolve the civilian mentality and rebuild a dedicated soldier.

Uniforms and rituals reinforce the sense of common identity and common purpose.

During army drills, soldiers, homogenized by their uniforms, march in perfect unison. All for one, one for all: they share a sense of identity, commitment and belonging. The camaraderie is, literally, vital: it's what binds them together during times of crisis.

The Church of Jesus Christ of Latter-day Saints was founded in 1830 by Joseph Smith in the state of New York. As a youth, Joseph claimed to have seen a divine vision in the secluded woods near the Smith home in Palmyra, New York in 1820. And shortly thereafter, he claims to have been visited by an angel, who told him of a book of ancient text, which he translated into the *Book of Mormon*. The *Book of Mormon* was published in March 1830 and the following month, Smith organized The Church of Jesus Christ of Latter-day Saints and became its first president.

Whether a result of collective interests or the Church's emphasis on proselytizing via missionary work, the Church has grown substantially since its foundation in 1830.

When it was originally founded, the Church had only six members. Almost 100 years later, in 1947, Church membership had grown to one million members. In 2009, Church membership was over thirteen million. In total, there are over 27,000 congregations in 177 countries, nations and territories around the world.

One avenue through which many are engaged to strengthen the congregation is the practice of serving a mission. The mission is described as being one of the rewarding ways that Mormons can dedicate their time to teaching others about their religion and is based on the

scripture found in Matthew 28:19–20 of the Bible which states, "Go ye therefore, and teach all nations, baptizing them in the name of the Father, and of the Son, and of the Holy Ghost: Teaching them to observe all things whatsoever I have commanded you: and, lo, I am with you always, even unto the end of the world."

At any one time, more than 50,000 missionaries are serving missions for the Church. Most of them are young people, under 25-years-old.

For approximately 18 to 24 months, Mormon missionaries – both males called Elders and females called Sisters – willingly leave behind friends, family and personal interests to temporarily provide service to others and to God.

While they are away, they serve under the guidance of a mission president who is married and typically older – often in their forties and fifties.

Benevolent, inspirational and wise, these men and their wives devote their lives for three years to support their young missionaries and preside over the missions – acting as role models or father figures while their missionaries are away from the families.

In turn, missionaries rely on the care and support of their mission presidents and reciprocate their president's devotion with obedience and respect. Mission presidents are supported by two assistants who organize the missions and oversee the training of the missionaries.

Missionaries are divided into geographic zones which are each led by a zone leader. Zones are subsequently divided into districts which are led by a district leader. This hierarchical structure ensures the safety, well-being and support of missionaries while they are away from their families as well as appropriate geographic coverage of region.

Before missionaries leave on their journey, they are required to attend a type of boot camp training at the Mission Training Center (MTC). This three-week program serves to transform previous college students into regimented missionaries. It prepares them for the demands of the upcoming mission and rigorous schedule as well as taking classes to learn how to study scriptures and preach the gospel. It is the first point at which would-be missionaries are immersed in the life they will lead for the next two years.

There is a very specific schedule and rules to which missionaries are expected to adhere.

First, missionaries are required to send mandatory monthly "Letters to the President" as well as conduct quarterly one-on-one interviews. This ensures that mission presidents are well-informed of their missionaries' needs and well-being. Missionaries are also required to provide both daily and weekly reports to their district leader discussing their overall progress.

Another strict rule is that missionaries must always work in pairs, called a companionship where there are two Elders or two Sisters per companionship. They must even abide by a relatively strict daily schedule:

6:30 am
Arise, pray, exercise, and prepare for the day

7:30 am
Personal study

8:30 am
Companionship study/planning for teaching

9:30 am
Proselytizing, teaching and service.
One hour each for lunch and dinner, often taken in the homes of church members or prospective members

9:30 pm
Plan the next day's activities

10:30 pm
Retire to bed

During the mission, missionaries are expected to follow a very strict code of conduct to help them stay focused on mission work. These rules are a critical part of the mission which must be obeyed; it is a severe offense to breach these standards. For example, missionaries:

- Must always stay with their companion.
- Are strictly told not to date or be alone with a member of the opposite sex.
- Are not allowed to watch TV, use the internet or view non-approved media.
- Are not allowed to make phone calls to home.

Along with the ever-present name tag, which is intended to always remind missionaries of their purpose, both Elders and Sisters are required to wear very specific, uniform-like attire on their missions. While each mission may have varied requirements, in general, Elders must wear white shirts, dark colored and conservatively cut suits, conservative ties, dark socks, comfortable, sturdy, thick soled shoes and a proper "missionary" haircut that's cut above the collar. Sisters are required to wear coordinated and properly fitting, full-length, modest skirts with kneehigh socks or nylons, and comfortable, conservative shoes.

Through the church, their beliefs, as well as through their missions, Mormons share a deep bond and common identity. They don a "uniform" that represents an easily identifiable, professional and clean-cut appearance, which in addition to their unique mission and message, helps distinguish themselves from others. In essence, they are all part of the same family with a shared culture and faith. The difficult experience of leaving home at a relatively young age combined with the challenge of the mission creates a deep commitment and sense of belonging to the church and each other.

In military settings, training and boot camp are supposed to be challenging, rigorous and even stressful. For example, recruit training is the initial indoctrination period which is intended to inculcate soldiers into the army mentality and prepare them for the challenges they are likely to face going forward. Though extreme, incoming soldiers develop a common bond with each other and with the military institution through the hardship they face. Their common identity is simply reinforced with shared symbols such as uniforms and specific rituals such as shaving one's head, conducting drills, and running a two-mile course.

So why do the Mormons fall into the General & Soldiers archetype?

For individuals that get sent on a mission, the ordeal provides an intense bonding experience not only between missionary companions, but also with the church as an institution. Going on a mission is not mandatory, but for those that decide to go, they must first pass various standards of worthiness, and thus demonstrate devotion to the religion including regular church attendance, scripture study, and personal prayer.

Potential missionaries are assessed to ensure that they are mentally, physically, and emotionally capable of full-time missionary service. In a sense, the church bishops ensure that each missionary is spiritually capable and mentally prepared to experience a wide range of challenges during the mission.

For up to two years, these individuals remain dedicated to their specific missions following a very specific schedule each and every day. They wear the missionary "uniform" and continue to practice personal study and prayer. While being on a mission can be an extremely difficult period for many young Mormons, the shared bond and sense of belonging ensure that, although the mission may be arduous, it will nonetheless be both spiritually and emotionally rewarding.

Is General & Soldiers
the right model for you?

Is this archetype right for your current situation? And, if it is, how can you be the best general you can be? The following sections will help you answer these questions.

Great if:

- You need to co-ordinate activities across large groups of people that cannot communicate with each other directly.

- You have full confidence that your strategy is ready to be implemented – and are willing to live with the consequences if you're wrong.

- You place a premium on high efficiency and fast deployment.

Think twice if:

- There is some conflict, confusion or doubt over who is in command.

- You cannot easily disaggregate your strategy into individual elements or components.

- The structure of your work and workforce does not allow for step-by-step progressions that celebrate individual achievements.

- Your hierarchy is so rigid that it cannot respond rapidly to changing conditions in the field.

How can you be a better general?

1. How clearly do you communicate your objectives and tactics?

Generals need to articulate the objectives of each mission clearly; soldiers must know what is expected of them and follow the tactics in the prescribed plan.

- Have you translated the overall strategy into specific missions and communicated them to the soldiers?
- Does each mission have specific objectives and operating parameters?
- Have you given a simple and clear explanation of the importance of the mission to the overall strategy?

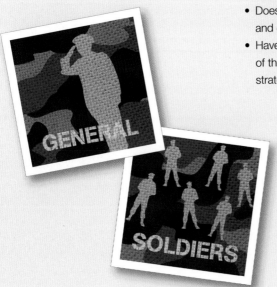

2. How clearly defined is your chain of command?

Generals are at the top of the hierarchy; they give strict orders, and expect unquestioning compliance, believing command and control to be "mission critical." The penalties for soldiers who don't comply are severe.

- How effective are you at communicating the importance of the hierarchy?
- How willing are soldiers to comply with the chain of command?
- Are the penalties for non-compliance serious enough?

3. How effective are you at disseminating information from the top down?

Information must flow efficiently and effectively from the top of the hierarchy to the bottom, from the generals to the soldiers. The communication system must be fast enough and efficient enough for today's rate of change.

- How easily is information disseminated?
- Do roadblocks in the hierarchy impede the flow of information?
- What tools are you using to make the communication system more effective and efficient?

4. How well does your recruitment program identify people who will be able to fit in with your culture?

Soldiers are cast from a very specific mold; they need to be mentally and physically tough. Your recruitment and training programs must only select those you can transform into specialized, highly skilled soldiers.

- How effective is your training program at developing the right skills?
- What criteria exist to evaluate the effectiveness of your recruitment and training programs?
- How are you evaluating recruits against the required skills once they've completed training?

5. Is there a clear career path to motivate recruits?

Soldiers are motivated by the ability to progress through the ranks to positions of authority. A clear career path encourages continuous learning and development, while creating opportunities for soldiers to mentor new recruits.

- How easy is it for soldiers to move up the hierarchy? How effective are your career paths at promoting soldiers?
- How effective is your leadership team at motivating and mentoring soldiers?
- Are there legendary leaders or success stories that you could draw on to inspire and motivate recruits?

6. How successful is your organization at developing "soldiers for life"?

Soldiers have a unique camaraderie and bond that lasts for generations. A strong alumni network allows soldiers to remain connected to the organization when they leave.

- How effectively do you maintain links with and support your alumni?
- Do you use your alumni network to help achieve specific strategic objectives such as the collection of intelligence?
- Are the benefits of an ongoing alumni association used as a recruitment and retention tool?

7. How effective are you at deploying soldiers for specialized missions as well as the general units?

Soldiers must have the skills for both general combat and specific missions. The most successful generals prepare their soldiers for the deployment of overall strategies – but they also train some of them for specialized duties.

- Do you have a plan that differentiates staffing and training for general deployments from that for specialized missions?
- How successfully do you select the right soldiers for the right missions?
- Do your specialized units have the right kind of stature in the organization? Are they seen as a deserving élite?

Chapter 6

Architect &
Builders

"I like to be on the edge of
 the possible"
 —*Jørn Utzon*

" Gentlemen, that's your winner! "

Jørn Utzon and the Sydney Opera House

"Gentlemen, that's your winner!" declared renowned American architect, Eero Saarinen, in 1956 as he sifted through the pile of rejected designs for the Sydney Opera House. The other three judges hovered over the sheets, curious to see what had so excited Saarinen. It was the design submitted by Jørn Utzon, a relatively unknown 38-year-old Danish architect. Compared with the other 233 submissions in the international competition, Utzon's sketches appeared preliminary, overlapping free-form black lines on a blank page. They were lacking in detail and depth, and didn't even meet the competition's entrance criteria. But Saarinen saw something that the other judges hadn't. Something remarkable. Behind those stark lines lay genius.

Many of the submissions had traditional layouts – some with square structures, others with circular designs. But Utzon's was different. As the son of a naval architect, he had grown up by and

studied the sea. His father had taught him to use nature and its power and beauty to inspire his designs. Saarinen was struck by Utzon's dramatic and organic roofline that arched up into the sky; its silhouette matched the graceful shape of spinnakers of a yacht under sail.

Utzon's layout also took best advantage of the narrow piece of land, Bennelong Point, upon which the Opera House would be built by putting the two largest venues side-by-side instead of one in front of the other. He understood that the environment and its location were key to showing off the building's beauty once complete: "This interplay with the sun, the light, the clouds is so important that it [will turn] the building into a living thing."

Utzon's vision of what the Sydney Opera House could be captured the imagination of the judges and public. Somehow, his raw sketches conveyed what the building could become – an icon of the 20th century.

The early stages

On January 29, 1957, Utzon was named winner of the Sydney Opera House competition. He envisaged the building to be "like a Gothic cathedral that people will never tire of and 'never be finished with.'" He received the equivalent of A\$10,000 for first prize and estimated it would take three years and approximately A\$7 million to bring his vision to life.

From the first, however, Utzon's design and his three-phase construction plan seemed overly ambitious. Thousands of diverse craftsmen would be needed to construct the Opera House: builders to lay the concrete foundation and the Swedish tiles of the roof's sails; stone craftsmen to create the pink aggregate granite walls, stairs and floors; carpenters to decorate the brush box and white birch plywood interiors; electricians to lay the 400 miles of electrical cable; and French glassmakers to make the windows and mouths of the roofs.

The biggest challenge was the advanced technology needed to breathe life into the sails. The roof design has been called "an adventure at the edge of what was technically possible." Utzon and his engineering partner, Ove Arup, spent countless hours redesigning the geometry. None of their solutions was successful.

Despite the setbacks, Arup remained committed in principle to the original design. As the engineer, it was his mission to bring the Sydney Opera House to life; Utzon's design – regardless of how technically challenging – would remain sacrosanct. But the foundation had already been started, and time was running out. After countless months of recalculating and redesigning, Arup's team finally and reluctantly admitted defeat.

Solutions – and more problems

It wasn't until October 1961, after two years of unsuccessful designs, that Utzon came up with a simple and elegant solution. He put forth a concept inspired by the act of segmenting an orange: the 14 sails of the building could be cut from a perfect sphere. Now the arcs of the sails could be replicated cost-effectively. In Utzon's own words, "After three years of intensive search for a basic geometry for the shell complex, I arrived in October 1961 with the spherical solution… I call this my key to the shells because it solves all the problems of construction… with this geometrical system, I attain full harmony between all the shapes in this fantastic complex."

The interior structure would be supported by similarly shaped reinforced concrete ribs. Peter Myers, one of Utzon's young architect disciples, saw these arrive on site: "The concrete was perfect, the edges were pure, there wasn't a blemish." Myers also recalled how he turned to see Utzon with tears in his eyes. "And then I saw that the tough Italian workers were crying, too. Their pride in workmanship was being acknowledged, and we were all transported by what had been achieved."

The construction of the Opera House broke new ground, leading to innovations such as an on-site "factory" to join the rib segments mid-air, a telescopic arch to eliminate the need for scaffolding, and the use of the world's largest cranes to maneuver the structural segments into place.

For the 1,056,006 Swedish tiles that would encrust the roof, Utzon had very specific ideas. He wanted a finish that "had gloss but did not have a mirror effect. A tile with a coarse structure that resembled hammered silver." "The material," he wrote, "would have to be sought in the building of the ancient world, which has stood up to many years' use without deterioration," and "in the hot sun of the day it will be a beautiful white shimmering thing." He had travelled to the Great Mosque in Esfahan, Iran, as well as to China and Japan to gather inspiration for his tiles. He had them painted off-white and beige to display their distinctive chevron shapes.

The sheer complexity of the project led to problems that impeded progress: sky high costs, government involvement, delays, and significant redesign of the interior.

Perhaps the biggest blow came in February 1966, when Utzon, dismayed not only by the many impediments to progress but also by the hostility of the press and by negative public opinion, resigned as chief architect and left Sydney. Dejected, he never returned.

The architect's and builders' achievements

Utzon's story would have been something of a tragedy – had it ended there.

Peter Hall was brought in to complete the unfinished work, and, on October 20, 1973, seven years after the architect's sad departure, the Sydney Opera House opened its doors. The Opera House ended up taking not three, but 16 years to build, at a cost, in today's money, of more than A$2.2 billion.

In 1999, after a gap of 33 years, Utzon was at last reconnected with his masterpiece, appointed to develop a set of design principles to preserve the integrity of his building. And in 2003, five years before he died, he received architecture's highest award, the Pritzker Prize. The jury said, "His work shows the world that he has been there and beyond – he proves that the marvelous and seemingly impossible in architecture can be achieved. He has always been ahead of his time. He rightly joins the handful of Modernists who have shaped the past century with buildings of timeless and enduring quality."

Few could have foreseen the impact that Utzon's daring vision would have on the world. When the building was added to the list of World Heritage sites in 2007, UNESCO stated that the Opera House "stands by itself as one of the indisputable masterpieces of human creativity, not only in the 20th century but in the history of humankind." Louis Kahn, the world-renowned Estonian architect said of the Sydney Opera House, "The sun did not know how beautiful its light was, until it was reflected off this building."

Utzon did much more than inspire the imagination of the public: he revolutionized the science and technology of construction. The Sydney Opera House is a model of innovation in both architectural form and structural design that required the dedicated collaboration and problem solving of both the architect and the builders.

In 1988, Arup wrote, "The Sydney Opera House is not the kind of building which often comes within the orbit of the structural engineer. It is an adventure in building ... It has created unique opportunities, both in the design office and on the site ... The structure now standing in Sydney Harbour is the result not only of much toil and sweat but also of an unprecedented collaboration between architect, engineer and contractor... We stretched ourselves to the limits of our skills."

Tata Nano
Building the Indian people's car

In 2004, Ratan Tata, the chairman of the Tata Group, currently India's largest conglomerate and the owner of Land Rover and Jaguar, was confronting one of the biggest challenges of his career – making a modern car for a minimal price.

He had just begun development of the Nano – the "tiny car with the even tinier price tag" designed to meet the needs of the masses. Like Henry Ford 100 years before him, Tata had seen a yawning gap in the car market: around 50 million to 100 million Indians get around on $1,000 motorcycles because they can't afford the $5,000 for the cheapest model on the market. "The Nano encapsulates the dream of millions of Indians groping for a shot at urban prosperity," reported the *Financial Times*.

To many of Tata's colleagues, however, the dream seemed impossible. Tata wanted the car to sell for just Rs 1 lakh (approximately $2,500) – a figure that sounded absurdly low, given the costs involved in automobile production and manufacture.

Tata's challenge was to convince not only a dedicated band of young engineers in the company but also its key partners that together they could revolutionize the automobile industry. If he could get the right team – a team that truly believed in bringing the Nano to life – he knew he could succeed. He knew that the expertise of the in-house team would need to be supplemented by the most innovative external automobile specialists and suppliers. It would be critical to get them to see the possibilities of this untapped market. With the Nano team planning the launch for 2008, he didn't have a lot of time.

Tata approached a long list of executives from the most innovative auto suppliers. One of them was Ashok B. Ramaswamy, president and managing director of Delphi India, a company that specialized in systems integration. Delphi, which would supply the dashboard for the vehicle, was known for "fit and lean" production, but Ramaswamy knew the success of the Nano depended not only on cost-cutting but also on new thinking about car design. He saw partnering with Tata as a chance to learn innovative development and manufacturing techniques that could be used across Delphi's global portfolio.

It was apparent in conversations with Tata that he focused not on detailed specs and process, but on the importance of overall functionality and price. The instrument panel, for example, needed to show only the basics such as a speedometer, odometer and turn signals – but it had to meet a specific price. The Delphi Team could be as creative as they needed to meet those requirements.

Tata forecasted that they could initially produce 250,000 Nanos a year, with the potential for an eventual one million units annually, including 500,000 assembled in markets such as northern Africa, Southeast Asia and South America. Successfully reinventing the automobile, however, was no easy task. The team couldn't just cut corners. The suppliers would have to work closely with each other to come up with new designs, new manufacturing processes, and new ideas to make their components lighter, cheaper, and compatible – slowly integrating their designs at each step of the plan.

Although many were intrigued by the proposition, not everyone bought into Tata's vision. Similarly, others didn't believe that they could adjust their manufacturing processes to meet Tata's requirements.

However, most suppliers were convinced they could make a unique contribution and did come on board. Some bet on the future. They saw the chance to partner with Tata Motors to make a profit (on slim margins but high volume) and tap into a potentially large, new market. Others, such as Delphi, saw the project as a learning opportunity.

Tata convinced suppliers to join him by appealing to each one's unique needs, emphasizing that their specialization was vital to the overall goal.

Tight control of the Nano production process was crucial. Girish Wagh – a stickler for perfection – was handpicked to manage the project. Having been with the Tata Group for more than 10 years, he coordinated the project meticulously, making sure things happened as – and when – they should. He coordinated the 500-strong Tata team, suppliers and vendors. He held team meetings daily: every morning, he would spend up to two hours on the factory floor, insisting on full attendance to speed up response times, decision making and problem solving.

No one, however, can plan for every contingency, and the Nano project met several complications along the way. Since the project challenged traditional automobile engineering orthodoxies, every step in the production process involved testing new concepts by trial and error. The engine had to be redesigned

"

From one believer to millions of converts,
Ratan Tata has proved that the $2,500 Nano
was not a personal fantasy

"

three times, and the body went through more than ten iterations.

But each time the team overcame a challenge, it gathered further momentum, and through this onerous process, the design innovations began to materialize. RICO created a 34-horsepower, two-cylinder petrol engine using aluminum instead of conventional heavy cast iron. Bosch used an external cooling fan to reduce the weight of its generator from 13 to 11 pounds.

Tata Motors itself designed a dashboard that only weighed 14 ounces, far less than the 2-pounds-3-ounces version typically found in North American cars. It cut costs by replacing screws with simple, snap-on panels and parts and by using a clear, curved plastic display panel to reduce reflections and glare, thereby eliminating the need for a more expensive anti-glare coating.

An average car has over 2,000 components, 30,000 parts, and nearly 10 million lines of software code. The Nano has as few moving parts as possible to increase the simplicity of the design. It's got one windshield wiper and one wing mirror; its smaller wheels have three bolts rather than four; there are only four gears plus reverse instead of five. Yet, it is a stylish car, spacious and comfortable to sit in and easy to drive on busy roads.

After a $400 million investment and four long years of collaboration and negotiation, the team was prepared to show the world what the Nano could do. Tata unveiled his new car at the 2008 Auto Expo in New Delhi to critical acclaim. Even before it was available, it was already on its way to becoming one of the most sought after cars of the year.

Demand for the little cars was so great that the first 100,000 were sold through a lottery to ensure all potential buyers got a fair chance. Over 200,000 cars were booked within a two-week period alone. And in July 2009, the first Nanos were delivered by Ratan Tata himself to the first three owners in Mumbai.

The delivery of the first Nanos was a dream come true for thousands of families in India. And Tata is now looking at selling to northern Africa, Southeast Asia and South America. There are even plans for designing modified versions of the Nano for launch in Europe and North America.

Ratan Tata recalls the initial skepticism that surrounded his idea, "There was a fair amount of ridicule when the project started that it is a pipe dream, and, in honesty, that would have extended into the company also... That it can't be done. And as one went along, it became clear that something was happening and we were going forward..." He adds, "I think, my friend [Renault and Nissan boss] Carlos Ghosn [was] the only person in the automotive area who has not scoffed at this. He has not ridiculed anything."

Now, from one believer to millions of converts, Ratan Tata has proved that the $2,500 Nano was not a personal fantasy. It may have taken millions of investment dollars, five years, and hundreds of iterations before they finally got it right, but in the end, Ratan Tata and his team were able to fulfill a seemingly impossible dream and bring "the Indian people's car" to life.

Key characteristics of Architect & Builders

The Architect & Builders archetype is a cross between the Landlord & Tenants and Producer & Creative Team models. Architects provide a strong, clear vision and direct people toward a goal. They rely on the innovation, ingenuity and diversity of the builders to achieve it.

Before they've worked out the precise details of the project and how the blueprint will be brought to life, architects use their own passion, vision and conviction to persuade the best builders to join their project.

Architects are visionaries with a goal that, at times, may seem like an impossible dream.

 Architects bring together a team of builders who have not only the right mix of skills but also a willingness to collaborate.

 "Revolutionary" problem solving is critical: the dream cannot be achieved by conventional thinking.

 Builders are given "freedom within a frame": they are expected to solve problems creatively but, at the same time, respect designated goals.

 Success is about completing defined, scheduled tasks on time.

 Builders, suppliers and other workers are interdependent links in a chain; their activities are synchronized.

1

Architects are visionaries with a goal that, at times, may seem like an impossible dream.

Great architects visualize possibilities others can't see. They are never dissuaded by the magnitude of the challenge they face. Their ideas are often so ambitious that they demand revolutionary thinking. Great architects inspire others to consider limitless possibilities and enlist their help in solving the associated technical problems.

In 2005, a group of the world's top thinkers under 40 across business, politics and the arts, were invited by the World Economic Forum to the tiny Swiss ski resort of Zermatt. For four days, they gathered in the small village to discuss ways in which they could make the world a better place by 2030. After returning home, delegates were asked to take a piece of what they'd learned to start implementing their action plans towards the "2030 Initiative." Some delegates have made significant progress against their plans. Others are driven to change the world. Forty-two-year-old Shai Agassi is one of those.

During his Zermatt sessions, Agassi focused on climate change. That's when something clicked for him. He learned that each year in the United States, automobiles emit more than 333 million tons of carbon dioxide, and yet, scientists have confirmed that enough solar energy falls on the surface of the earth every 40 minutes to meet 100 percent of the entire world's energy needs for a full year. How could we make better use of sustainable energy sources in a practical and impactful way?

Though he first considered other options, Agassi believed electric cars were the answer. In fact, their loaded cost is cheaper than gasoline cars by about $1,000–$2,000. The problem is that electric car batteries cost about $12,000 each. Right now, they are neither affordable nor

convenient. His solution is to separate the battery from the car and use what he calls an Electric Recharge Grid Operator (ERGO) or recharge station. Similar to gas stations, electric cars can recharge at ERGOs at various points in a journey. Using this concept he believes electric cars can be viable – even profitable.

Though considered the whiz kid of the world's biggest business software company, SAP, he decided to quit. He made the eradication of fossil fuels his mission and in May 2007, launched Project Better Place (now called Better Place).

Better Place is building global energy networks so that electricity will replace gasoline and electric cars can be widely used around the world. Do you believe it can happen? It's a visionary plan that's decades in the making, and Agassi can't do it alone. So he's been talking to different regions around the world in hopes of getting them on board. So far, Denmark, Australia, Israel, Hawaii, Canada, Oregon and California have agreed to join the project.

Within a matter of five years, how has Agassi accomplished all of this? As ambitious as Agassi's vision may be, achieving it is closer than we think. His biggest challenge hasn't been to create or evangelize the concept. The hardest part has been to convince people from across industries and countries to join in his mission including governments, politicians, car manufacturers, businesses, insurance companies, investors, energy companies and the

"

Architects have a crystal clear idea of what the future could be and their insatiable drive to achieve it

"

public. Renault-Nissan has already partnered with Better Place and three prototypes are in production. One hundred thousand vehicles will be available on a per-use basis by 2016. Pilot programs will be running in Northern California, Hawaii, Denmark and Israel. Better Place's first two projects in Denmark and Israel are on track to go online in 2011 using the all-electric Renault sedan. If Shai Agassi has it his way, we'll all be driving electric cars by 2012.

What makes people like Agassi architects? Obviously, architects are ambitious and intelligent. They can speak persuasively and passionately. But they also have a crystal clear idea of what the future could be and their insatiable drive to achieve it. Agassi is what you'd call a visionary.

As Daniel Roth, senior writer at *Wired* magazine said of Agassi in 2008, "[He] has only one car, no charging stations, and not a single customer – yet everyone who meets him already believes he can see the future."

Architects can grasp onto a big idea but not just any idea – it's something that no one thinks can be accomplished, or an idea that no one has ever conceived. Their visions tend to be long sighted in nature – but that's just part of the challenge architects face in the beginning.

What sets architects apart is an ability to inspire people to follow their vision. It's a charisma and enthusiasm. They inspire others to consider limitless possibilities and enlist their help in solving the problem. They are never dissuaded by the magnitude of the challenge. Instead of focusing on failure, they learn from it and focus on the potential. Ever optimistic, they challenge and motivate others to consider limitless possibilities then enlist their help in solving the bigger challenges. Architects' optimism is so infectious that it makes them very effective at gathering a circle of dedicated followers and convincing them to join the daring ride.

Architects bring together a team of builders who have not only the right mix of skills but also a willingness to collaborate.

Architects need a team capable of solving problems in a collaborative spirit. Subsets of the team, formed to tackle specific, specialized issues, must never forget the overall project aims. Builders will be motivated by the iconic vision of the architect but they need to know they are critical to the task. The innumerable challenges of the project are resolved through intensive joint problem solving.

When Englishman Thomas Austin introduced 24 wild rabbits into Australia in 1859, he never fathomed the devastating impact that the cute creatures would have on the Australian ecosystem. But the rapid spread of the rabbits led to the extinction of many plant species. A century after their unfortunate introduction to Australia, their numbers were estimated at 600 million.

To solve the burgeoning problem, the Commonwealth Scientific and Industrial Research Organisation (CSIRO) was called to the rescue. Twice, in fact. In the 1950s, the virus, myxomatosis, was first used to successfully kill off 99 percent of the rabbit population. But the rabbits soon developed resistance to the virus, and again in 1995, CSIRO had to step in. It introduced rabbit haemorraghic disease virus (RHDV), and successfully combated the rising population.

The organization is so iconic and nationally treasured that every Australian schoolchild learns of its role and major success stories. Over the years, it has built up this long list of remarkable discoveries and research by quickly gathering together some of the most diverse and intellectual groups from across various scientific disciplines to

Big science for challenging times | National Research FLAGSHIPS CSIRO

solve some really big problems. But in 2001, Dr Geoff Garrett, CSIRO's new CEO, wanted to take this capability to a whole new level.

Garrett thought it was time to reinvigorate CSIRO. He wanted the organization to draw excellence, not just from the scientific communities within CSIRO and Australia, but globally and across multiple disciplines including business, healthcare, public sector, and universities. Garrett's passion and energy succeeded in transforming the organization, and his efforts culminated in a new scientific research paradigm called the National Research Flagship Initiative. The Flagships weren't going to simply collect existing research and bundle it together. Their impact would be far reaching, as their objectives would be of extraordinary proportions akin to a "BHAG" or Big Hairy Audacious Goal.

For example, Australia is currently facing the worst drought in recorded history. In fact, there are localized regions that are experiencing the lowest rainfall levels since the Australian government started monitoring them in 1900. Recognizing this issue, CSIRO created the Climate Adaptation Flagship to help Australia adapt its cities, industries, ecosystems and people to future climate change issues. This is just

one of ten Flagships that have been created over the last decade. Other Flagships have been established to monitor energy consumption, sustainable agriculture, preventative health, and ocean sustainability.

Ultimately the Flagships have forged new identities in CSIRO. Collaboration has been critical to the success of the Flagships. The best and brightest from across Australia and the international research community have been called upon, bringing their unique and specialized knowledge, to work on developing solutions to complex national issues. External collaboration has further engaged outstanding global researchers into the Flagship family. In a review of the initiatives, an external panel stated, "[The] Flagships offer the most promising mechanism yet to drive large-scale activity addressing National Research Priorities in a collaborative and intensively managed manner."

Architects have the vision, conviction and the passion – they know their dream can be attained, but they also realize that they can't achieve it alone. Architects use their power to convince and connect builders to achieve the impossible dream. Architects are dependent upon the builders to bring their specific skills across diverse disciplines. They need engineers, electricians, glass cutters, wood workers, brick layers, and the more complex the structure, the more diverse the skills required. Each builder has the specific disciplinary depth required to enable architects to achieve their unique dream. But the archetype can also be about tailoring the architect's blueprint to create localized success while staying true to an overarching vision. Here are a few more examples to explain.

In 1985, a small group of West African businesses believed that forming a bank would bring a measure of control back to African hands and drive the economic integration of the continent. Today, Ecobank Transnational Inc. employs over 11,000 staff in over 30 African countries using 50 different regional and national languages. Remarkably, it has the largest banking network than any other bank in the world.

Its success is in large part due to the geographic expansion strategy which enables its diverse subsidiary banks to access the bank's common technology platform while tailoring local delivery models to the specifics of each local market. The centralized technology platform acts as the common bond across the diverse regions; it ensures standardization, efficiency and adherence to Ecobank's overall blueprint. On a continent where technology and banking performance tends to be unreliable, Ecobank's model focuses on delivering consistent services regardless of time zone or location.

Leveraging its strong ground presence and local knowledge, Ecobank has taken the lead in introducing innovative retail products as part of its "Taking banking to the people" campaign. They've constructed over 120 kiosks near markets or high-traffic-density areas and they've employed a sales force of over 700 direct agents to take banking products and services to where customers are: in homes, offices, markets, factories, restaurants or along the street. This unique practice has enabled the organization to be successful at tailoring its branches to some of the world's most diverse environments – transcending language, culture, economies, and politics.

"Revolutionary" problem solving is critical:
the dream cannot be achieved by
conventional thinking.

Architects' visions are so ambitious that they can't be
achieved by incremental innovations. The builders often
completely reinvent and rethink ways of doing things. They
challenge, and sometimes reverse, received wisdom.

Architects work hard to convince the right builders to
join, knowing that once the team hits its stride, they will
be able to solve the critical challenges together. It's the
combination of the architect's vision and the builders'
skills that enable them to look at something and see it for
much more than what it is. In Ratan Tata's case, he had
the overall vision and defined the guidelines. He knew
there was the opportunity to take advantage of this market, but the builders were the ones that created the
remarkable breakthroughs.

Often one of the biggest challenges for builders is that
leading-edge innovation and disciplined, trial-and-error
testing go hand in hand. Since builders are experimenting
with new ways of working, technologies, or designs as
they go along, often multiple painstaking iterations and
even failures are often experienced before a final product
is achieved.

Take for example, Capital One. The financial institution is known for its innovation and experimentation.
Since 1994, it's grown from a Signet Bank spin-off with
only 2,000 employees to one of the largest diversified
banks and credit card issuers in the United States. From
the very beginning, CEO Rich Fairbank has viewed
Capital One, not as a traditional credit card company, but
a technology company. The heart of Capital One's credit
card strategy uses a highly analytical approach to market-

ing called information-based strategy or IBS. This strategy leverages sophisticated, technology-based analytics to tailor products that will appeal to specific customer segments. Fairbank is oft-quoted as saying, "Credit cards aren't banking – they're information."

One of Capital One's claims to fame was the brilliant concept of balance transfers. Through its advanced analytics strategy the company had identified a potentially high-value customer segment: consumers who run up high debt on their cards but eventually pay it off. By targeting this group through proactive tailored marketing campaigns, Capital One was able to capture market share by shifting these customers' balances from other high-interest credit cards to Capital One cards.

It was through innovative concepts such as the balance transfer and other products that Capital One experienced significant growth in the late 1990s and early 2000s. For example, from 1996 until 2004, Capital One's annual return on equity never slipped below 21 percent.

How has Capital One been able to create an environment and culture that supports innovation? The answer is embedded within the company's 1996 annual report: "Many of our business opportunities are short-lived. We have

to move fast to exploit them and move on when they fade." So, before they roll out any major campaign, Capital One employees, called associates, rigorously test products and marketing ideas to understand potential outcomes under various circumstances. For example, it might divide the customer segment into smaller ones, and pitch a slightly different offer to each to understand what works and what doesn't on customer response rates.

––––––––––

Architects' visions are so innovative and ambitious that they can't be achieved simply by using conventional means. Builders often need to reinvent and rethink ways of doing things to build from the architect's blueprint. They have the unique capability to solve some of the architect's most challenging problems by using innovation, experimentation, and failure. The blueprint guides the builders' work, but they can't always use the same conventional techniques to achieve the architect's dream. Think of Thomas Edison and the light bulb. When Edison was interviewed by a reporter who asked if he felt like a failure, Edison purportedly retorted, "I now know definitively over 9,000 ways that an electric light bulb will not work. Success is almost in my grasp." And shortly after that with over 10,000 attempts, Edison finally got it right.

Builders are given "freedom within a frame": they are expected to solve problems creatively but, at the same time, respect designated goals.

Builders need license to use their craft, the freedom to decide how they can use their specialized skills. At the same time, however, they follow the design direction set by the architect. The architect has the overall vision; the builders are accountable for their part in it.

Robert Henderson had a big responsibility. In the early 1990s, he was tasked with opening up a new GE Aviation plant. He wasn't daunted by the job as he'd actually built a plant from scratch before, but this time, the stakes were much higher: GE Aviation's goal for the factory was to manufacture the largest commercial jet engine in history.

The GE90 was and still is one of the most powerful air-breathing engines ever designed. It holds two Guinness World Records for the highest thrust (127,900lbf or 569kN), and the world's longest flight by a commercial airliner (13,422 miles or 21,601 km in 22 hours 42 minutes). GE Aviation had invested over $1.5 billion in the engine's development, and the job of building the plant to manufacture these behemoths rested squarely on Henderson's shoulders.

From previous experience, Henderson knew he wanted to run things differently. On building the plant, he said, "My outlook was 'Let's push the envelope as far as we can at the start, because it's the only chance we'll get to do that. What you establish is what gets perpetuated. Starting a culture is so much easier than changing a culture." So he began to tour other GE plants to pull out the best ideas to implement them in his soon-to-be identified location. GE's CEO at the time, Jack Welch said, "We now know where productivity comes from. It comes from challenged, empowered, excited, rewarded teams of people." Henderson decided to follow that philosophy and looked for ideas that would be implemented to empower people on the factory floor.

With a small team of managers, Henderson selected one of GE's empty plants in Durham, North Carolina. Culture wasn't the only aspect that would differentiate this plant from others. They decided that all employees required FAA-approved mechanic's licenses so that the caliber of recruits would be higher. But what really set the Durham plant apart was that each never-before-made engine would be built by a single group of nine people.

From its initial 10,000 parts until it's loaded on the truck, the engine is owned by those individuals. And what's more remarkable is that the only piece of instruction they are given is the date that their finished engine must be loaded on the truck.

There are no set processes around how to assemble the engine. They are given "freedom within a frame" to decide the best way to work as long as they meet their deadline. Working against the clock, employees can deliver a new jet engine in a mere nine weeks. Each team member signs off each component that is installed for which they are responsible.

Considering the safety measures and risk associated with building the engines, how can these employees near-perfectly assemble the world's most powerful engines with no rules, no guidelines, and no boss?

The short answer is that the builders own the engine. At the very beginning, Henderson had a plan. He knew that if he could get the right team of skilled people together and give them the right environment to work in, the Durham plant could be one of the best among GE. And he was right.

The only plant in the entire GE fleet that builds GE90s is the Durham plant. The external turnover rate there is less than 5 percent per year. Its 170 employees are overseen by one person: the plant manager. The builders are given full freedom in their teams of nine to decide how they are going to build their engine. They are not at the whim of anyone but themselves. They are responsible for their own components, and they rely on each other as a team to make sure that each person does their job.

Though each team may work very differently from one another, each team member is part of a self-motivated and dedicated group that wants to see the best engines delivered from GE.

Success is about completing defined, scheduled tasks on time.

If any part of the team fails to perform, the project will flounder. Builders strive to meet ambitious deadlines and milestones. As each milestone is completed, they become one step closer to turning the architect's dream into a reality.

Sir Terry Leahy is the CEO of Tesco, the largest supermarket chain in Britain and the third-largest in the world behind Walmart and Carrefour. Leahy started off his career at Tesco as a shelf stacker before going to university and has risen through the ranks, first through the company's marketing department before becoming CEO in 1997. He's practically lived his entire working life there.

Leahy attributes Tesco's success in part to a simple four-pronged strategy based on increasing the core UK market, diversifying into non-food, moving into services, and expanding internationally. Sounds pretty basic and Leahy admits that. However, Tesco's success is not based on strategy, but how it's been executed.

Part of Tesco's challenge is to deliver a consistent buying experience to consumers in every store, which is particularly difficult when you have more than 468,000 employees in multiple countries. How could Tesco ensure that all employees from its executives to its in-store employees were working together to achieve the four components of the company's strategy?

Leahy decided to break the strategy down into easy-to-understand, achievable and measurable goals and milestones. Intrigued by Kaplan and Norton's Balanced Scorecard concept, one of his first moves as CEO was to implement the "Tesco Steering Wheel." The steering wheel has allowed him to track and communicate progress

at all levels of the organization across its 4,300 stores. Every store gets a monthly steering wheel update so that all employees across its 15 countries get feedback on their performance. "Shopping lists" are used to break down the strategy into simple terms so employees can make changes in their everyday activities. Aggressive as the milestones and metrics may be, they provide common goal posts for the entire organization to work toward. Over the past 13 years, the steering wheel has helped Tesco remain on track as it experienced its rapid growth phase. Leahy explained, "Tesco doesn't want one leader. We want thousands of leaders who take initiative to execute the strategy."

We often spend considerable time thinking about the overall strategy, and less so about the details on how to get there. Architects set aggressive deadlines mapped to progress against the blueprint – similar to natural, built-

in progress points along the way such as the establishment of foundation and the completion of the roof.

The goal of every leader is to get their followers on the same page. But if any part of the team fails to perform, the dream will not be achieved.

Builders strive to meet ambitious deadlines and milestones mapped to deliberate work cycles. As each milestone is completed the builders become one step closer to bringing the architect's dream to reality. But it's easy for builders to become discouraged if tangible progress is not made against the long timeframes. Experimentation and the trial-and-error process can often wear down motivation. Thus it's helpful for architects to articulate aggressive milestones that maintain momentum. The project milestones should provide future points of reference for builders to work toward.

Builders, suppliers and other workers are interdependent links in a chain; their activities are synchronized.

The architect's design is made up of discrete parts that are worked on separately but, ultimately, come together to form a perfect whole. This makes synchronization of work essential. The architect sets a rhythm for the project and provides, in the blueprint, a "road map." Any changes to the design are communicated clearly to everyone involved at the same time. Each builder works from the "master" version of the blueprint. Without this synergy, the project disintegrates.

In the 1970s, the psychologist Ulric Neisser conducted a well-known experiment to highlight what is known today as "inattentional blindness." This means that when individuals are playing close attention to one thing, they can fail to see something unexpected even when it passes directly through their field of vision.

Neisser showed a videotape of two visually-superimposed teams passing basketballs, one wearing white shirts and the other wearing black. He asked participants to count the number of passes made by one team, and to ignore the other. To score accurately, participants were told to pay careful attention to the task.

When asked at the end of the tape whether they saw anything noteworthy, only one-fifth of participants reported seeing a woman walk through the players with an open umbrella; though she was on screen for several seconds.

Two decades later, subsequent tests by other researchers repeatedly demonstrated the same phenomenon. In one instance, 50 percent of the participants failed to notice a person wearing a gorilla suit walk into the middle of the basketball game, face the camera, and thump its chest, though it was on screen for a full nine seconds. Why did so many people not see the woman or the gorilla?

The answer can be attributed to an overarching management concept identified by Max H. Bazerman and Dolly Chugh called "bounded awareness." Similar to inattentional blindness, Bazerman and Chugh imply that when making decisions, people often fail to perceive and process information that is easily available to them.

Most people's reactions to these concepts are: "How could I have missed that?" We think that just because our eyes are open, we can see. The shocking results of this research demonstrate how little we actually see when we're not paying attention.

What does this mean for architects and builders, and how can bounded awareness impede builders' progress?

Clearly, we see far less of our world than we think we do, so when builders focus on their specialized task to create their individual "component," architects must schedule deliberate "moments of synchronization" to ensure the builders' designs are aligned both with each other and against the architect's blueprint.

Each of the pieces of the builders' components must fit together perfectly. It is too easy to remain in your specialized domain focused on your piece of the puzzle and not see how your piece needs to fit in with the others, let alone the big picture puzzle you are assembling. When you consider the number of trial-and-error iterations that each part goes through, it's an entire challenge in itself to keep the builders on the same page.

Synchronization is crucial for the builders to integrate their designs and pool their learning. But it's not always easy to get large groups of people lined up in the same direction and following the same blueprint, especially if the blueprint is changing on a daily basis. Adding to the challenge is that builders must collaborate to build something new; something that's never been done. Thus, to be successful, they must work across new boundaries and take on new challenges as a team.

Architects establish the rhythm top-down and provide the blueprint and guidance to keep everyone on track. The difficulty is that because each of the builders works on a separate part of the architect's design, it's easy for them to focus on individual tasks at hand, forgetting how their work impacts others. In the end, the pieces must to fit together perfectly. Information must be must kept current and transparently shared across the builders, so each time the vision gets refined, each builder works from the same version of the blueprint.

To be successful, builders must work across new boundaries and take on new challenges as a team

Is Architect & Builders the right model for you?

Is this archetype right for your current situation? And, if it is, how can you be the best architect you can be? The following sections will help you answer these questions.

Great if:

- You have a BHAG (big hairy audacious goal); a dream of building the impossible.

- You want to do something that's never been done before.

- You have a concept that needs to be refined by local experts to make it fit for expansion.

- You have a model of continuous innovation that requires people to push beyond normal boundaries.

Think twice if:

- You believe in "creative tension" and, to cut costs, would like to see different teams of builders compete with and usurp each other.

- Your builders are primarily driven by short-term financial incentives.

- Your vision is too wild and too personal to inspire others.

- Your vision is not clear enough or developed enough to inspire others.

How can you be a better architect?

1. Is your dream impossible or insane?

There's a big difference between a dream that seems impossible and one that seems so wild it's doomed. People want to succeed. You'll need to challenge and inspire them without alienating them and, crucially, you'll need to convince them that they can make a difference.

- Does the way you communicate your goals inspire and motivate people?
- How successful are you at enlisting others to help you achieve your dream?
- What tactics are you using to win commitment from your builders?

2. Have you broken the project down into a coherent set of challenges that draws on different capabilities and experience?

The vision will seem less daunting "piece by piece." Successful architects define the project in terms of a collection of specific challenges that must be resolved by the right groups of expert builders.

- Have you translated your vision into distinct yet mutually reinforcing challenges?
- Have you assembled the right team of expert builders to take on each "module"?
- Have you told each builder that they're as important as the next; have you discouraged competitive tension between subsets and groups?

3. How successful have you been at convincing the builders about the critical nature of their contribution?

Architects establish the collaborative environment that supports the builders' work. The builders need to be able to understand precisely what they bring to the table.

- How effective are you at tailoring your messages to reflect different builders' strengths?
- How do you convince builders that every one of them has something special to contribute?
- Is your relationship with your builders built on respect and trust – or have you hinted there's a contingency plan if they don't deliver?

4. Are your builders "licensed" to innovate and reinvent designs?

If builders are to break away from traditional thinking, they need to have the freedom and environment to apply their skills and experience. They need to feel "empowered" by you.

- How successful are you at creating the conditions for innovation and reinvention?
- Are your goals ambitious enough to encourage radical thinking?
- How do you ensure cross-innovation; how are different ways of problem solving shared by the different teams?

5. How well do you inform builders of changes to the blueprint and their consequences?

Cross-team links are essential for ensuring that everyone is working to the same blueprint and that pieces of the plan fit together. Updates to the design must be communicated across the entire team. Frequent integration points are usually needed to keep all the builders on the same page.

- How frequently do you hold meetings or calls to integrate learning across the group?
- Are you using a systematic time-pacing methodology to accelerate major releases of and minor upgrades to the blueprint?
- Are you developing a culture that thrives on collaborative information exchange; is the team self-motivated to openly share information?

6. How clearly are you communicating the teams' progress so that everyone knows what's working and what isn't?

Performance and progress must be made transparent across the team so that the builders understand how other people's changes will affect their own work.

- What tools are you using to track individual progress and how effective are they?
- Can builders update their own information and tell others of their progress?
- Are you communicating with those who are not keeping up with the schedule and are causing delays?

7. How effective are you at communicating across the whole group?

You need a communications platform that connects all the teams. Transparency of information is crucial. The builders must be able to update others of any changes made to the design.

- How effective and efficient are your current communication channels and tools at disseminating messages in real time to the group of builders?
- Are you using the best collaborative technologies to enable different teams to work off a single version of the blueprint?
- Does your information system communicate bad news and warn of pitfalls as quickly and as clearly as possible?

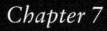
Chapter 7

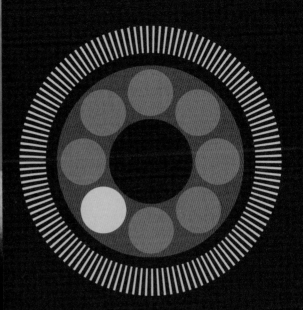

Captain & Sports Team

"I am a member of a team, and I rely on the team, I defer to it and sacrifice for it, because the team, not the individual, is the ultimate champion"

—*Mia Hamm, US soccer player who scored more international goals than any other player, male or female*

" Look around you. See those flags? Play for those people. This is our one chance "

François Pienaar: Working for a new South Africa

When François Pienaar, captain of the South African rugby team, the Springboks, between 1993 and 1996, was first introduced to Nelson Mandela, few people would have described the meeting as momentous. Pienaar was a nervous 27-year-old; the 77-year-old Mandela had recently been elected president. It was hardly, you'd have thought, the kind of encounter that would make history; hardly a landmark in world politics. Yet that day, June 17, 1994, for the president at least, symbolized the start of a new South Africa.

Born into an average working class Afrikaner family in Vereeniging, an industrial town south of Johannesburg, Pienaar didn't think of himself as anything particularly special. But he made a deep impression on the president. Mandela recalled, "He did not seem to me at all to be the typical product of an apartheid society. I found him quite a charming fellow and I sensed that he was progressive."

Mandela wanted to use rugby to unite the nation; and he knew, from that day, that Pienaar was the man to help him do it. At the time the new president took office in 1994, non-white South Africans still saw the Springboks as a symbol of apartheid. At matches, the whites had typically sung out racist fight songs; and the blacks had cheered for the opposite side. Only small areas of seats were designated for black spectators; 99 percent were "reserved" exclusively for white fans.

Mandela wanted to build one team, one country, one South African people. He told Pienaar that June day: "Let us use sport for the purpose of nation-building and promoting all the ideas which we think will lead to peace and stability in our country." By the time their afternoon tea was finished, the captain understood his message: "get out there and win, wear that shirt with pride, certain of my support."

Pienaar left Mandela's home knowing he'd remember those words. And, almost a year later, they once more rang in his ears. Pienaar and his team faced the toughest challenge of their lives: the 1995 World Cup final in Johannesburg versus the formidable New Zealand All Blacks. It would not only test their sporting abilities, but open the eyes and minds of their fellow countrymen and result in bringing blacks and whites together in the streets.

Two leaders; one cause

Though the unassuming Pienaar would probably never say so himself, he had certain things in common with Madiba (Mandela's honorary title). As captain of the national rugby team, he had to be a leader and a role model. He had always to do more than expected – run farther, play harder. He had to be on the field influencing the strategy in real time, motivating the team, raising their morale, in bad times as well as good. He had to demonstrate patience and composure on the field, and understand the players and their strengths.

As John Carlin, author of the book, *Playing the Enemy: Nelson Mandela and the Game that Changed a Nation*, describes, "The role of captain in other sports often has a token or ceremonial quality to it, but in rugby it carries real weight. Not only does the captain exercise a great deal of tactical authority during a game, calling moves that in American football, say, would be made by coaches on the sidelines, he also carries, by rugby tradition, a special mystique."

On June 24, 1995, the day of the World Cup final, Pienaar needed all the mystique, all the strength, all the special skills he could muster. Against the favorites, the All Blacks, the Springboks' chances of victory seemed remote. Nine out of ten times, Pienaar recalls, the All Blacks would beat the Springboks. The day was filled with tension; some of the players were physically sick. "The pressure," says Kobus Wiese, part of the Springbok team, "was absolutely hectic. It was massive… I felt fear, fear that we would disappoint all those millions of fans."

What we saw that day was a revolution…
[That match] galvanized us; it made us realize that it
was actually possible for us to become one nation

That this was no ordinary final became startlingly apparent when Mandela arrived at Ellis Park for the match. The crowds were singing "Shosholoza," the song originally sung by black migrant workers who toiled at the gold mines near Johannesburg. It had been adopted as the official World Cup song, and now both black and white fans belted it out.

Then, as Mandela stepped on to the field to shake hands with the players, the world stood still for a moment. He was waving and he was laughing, smiling his famous wide smile – and he was wearing what to black South Africans symbolized everything they hated: the Springbok green jersey. South African rugby and the South African team somehow seemed transformed, and, in reality, Mandela underwent his own form of transformation. It was no longer a matter of using sport, he became part of the rugby. That is why it was so credible.

"Now suddenly before the eyes of the whole of South Africa, and most of the world, the two negative symbols had merged to create a new one that was positive constructive and good. Mandela had wrought the transformation, becoming the embodiment not of hate and fear, but generosity and love."

Victory against the odds

As the match progressed, the pressure on Pienaar and the players became intense. At the end of the first 40 minutes, the score was 9–6 to South Africa. Then the All Blacks equalized in the second half. During one interval, Pienaar told his weary team, "Look around you. See those flags? Play for those people. This is one chance. We have to do this for South Africa. Let's be world champions." The sports team's success became the symbol for hope, change and uniting a nation.

Ten minutes before the end of the game, the score was 12–12. Then, in extra time, the Springboks' Joel Stransky scored a drop goal to win the match. Stransky described the moment, "I received the ball, clean and true, and I kicked that ball so, so sweetly. It was holding its line. It was spinning truly and it didn't veer at all... And I felt absolute jubilation."

Afterwards, the streets of South Africa teemed with celebration and life. Archbishop Tutu joyously recalled, "What we saw that day was a revolution... [That match] galvanized us; it made us realize that it was actually possible for us to become one nation."

Through inspired teamwork, the Springboks had beaten all odds to win the 1995 World Cup. Despite their strength and speed, the All Blacks hadn't found a way through their defense. Their triumph transcended all the differences of race, politics, and religion. Crucially, it was a national triumph.

Mandela – still sporting the Springboks jersey – handed the William Web Ellis trophy to Pienaar and said, "Thank you very much for what you have done for our country." "Mr President," replied Pienaar, "it is nothing compared to what you have done for our country."

Mandela once said, "Sport has the power to change the world. It has the power to inspire, the power to unite people that little else has…" The leadership of the team captain and his ability to connect, drive and motivate his players, took the Springboks to an historic victory. François Pienaar – an average man from Vereeniging but one of the greatest team captains in the history of rugby – worked hard for one team, one country; for the new South Africa. He and his Springboks team epitomize what can be achieved through vision, discipline and, perhaps most importantly of all, hope.

*Sport has the power to change the world.
It has the power to inspire, the power to
unite people that little else has…*

Dabbawalas
Even during the monsoon

For over 125 years, every business day of every year, something remarkable has been happening in Mumbai. Come rain, shine, monsoon or blazing heat, nearly 5,000 dabbawalas, or lunchbox men, wake up every morning with one primary purpose: to deliver nearly 200,000 hot meals directly from the Mumbai suburbs to hungry office workers downtown.

This isn't just any meal distribution system. Some of these men travel up to 80 miles a day carrying loads that weigh up to 100 pounds. What really sets them apart, though, is their breathtaking efficiency. Out of every 16 million planned deliveries, only one fails to arrive; only one lunch remains undelivered every two months. For this achievement, the dabbawalas were certified Six Sigma in 1998.

With eight out of ten white-collar workers living too far from their offices to go home for lunch, and restaurant meals costing five to 15 times more than home-cooked food, the dabbawala trade is an essential fixture of Mumbai – woven into the fabric of the city's culture. Monthly delivery costs are just US$5, making the service affordable to the middle class in Mumbai, where wages are low.

The dabbawalas' delivery system is complex in its flow of lunchboxes from the Mumbai suburbs to downtown and back, yet simple in the way that each dabbawala operates. The dabbawalas form a dynamic network so that – at multiple checkpoints along Mumbai's elaborate train system – hundreds of lunches are sorted and redistributed to reach their destinations. One lunchbox can easily change hands at least four times along its journey. Yet, the dabbawalas accomplish this striking feat using the most basic means of transport – bicycles, trains, and pull carts – to move the lunchboxes to their final points.

The dabbawalas collect the same lunchboxes and return them the same afternoon to their original locations, so that the process can be repeated the next day. For an organization that has no IT infrastructure and a workforce where illiteracy levels are 85 percent, it's a remarkable operation.

A day in the life of a dabbawala

Each wearing a white, Gandhi *topi* hat and dressed in a white, cotton *kurta* pyjama, the dabbawalas start their morning around 8:00am by going out into the suburbs to pick up the home-made meals that are packed in the dabbas. Each dabbawala will pick up 30–40 dabbas, and bring them to the train station.

At 9:00am in the train stations, dabbawalas meet to sort the dabbas and move them to the right train. The railways even have special reserved compartments for the dabbas, with 700 to 800 neatly packed for the ride. Further sorting takes place in the trains – sometimes by hundreds of dabbawalas.

At approximately 11:30am at the right train station, a dabbawala will jump out with their dabbas, which will get sorted and delivered to the neighborhood, building and floor they're meant for.

From 2:00pm to 6:00pm, the entire process reverses as empty dabbas are returned to their original locations out in the suburbs of Mumbai.

The language of the dabbas

Each dabba, also known as a tiffin or lunchbox, is marked with colored codes (symbols, numbers, and letters) to denote where the dabba comes from, which railway station it must pass

through, and which specific office the dabba should be delivered to in downtown Mumbai. Raghunath Medge, president of The Mumbai Tiffin Box Suppliers' Association, which runs the service, says, "The beauty of the system is the color coding used on the top of each tiffin box. The home address, office address, railway stations of delivery and pick-up are all crunched into a small series of letters and numbers, painted by hand."

Every dabba has the mark of a circle or a flower of a specific color and a digital identity number. Take this Tiffin Mark, for example: "K-BO-10-19/A/15." "K" is the identity letter of the dabbawala. "BO" means Borivali, the area from where the tiffin is to be collected. "10"

refers to Nariman point area. "19/A/15" refers to the 19th building and the 15th floor in Nariman point area where the dabba is to be delivered.

Today's existing coding system was developed in 1974, and allows the workforce to communicate quickly with one another to determine the sorting process for each dabba. It not only tells dabbawalas where dabbas should be routed, but also provides messaging about prioritization, key in a fast-paced environment where lead times are so tight.

A single DNA

The origins of the dabbawala, literally "one who carries a box" in Marathi, a language of west and central India, date back over a century to

"

*Not just anyone can be a dabbawala. You need to be physically fit,
dedicated to your work, punctual, and sociable*

"

1890. An Indian entrepreneur, Mahadeo Havaji Bacche, invented the meal distribution service to meet the culinary needs of the British and Indian working population. Over the years, the codes became simpler, and the dabbawalas more popular. And by the 1950s and 1960s, around 200,000 dabbas were being delivered a day.

Not just anyone can be a dabbawala. You need to be physically fit, dedicated to your work, punctual, and sociable. And coming from a specific farming village near Pune helps. Almost all of the dabbawalas come from this village, which is about four hours away from Mumbai. In fact, most of them are related to one another. They have similar beliefs, customs and traditions and share a close cultural and social bond. Some of them come from four generations of dabbawalas. "They are a single DNA. Everyone is a Marathi, they are made from the same cloth, speak the same language, everyone's lunch is the same, everyone's god is the same. So there's a high degree of coordination and commitment," says 33-year-old dabbawala Manish Tripathi.

Dabbawalas are self-employed. Their pride in their role not only comes from their heritage and tradition, but also from the fact they are partners in the business.

Dabbawalas receive 5,000 rupees (about US$123) a month – a good salary by Indian standards – and a job for life. To become a dabbawala, you must provide a donation to the dabbawalas' union, a minimum initial investment of two bicycles, a wooden crate, at least one *kurta* pyjama and a Gandhi *topi*, all costing a little over 4,000 rupees, most of your first month's pay.

The inner workings of the dabbawalas

The dabbawalas have developed a culture of inter-dependence and inter-reliance based on three roles. There are dabbawalas that collect, unload, and deliver dabbas. They're dependent on each other to ensure the dabbas are delivered on time. According to Natarajan Balakrishnan and Chung-Piaw Teo of the National University of Singapore, "Every dabbawala understands the need to race against time to reach his destined station to meet his *badli* (counterpart) who will board the local train with his quota at the precise hour at a given station. The effect of slip delivery is immediately discernable."

When interruptions occur, the dabbawalas, supervised by *mukadams*, old-timers who know the system, respond instantly to ensure that delivery remains on schedule, relying on the simplest means of communication and transport.

When a dabbawala on his bicycle was hit and killed by a large truck, news of the incident traveled fast in the network and, within minutes, the *mukadam* contacted the secretary of the Association who took care of the police formalities. The *mukadam*, familiar with the coding, then raced into action, collected his fallen team member's dabbas and personally delivered them to their final destinations – just 30 minutes behind schedule.

The dabbawalas adapt to accidents, to traffic jams, and also to the weather. During monsoon season, when the railway tracks get flooded, they are known to get off trains and make their way several kilometers to their checkpoints by foot, carrying the dabbas in large trays on their heads as they wade through the water.

So "natural" is the Mumbai tiffin business that it almost seems to run on instinct. As Paul Goodman, a professor of organizational psychology at Carnegie Mellon University puts it: "Most of our modern business education is about analytic models, technology and efficient business practices. The dabbawalas, by contrast, focus more on human and social ingenuity."

Nonetheless, the dabbawalas have entered the "20th century," launching an official website in 2003. They have slowly started to adapt to high technology, despite the high rate of illiteracy among the group. Now you can contact them by text message and via their website in order to have hot lunches delivered in Mumbai. The site gets about 10 to 15 new enquiries a day.

A modern-day contradiction

The dabbawalas, in some ways, are a paradox. They follow dynamically complex routes using the simplest means of transport. They operate with more precision, accuracy and efficiency than most modern organizations, yet none of them has above an eighth grade education. They form a complex, adaptive system yet they rely on strict rules, roles, and timing. They are based on traditional practices – with virtually no technology – that haven't changed since their inception, but they successfully operate in India's modern commercial capital.

Their integrity and discipline are world-renowned, yet they remain dedicated to their simple, local tasks.

Mr Chaudhary, a 65-year-old dabbawala, says, "The most important thing for us is to be on time. If we are late with the lunchboxes then office workers don't get their lunch... By lunchtime, everyone should have their tiffin."

Key characteristics of
Captain & Sports Team

The Captain & Sports Team is a hybrid between the Community Organizer & Volunteers and the Conductor & Orchestra archetypes, meaning that scripted processes and specific rules are followed even though there is no set strategic direction. Though a playbook exists, strategy and direction emerge over time based on interactions in the field of play. Therefore the sports team needs to adapt judiciously to unpredictable situations.

Members of the sports team have a high shared identity and come from a very small talent pool. Thus, there is a strong camaraderie and trust amongst the sports team. The captain does not manage strongly from the top down; his or her primary role is to be the catalyst on the field as part of the team to interpet and disseminate information and coordinate the team's actions. The task of the team is shared by all its members.

Sports teams have a strong sense of shared identity; members are recruited from a narrow pool.

 Recruits primarily join to achieve their personal goals.

 There is minimal hierarchy and sometimes no apparent leader.

 Tasks and processes are clearly defined, often learned through repetition.

 Internal communications are extensive, networked and made in real time.

 Strategy emerges gradually – developed largely in response to the environment.

Sports teams have a strong sense of shared identity; members are recruited from a small pool.

Recruits typically come from a very specific talent pool. Sometimes members of the same community, they identify strongly with each other and often remain on the team for a long time. They wear the same uniform, know precisely what role they perform and share the same culture or corporate identity.

In the 1970s, the world began to see a different type of violence with extremist groups such as the Red Army Faction the Palestinian Liberation Organization and the Red Brigades in Italy.

In 1977, inspired by his experience as a Green Beret in Vietnam and in response to the rise of terrorist activity, Colonel Charles Beckwith proposed that the US government create the ultimate tactical team capable of responding with deadly force to terrorist activities. It was called Delta Force.

Comprised of top recruits from the Green Berets, the elite Army Rangers, and the Airborne divisions, Delta Force was activated on October 9, 1977. It is a unique unit of handpicked and specially trained soldiers, or operators, based at Fort Bragg in North Carolina.

Within the military, the group is considered altogether unique, practically undetectable and virtually untouchable. They don't follow traditional philosophies of military life.

Unlike much of the rest of the military, Delta Force has no distinct outward uniform or insignia, and to protect their identity they wear civilian clothing. The *New York Times* reported that "Delta [Force] is organized for the conduct of missions requiring rapid response with surgi-

cal applications of a wide variety of unique skills, while maintaining the lowest possible profile of US involvement."

And because of their role in protecting the nation, not just anyone can be recruited to join Delta Force. They are selected through a rigorous and challenging assessment process based on mental toughness, motivation and sheer physical ability.

Sergeant Major Eric Haney who served with Delta Force in the 1970s and 1980s, and was one of the founding members, states, "Well, first of all, the selection process is what's so important because we're looking for a very particular kind of individual, a man with great tenacity, that's intelligent, that has an ability to learn. He's curious. He operates alone. He likes himself but he also likes other people and though he enjoys being by himself he's not alone and he works well with other teams and

other members of the organization. And just a real mental toughness and a mindset that he won't quit no matter what. He's just not going to quit. He's going to prevail and he knows he'll prevail."

In general, the minimum profile of a Delta Force recruit is that they must be male, at least 21-years-old, a US citizen in active army duty holding a rank of sergeant, captain, or major, have no limiting physical profile, pass a HALO/SCUBA exam, either have airborne qualifications or volunteer for airborne training, pass initial background security checks, hold a college degree, have no history of recurring disciplinary action and pass the five-event physical fitness qualification test while wearing boots and battle dress uniform.

Upon selection, the recruits are involved in a grueling two-part physical and psychological assessment over a three- to four-week period modeled on the British Special Air Service selection. The process includes a series of navigation tests where the length and the route changes every day and the recruit must carry increasingly heavier loads. Elements of the physical assessment include a timed 18-mile night march where recruits carry 35 pounds in their rucksack, and a timed 40-mile march that often extends over 48 hours, while carrying a 45-pound rucksack over rough terrain with little or no sleep.

In Delta Force's founder Beckwith's book, *Delta Force: The Army's Elite Counterterrorist Unit*, he wrote, "The endurance march revealed clearly those candidates who had character – real determination, self-discipline and self-sacrifice – and those who did not."

After the physical testing, the psychological portion begins where the men must confront a board of Delta instructors, psychologists and the Delta commander who ask a barrage of questions, ranging from simpler historical and family background questions to more intellectually demanding ones that test judgment, ethics and ability to withstand pressure.

They must be mentally stable and readily able to adapt to both working as part of a team as well as independently. After this rigorous assessment, the commander will then divulge whether the candidate has been successful.

The recruit is then entered into an intense six-month Operator Training Course, where he will learn the art of counter-terrorism including munitions, commando assaults, combat theory, close-quarters battle, rescue operation, and marksmanship.

Due to the caliber of assets, or individuals that are ultimately chosen, some state that selection statistics and attrition rates are never published. The Canadian Broadcasting Corporation estimated that "a quarter of those who volunteer – and these are top soldiers – are routinely washed out. Of those who go on, one in 10 makes it to the elite unit."

For the Captain & Sports Team, this degree of shared identity is needed on the team to support a culture of trust and camaraderie. Often, sports team members are subject to situations that are both fast paced and demanding. There is little time to second-guess one's actions, let alone those of your team members. They must all work together as a tight-knit unit, understanding the special language which only they comprehend. Through intense training, sports team members interact fluidly and see themselves as part of a special society where it is their duty to carry out a specific activity.

Recruits primarily join to achieve their personal goals.

Sports team members take great pride in their personal performance and achievements. They work hard to ensure they don't let other team members down, but often their primary motivation is personal pride. They don't join the team out of altruism – or a desire to change the world. They want to make a living doing what they do best.

Owned by an Australian-based company, CHEP, or the Commonwealth Handling Equipment Pool, got its start during World War II as a way to handle defense supplies. After US forces returned home, leaving behind vast piles of pallets and loading equipment, the organization continued to operate for a few years under the Australian government but was then privatized in 1949. In 1958 Brambles Limited, a company founded in 1875 that was familiar with logistics, bought CHEP and brought it into its portfolio. The company continued to grow and in 1973 expanded its operations to other countries outside of Australia. Today, the company is viewed as the global leader in the container and pallet pooling industry.

You may be wondering what exactly are pallets? We've all seem them before – they are wooden-framed transport structures that warehouses and retailers use to move large stacks of products from one place to another. The basic wooden ones are relatively simply constructed – made of 25 pieces of wood and 150 nails. Today you can get the classic wooden ones, plastic or galvanized steel. Their dimensions are often very specific depending on the industry which is using them, but essentially for the last 70 years, their basic design has remained relatively unchanged. While most pallets get traded back and forth amongst shippers without a real owner until they ultimately break, CHEP has turned the humble pallet into big business.

So how exactly does CHEP make money? CHEP basically rents out pallets for companies to use. They also collect, repair and re-issue the pallets so that at any point in time customers can access as many pallets as they need. With a global network of over 550 service centers, their customers have just-in-time pallet access to transport their products efficiently and safely.

In the US, CHEP charges its customers a one-time fee, usually $5 per pallet, plus a rental fee of less than a penny a day per pallet. In other markets, CHEP also makes money by

charging manufacturers a transfer fee when they ship pallets to a retailer. The pallets are, in turn, transported from the retailer to one of CHEP's service centers where they are inspected for quality, repaired as necessary, and made available for the next job.

What's interesting is that CHEP has amassed a pool of 250 million pallets worldwide that it rents to companies. While there's no centralized "home" or return address for the pallets, there is a sophisticated tracking system that monitors the overall efficiency and routes of the pallets so that as few as possible get "lost in the mail" and that they get rented by the next manufacturer in the most efficient manner. In

the process, CHEP has developed a network of customers that benefit from this seemingly random pallet sharing simply to ensure their individual business needs are met. On average, when a no-name new pallet costs mere dollars, why wouldn't a manufacturer simply buy new pallets?

Around 2000, the pallet renting industry was on the rise. Companies decided that renting pallets was more cost-effective and efficient; they were better quality and less hassle. Since they didn't own the pallets, companies didn't have to worry about disposal or repair, and large pallet rentals can provide improved service to national accounts.

Big retailers all need pallets to deliver their products. So CHEP made a smart decision and approached the biggest of them. It is reported that CHEP and Walmart have worked together since 1999 when CHEP put its rental pallets into about 40 Walmart distribution centers.

CHEP's ability to meet the business needs of their customers extends overseas to Europe as well. In continental Europe, the traditional white pallet exchange has been the standard, but the limited standardization in pallet size, material type and quality increased inefficiencies. Transportation costs were increasing across Europe. As a result, Agora Network, a company comprised of four leading distribution chains in Northern Italy, decided to switch to CHEP.

Febrizio Carboni, Agora Network logistics operator, said, "While Pallet Exchange seems straightforward on paper, however, in reality it can generate significant problems like unneces-sary capital expenditure, administrative cost and environmental impact... We are opting to switch to equipment pooling providers such as CHEP because equipment pooling provides an environmentally sustainable solution which eliminates the need for costly recovery transportation of empty pallets. Pallet pooling also avoids disputes between manufacturers, transporters and retailers relating to the pallet quantities that have been exchanged... We are a local group and have come to understand that working with CHEP allows us to be more efficient and competitive. We hope that the other national distribution chains see it this way."

In this instance, the Captain & Sports Team model refers to actions that CHEP's clients, such as Walmart and Agora Network engage in to rent CHEP's pallets. Although Walmart may be the world's largest retailer, it heavily relies on its supporting suppliers, such as CHEP for the efficiency and cost savings for its delivery and logistics. Walmart's primary goal has always been to focus on lowering prices. CHEP enables them to do that.

It's in CHEP's customers' best interests – for efficiency, cost savings, convenience, and environmental impact – to become part of CHEP's pooling system. Individual customers are interested in reducing their supply chain costs and by joining CHEP's unique system, companies can reduce their overhead costs and focus on their core businesses by not having to purchase their own pallets or containers.

To further highlight the Captain & Sports Team dynamic, let's imagine a national car rental company, say Avis. When you rent a car, you don't know exactly where you're going or how you're going to get there. Perhaps you're driving to Miami from New York City. You know what your final destination is, but you could get a bit lost along your way. You may pick up the car from one of the Avis depots in NYC, but you can return it to any number of Avis locations within Florida.

Each car that is available is monitored and easily tracked within Avis's car rental system but that doesn't really matter to you. Your primary concern is getting to Miami and you let Avis sort out the rest. For instance, does the car that came from NYC have to be returned there? Does the car need a tune up? What happens if there are too many cars dropped off at the Miami location? The good thing is that you don't need to worry about the long-term costs associated with that car you've just rented. CHEP and their blue pallets work in the same way.

One of the ways CHEP meets customers' business needs to save money is by increasing efficiency through its use of technology. While customers can access pallets from a number of locations, CHEP often doesn't know exactly what the demand will be; they need to be adaptable to provide their products based on unpredictable customer demands. They also need to be flexible enough to redistribute their pallets where they are needed across their national facilities.

CHEP's system can anticipate pallet usage and reduce the distance pallets must travel. For example, while a typical supply chain outfit would look at 200,000 variables, CHEP's advanced system considers 1.8 million variables when deciding how to redistribute pallets to customers. As a result within the US, while an average CHEP pallet travels 100 miles carrying goods, it only travel 40 miles getting back-hauled. The company states, "While the CHEP pallet pooling model is strong, CHEP continues to drive a culture of continuous improvement by using a program called Perfect Trip. Perfect Trip [uses] facts, data and statistical analysis to improve and reinvent business processes – to grow sales, reduce costs and improve quality and customer satisfaction."

There is minimal hierarchy and sometimes no apparent leader.

Relying on their innate abilities, teams often seem to work and function by instinct. Captains, however, provide a pivotal role, acting as role models and directing the tactics of a game. They do not tell the team what to do, but they co-ordinate activities and communications. Crucially, they motivate members and raise their morale, helping them to achieve their personal best.

Of all the *Star Trek* adversaries, the Borg were one of the most powerful and most feared. Q, the *Star Trek* character who first introduced Captain Jean-Luc Picard and his crew to the Borg said, "[They are] the ultimate user. They're unlike any threat your Federation has ever faced." Imagine a humanoid form sheathed in a black-plated exoskeleton, armed with daunting mechanical implants and forearms attached with robotic prosthetics and injection tubules. Their prime directive is to assimilate all other species and to add others' biological and technological strengths to their own; their imperative, "Resistance is futile."

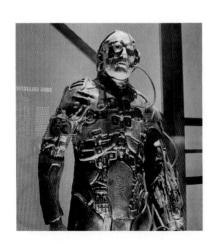

The cybernetic implants are the key to the Borg's power, super human ability, and their ability to proliferate. The implants have multiple functions that not only connect the drones to the collective, they also increase their strength, mental ability, physical capabilities such as sight, and eliminate dependence on basic life elements, such as food, water, and oxygen.

Memory Alpha, the wiki reference site dedicated to *Star Trek* states, "The collective form of organization allows for tremendous efficiency in action and deliberation. With each drone functioning separately according to its instructions, it may at any time be processing information, performing physical actions, or focusing its energy toward other collective goals. The best example of this is the Borg ability to "adapt" nearly instantaneously to any type of attack or threat… The collective state of organization also greatly decreases the chance of error that exists with the decision making of individuals or the conflicts of opinion that are a factor in hierarchical organizations."

The Borg collective is modeled after a super-organism, which is often compared with a colony of ants or a hive of bees where individual insects work together to achieve common objectives and are governed by the collective. They instantly adapt to any threats. An individual Borg's shield protects it from phaser fire, and strategic tactics, such as rotating frequencies, only serve to delay the onset of defeat. Though the Borg are vulnerable to weapons that they have not previously encountered; they can instantaneously adjust their defense capabilities to improve their positioning and overpower any other species.

Similarly, there is no form of governance with the Borg; all Borg share the same mind in the pursuit of their single goal. Aside from this structure, there is virtually no hierarchy amongst the collective and no Borg leader or even central command center on their ship; only drones and the Queen. With the sheer numbers of drones, the Borg – like a super computer – are able to process millions of options, recalculating and instantaneously adapting to new circumstances as a single entity. Decision making does not occur at the individual level but in response to the needs of the collective.

With their networked collective mindset, any individual Borg's needs or independent thoughts are overridden by the collective's needs.

Unlike other hive-like societies, the Borg Queen is not a breeder of new drones. She represents the personified central hub of the hive – her purpose is to "bring order to chaos"; hence she disseminates and gathers information from the billions of voices in the collective and deploys the drones for their various tasks. She is "the beginning, the end, the one who is many."

For adventurous Federation star ships, helpless species, and countless Trekkies that delight in the Borg, the threat persists… "You can't outrun them," says Q. "You can't destroy them. If you damage them, the essence of what they are remains – they regenerate and keep coming… Eventually you will weaken – your reserves will be gone… They are relentless."

———

Though science fiction, the Borg are a near-perfect example of the Captain & Sports Team archetype. Like a single swarm of bees, the Captain & Sports Team work together to overtake any opponent, adapting instantly to environmental factors, and adjusting their strategies as they encounter new ones. Together, the sports team members decide on and set their direction, while the captain is the team's mouthpiece, co-ordinating activities and communications.

But the captain does not control the sports team; they work together like a collective mind and move on the field like a single entity. Individual team members will do whatever it takes to protect and defend the team even to the point of sacrificing themselves to clinch the win.

Similar to the Captain & Sports Team mode, scientists from the Universities of Edinburgh and Oxford have recently discovered that cooperative groups of animals, called superorganisms, like ants and bees actually have the best interests of the group at heart and strive to protect the genetic line within the community. Evidence suggests that, similar to the Borg, these communities subjugate their own individual personal interests for that of the greater good of the collective; a notion that is reflected in the conformist hive societies portrayed in the animated films such as *Antz* and *Bee Movie*.

There are two specific examples in which superorganisms clearly demonstrate collective behavior: 1) when members are closely related, they act together to ensure their genes are passed on to the next generation, and 2) when members need to protect their community or gene line. For example when worker honey bees destroy eggs not laid by the queen. On both occasions, the individual insects act in a coordinated manner, united in a common purpose.

Dr Andy Gardner, from the School of Biological Sciences, University of Edinburgh, said: "An ant nest or a beehive can behave as a united organism in its own right. In a beehive, the workers are happy to help the community, even to die, because the queen carries and passes on their genes. However, super organisms are quite rare, and only exist when the internal conflict within a social group is suppressed...."

Another breathtaking example is the largest mass movement of land mammals on the planet. Every year, over 1.3 million wildebeest and hundreds of thousands of gazelles and zebras follow an annual migration route from the Southern Serengeti to the northern edge of the Masai Mara National Reserve, their bodies cover the plains like a moving sea in their search for food and water. The Great Migration takes an entire year to complete and covers over 1,500 km.

In February, female wildebeest give birth to over 500,000 calves all synchronized within a two- to three-week period. Within 10 minutes the calves are on their feet looking to nurse. The herds consume up to 4,000 tons of grass daily and when the dry season arrives in June, the herds must begin their multi-month march northward toward Kenya. However their path is replete with threats and dangers for the weaker, younger, or older animals.

When leaving the northern plains, lions and cheetahs often follow the herd waiting to pounce. As the herds cross the Mara River, crocodiles and swift currents threaten to eliminate thousands more. Over 250,000 wildebeest will die along the journey. The only dependency in the herd is between cow and calf; there is no logical leadership structure. However, every day a different wildebeest will take the lead despite the various risks, setting the pace in crossing the waters. Driven by the objective of survival, the rest follow. This is a classic example of the Captain & Sports Team archetype.

Tasks and processes are clearly defined, often learned through repetition.

After many hours of practice, the reactions of members become reflexes. Team players adapt to various situations through learned behaviors and interactions with others: they memorize the same playbook. In any situation, they know exactly what role to take on the field.

Officially known as the hackney carriage, the distinctive shape of the modern black cabs is a common sight on the streets of London.

The origins of the London black cabs lie in the early seventeenth century. By the mid-1600s, cab driving in London had become a formalized profession. With a 300-year history, it's no wonder that London's 24,000 cabbies have earned the reputation of providing the best taxi services in the world. In essence, they are members of a highly-trained and professional team that can easily navigate their way through the ins and outs of chaotic London streets.

The reason their reputation precedes them is that to belong to this elite club, drivers must pass a grueling exam known as "the Knowledge" to obtain their "green badge," which enables them to navigate the web of London streets. In fact, only three out of every ten people who begin the Knowledge finish and receive the coveted green badge. The Knowledge originated in 1851, introduced by Sir Richard Mayne, the head of the London Metropolitan Police, after complaints that cab drivers did not know their way around London.

The amount of information drivers must absorb is staggering as they must memorize close to 25,000 streets within a six-mile radius of Charing Cross, 320 routes and every single one of the 1,400 landmarks along those routes. Cabbies will tell you however, there are infinitely more.

The 320 routes are in a reference document called the "Blue Book" or more formally "The Guide to Learning the Knowledge of London."

Training starts off simply enough. If you travel the streets of London, you can often see people, typically men, on scooters with a clipboard and map driving around London; it's likely they are in the Knowledge training.

It takes on average three to five years, and sometimes up to a decade, to pass the Knowledge exam, and test takers take anywhere between 19 and 12 "appearances" or pre-Knowledge tests before passing it. During the appearances, the examiner asks a series of point-to-point questions where the examinees, without the aid of a map, must provide the shortest and sensible route possible. Applicants must recite from memory "the names of the roads used, when they cross junctions, use roundabouts, make turns, and what is 'alongside' them at each point."

The intense mental exercise to memorize all of that information actually translates into significant changes in the brain. Scientists at the University College London discovered that drivers have a larger hippocampus, a part of the brain associated with navigation and geography in animals, compared with other people. And more remarkably, the longer a cabbie stays on the job, the larger the hippocampus grows.

———

The most successful sports teams instantly know how to react to unexpected situations based on their background and intense training. As elite athletes, team members have dedicated their lives to understanding, calculating and predicting various situations that they may encounter, and they rely on the same dedication and adaptability in their fellow team members to effectively adjust to their changing environments. In certain sports such as football, the playbook is considered "a sacred hardbound diary of trust." Elizabeth Merrill, an ESPN journalist writes:

> It's an accumulation of decades' worth of knowledge, tweaked and perfected, sectioned off by scribbles and colored tabs. It's the first thing the fresh meat get when pre-season workouts start in the spring and the last thing that is pried from a player's sweaty mitts...
>
> No two playbooks are alike. Some are as massive as 800 pages; others are thinner than the Mankato, Minnesota, phone book. No layman or superfan could get through the first section without being completely confused. But therein lies the trick, to sort through the clutter, learn fast and play faster.

Sports teams rely on their playbooks to make sure their plays become second nature – even if they aren't required to execute 100 percent of the maneuvers during games. While the instructions may appear to be overly detailed, they prepare the sports team, under the direction of the captain, to understand how to react to and predict each other's moves on the field. Preparedness, practice and access to information ensure that the sports team members are in sync when they are confronted with an opponent.

Similarly, the London black cab drivers have their own playbook from which they learn some of the most complex and mentally challenging navigation activities in the world.

With the popularity of global positioning system devices (GPSs), there is some concern that all the hard work and prestige of passing the Knowledge will become a thing of the past. Black cab drivers are vehemently against using this technology stating that it will never be able to replace the knowledge, instinct and judgment of a cabbie.

One London cabbie muses, "I cannot help but think we London cabbies have it right: we know the streets better than just about any [GPS] device. We don't try and drive the wrong way up a one way street, we don't think we should turn left even when it's obvious the car isn't going to fit down that alleyway, and we don't get stumped when a roundabout has been constructed that isn't yet on the map.

Independent writer Ed Caesar agrees, "While GPS systems are enhancing the possibilities for taxi drivers outside the capital, they are [still] nowhere near sophisticated enough to compete with the common sense and detailed knowledge of the London black-cab driver."

Internal communications are extensive, networked, and made in real time.

Members are so attuned to each other that they can appear to predict each other's reactions. Through training and hard work, they develop a common language. Coordination and collaboration are critical to overcoming opponents. On the field, team members must send signals to each other to adapt to new challenges.

It has long been known that if a fighter pilot can survive the first 10 missions, the chances of them surviving throughout their careers improve dramatically. Between four to six times a year, over the Nellis Air Force Base north of Las Vegas, a group of the best fighter pilots flying the most powerful fighter aircraft ever built across approximately 30 allied countries get together for an intense aerial war game exercise.

This two-week advanced simulation is often cited as more challenging and dangerous than war itself and is intended to give the best fighter pilots in the world the opportunity to survive those first ten missions. Called Operation Red Flag, the exercise tests hundreds of pilots in preparation before being sent into actual combat. It is the largest most sophisticated air combat exercise in the world.

Established in 1975 in a response to the declining USAF air combat effectiveness during the Vietnam War, the object of Red Flag is to simulate realistic combat scenarios and implement dramatic changes in aircrew training. With over 120 aircraft from multiple countries, pilots gain firsthand experience in the precision, complexity and chaos required for a battle in the skies.

The exercises are set up across three teams: two opposing Blue and Red teams and one White "surveillance"

team. "Blue" forces are considered the "good guys." Their mission is to attack ground targets such as "mock airfields, vehicle convoys, tanks, parked aircraft, bunkered defensive positions and missile sites." But these targets aren't static and they are defended by a wide range of simulated ground and air threats.

The "Red" forces are the "bad guys" or aggressors who are deployed to attack the "Blue" forces. Threats that the Red forces must face include simulated surface-to-air missiles and anti-aircraft artillery, communications jamming forces and an opposing enemy air force composed of 64th Aggressor Squadron pilots. About a dozen of the Red pilots are specially trained to replicate the tactics and techniques of potential adversaries.

What is most interesting about the simulation is the sophisticated tracking and surveillance equipment used by the White team. On the AWACS (Airborne Warning and Control System) aircraft, the White forces utilize the Nellis Air Combat Training System (NACTS) to monitor this mock combat between the Red and Blue teams.

For Red Flag to be successful at providing realistic training, the military had to develop a sophisticated real-time assessment system; one that enabled pilots to see for themselves their exact maneuvers and analyze their actions after the mock missions. The NACTS allows simultaneous monitoring of up to 100 aircraft and 70 electronic simulated threats at a time. It's the world's most sophisticated tracking system for combat training exercises. Commanders can monitor the individual cockpits of each plane tracking an aircraft's speed, altitude and line of sight, as they are occurring.

Each plane is equipped with an Airborne Instrumentation Subsystem (AIS) pod that contains a GPS transponder from which information is then transmitted to the ground crew and relayed back to AWACS or White crews that monitor from the air. Each aircraft broadcasts real-time telemetry that appears as 3D imagery onboard the AWACS. From this position, the White team can relay information directly to the pilots providing them with the intelligence they need to make complex mid-battle decisions. While F-15s can reach an altitude of 30,000 feet within 60 seconds, the technology of the NACTS enables AWACS crew to monitor and provide real-time information to the pilots as well as see the planes' locations with an accuracy of 15 feet or less.

As planes are targeted and hit, they turn white on the AWACS' screens. Blue team members are then told to disengage and return to base. Red planes are regenerated and returned to the fight; further increasing the danger and challenge for remaining Blue planes. AWACS crews must use the tracking system to prevent over 100 of the world's fastest planes from crashing into each other in the skies. During a post-flight debrief, information collected during the simulation is then analyzed with all of the participating teams.

––––––––

Real-time communications are critical for the success of the Captain & Sports Team archetype. Operating in environments which require instant adaptability and adjustment to changing circumstances, the team must have the ability to transmit accurate information on their surroundings. With minimal time to react, the captain and sports team must stay coordinated at all times. Members must be kept constantly updated and in sync with the rest of the team in case substitutes are required or if threats endanger the team's activities.

The success of the program and the NACTS is based on the team's ability to accurately capture complex simulations in real time, and then debrief on the activities within the simulation. In fact, the simulation isn't just for pilots; the program invites the finest ground crews, mechanics and rescue personnel from each country and pushes them to the limits of what they can handle. To date, over 400,000 elite military personnel, including more than 132,000 aircrew members flying over 350,000 missions and logging over 600,000 hours flying time have undergone Red Flag training exercises.

6

Strategy emerges gradually – developed largely in response to the environment.

The Captain & Sports Team archetype is highly organic and adaptive. Success is not about setting a direction: it's about agility and flexibility. Members are acutely aware of their teammates' actions as they are making plays on the field. They adjust their own movements and they react to opponents based on "live" outcomes.

Paul "Red" Adair, the son of a Houston blacksmith was arguably the world's most famous firefighter. In 1938, aged 23, Red was hired by the Otis Pressure Control Company, his first oil-related job. In the same year, his first claim to fame occurred when a valve blew on an oil derrick and instead of running for cover, he stopped to fix the damage. "I don't know, maybe a valve blew that we was working on," he recalled. "Everybody else runs but me, and I stayed up there and put the valve back on and almost got fired." Since that time, Adair continued to risk his life by using his calm, cool and collected judgment to control massive oil-well fires across the globe.

His lifetime achievements include extinguishing more than 2,000 land and offshore oil-well fires. In 1961, Adair extinguished one of the most spectacular fires in history, the "Devil's Cigarette Lighter" in the Sahara desert. But perhaps Adair is best known for his heroic actions to extinguish 117 of the burning oil-well fires during 1991 during the Gulf War. That's when he became a household name.

Every day, firefighters encounter a variety of life-and-death situations. And they often use the term organized chaos to describe the state in which they operate during rescues where they must rely on their years of training and conditioning to remain disciplined and to keep their emotions in check.

While education and training form the foundation of knowledge, nothing can truly prepare a firefighter for a real-life emergency. No situations are the same and little can be predicted. The best rules of thumb that firefighters can follow are to be prepared for the worst and be ready to adapt to any situation.

Firefighter training involves learning a basic framework called an incident command system (ICS) which lays out a step-by-step procedure for responding to various emergency situations. It's basically a standard decision-making process or protocol that provides flexible guidelines to enable firefighters to know what the right basic actions are, but can apply their judgment depending on the situation.

For firefighters to work together effectively as a team and for an ICS to be used properly, each member must fully understand the ICS as well as be able to gauge their level of experience and their role based on the situation. In recent Canadian research conducted on policy versus practice for emergency response teams, firefighters were quoted as saying, "Everything's great on paper, but nothing ever goes that smooth [in reality]" and that the key for survival under such strenuous conditions is to "adapt, adjust, adjust, adjust."

Part of the challenge is that you can't simply describe what needs to be done in an emergency situation, it needs to be experienced. That alone lends itself to problems of passing knowledge and experience down to new firefighters. As the previous researchers state, "The ability to tackle problems and adapt is key, and the only way to adapt is through experience. Firefighters must learn by doing, with jobs of increasing skill, decision making, and complexity."

Like firefighters and other emergency teams, the sports team is a unique organism that faces unpredictable circumstances. It has to be prepared for anything that comes its way. It moves as a single unit – shifting to respond to the emergent strategy of the plays, adapting to whatever the opposing team sends its way. As Scotty Bowman – the National Hockey League Head Coach who holds the record for most wins in league history, said, "I found out that if you are going to win games, you had better be ready to adapt."

The team members are adaptable and homogenous – both from the perspective of how they interact and adjust to counter-plays. If a team member gets injured, he or she is immediately replaced and the replacement is virtually indistinguishable from the others. Their strength is in their ability to seamlessly and effortlessly adjust to new environments and situations as they arise. The captain's role isn't to tell his or her team what they need to be doing. Each team member is highly autonomous and uses their own innate problem-solving skills to determine the best immediate course of action. The captain keeps the team coordinated and motivated under situations of duress, but essentially relinquishes his or her authority once the game starts because the game cannot be stopped and the continuous action on the field begins to drive the team members' behaviors.

Is Captain & Sports Team the right model for you?

Is this archetype right for your current situation? And, if it is, how can you be the best captain you can be? The following sections will help you answer these questions.

Great if:

- You work in a dynamic environment and depend on distributed intelligence to adapt quickly to changing conditions.

- Parts of the group are currently isolated and need to be more closely connected to others.

- You have a very high degree of trust in the skills and judgment of those around you.

- There are well-understood rules that shape local actions and decisions.

Think twice if:

- You work in a very dynamic environment, where disruptive change is likely to throw out the rules.

- You do not have systems for real-time, networked communications.

- There are mavericks or factions that will pursue their own agendas.

How can you be a better captain?

1. How strong are your connections to the right talent pools?

The team relies on the ability to recruit people of the right profile. Therefore, it's important to develop free access to and close relationships with specific sources of talent.

- Do you have close links to the right recruitment pools?
- Do you have a sufficient pipeline of qualified candidates?
- How do you test candidates for "chemistry" and "cultural fit"?

2. What traditions and rituals (eg, uniforms, initiation ceremonies) are you using to build a shared identity?

Captains can use various symbols to increase the cohesion of the team and members' sense of belonging.

- What system do you use to measure members' sense of common identity?
- How effective are your existing mechanisms for creating unity and camaraderie?
- Have you devised ways to increase members' sense of belonging?

3. Is there a "master-and-apprentice" culture that allows for the transfer of skills, knowledge and experience?

Members learn through on-the-field practice, interacting with each other and watching more experienced members.

- What formal measures have you taken to encourage the apprenticeship culture?
- How effectively do seasoned members transfer knowledge to more junior members?
- Do you have specific rites of passage to record and celebrate levels of achievement?

4. How successfully have you introduced a "flat" organizational structure where people's contribution means more than their rank?

Since both the captain and the members of the team make decisions on the field, there is virtually no room for hierarchy. No-one tells the team members how to play or where to run; they use their own judgment to react to opponents.

- Can you remove another level of hierarchy from your organization?
- Have you successfully devolved decision making to increase efficiency and agility?
- Do team members feel they have the power to make real-time decisions on the field?

5. How effectively do you use real-time, networked communications across the team?

Whether through words or body language, the captain and the sports team need to communicate "live" on the field. They must develop a common language of strategic plays, watch their own and their opponents' movements, and adapt instantaneously.

- How effective is your common language at conveying real-time messages?
- How successful is your team at receiving and interpreting real-time communications on the field?
- What's the contingency plan if real-time communications fail?

6. How easily does your organization adapt to small changes in the environment?

Part of the success of the captain and sports team is the ability to respond to subtle, but significant, change in real time.

- What methods do you use to anticipate changes and to communicate them across the team?
- How successfully have you adapted your activities to counteract small shifts in the environment?
- How effectively have you developed a team culture that readily perceives and reacts to changes?

7. How effective are you at adapting to dramatic external changes?

The homogeneity of the sports team and the repetitive nature of its work mean it does not always adapt easily to significant environmental disruptions. Captains must keep an eye on the horizon to anticipate shifts in the "marketplace."

- What big changes could disrupt your organization?
- What mechanisms are you using to identify and monitor potential shifts?
- What's your strategy for coping with unexpected changes to market conditions?

Chapter 8

Senator &
Citizens

"Democracy is the government of the
people, by the people, for the people"
—*Abraham Lincoln, 16th president of the United States*

> ## He came to stand for future generations as a model of defiance against tyranny

Marcus Tullius Cicero: Father of the free state

Marcus Tullius Cicero was only 25 when he decided to take on Sextus Roscius as a client in his first public criminal case. One late summer evening in 81BC, when returning from dinner, Roscius's father, a well-to-do farmer, connected to some of the noblest families in Rome, had been attacked and murdered near the public baths. Convicted of patricide, Roscius faced the death penalty.

Cicero crafted a meticulous and painstakingly researched defense, turning the tables on one of Roscius's accusers, who, as a relative, stood to gain from the murder. He caused a sensation by claiming that Chrysogonus, a favorite of the ruling dictator Cornelius Sulla, had helped cover up the crime and, in return, been sold the bulk of the dead man's estate for a rock bottom price.

After his closing arguments, Cicero received thunderous applause from the court. Roscius was acquitted; and his lawyer left the courtroom a famous man.

Cicero's courtroom display secured his place as one of Rome's greatest orators. It also showed him to be a passionate supporter of the values that underpinned Roman citizenship. By defending not only an individual but their moral rights, he put forward arguments that were incontrovertible. By risking the opprobrium of Rome's most powerful politician, he proved his own integrity.

Life and times

Cicero, lawyer, philosopher, orator and statesman, lived from 106 to 43BC, during the twilight years of the Roman Republic. He was one of the most notable Roman senators, not only because of his legendary eloquence, but also because of his contributions to advancing the political, moral and philosophical thinking of the time.

To understand him and the position he took, you have to understand the times he lived in.

The Republic was Rome's equivalent of a democracy: an era where freedom of speech was seen as a right of citizenship and where the state was governed by the people. It originated when the citizens of Rome rebelled against King Tarquin the Proud, a vindictive tyrant who'd ruled by oppression and fear.

Tarquin was exiled, and the newly formed Republic was founded on the segregation of power, such that the fate of the citizens could never again be held by just one man.

271

The new Republican state consisted of multiple bodies with varying degrees of authority and responsibility. The Senate, comprised of 300 land-owning men from the aristocracy, was the guardian of the state and the people. It had no executive or law-making power but it exerted considerable influence through the *senatus consultum*, advice given to the Roman magistrates and the two heads of government, the consuls. During the era of the Republic, the slogan *Senatus Populusque Romanus* (SPQR) – "the Senate and the People of Rome" – was used to reassure the citizens that Rome was no longer under the rule of one person. Dictators like Sulla were "masters of the people," magistrates given the authority by the Senate to perform particular state business. Their term in office was generally limited to six months, as a check on their power.

Political career

Around 50 years after the Roman Republic was formed, its elected leaders formalized the constitution. The laws that applied to every Roman citizen regardless of wealth or standing were engraved on tablets of metal and displayed in the Forum. Today, they are referred to as "The Twelve Tables."

Of the constitution, Cicero wrote, "Though all the world exclaim against me, I will say what I think: that single little book of the Twelve Tables, if anyone looks to the fountains and sources of laws, seems to me, assuredly, to surpass the libraries of all the philosophers, both in weight of authority, and in plenitude of utility."

The Republic became a society ruled by law rather than by the whim of the aristocracy. The constitution laid down guidelines for good and moral behavior, for a code that could be spread through the citizens' "collective".

Cicero's works cling to the moral traditions and principles of the Republic during times of social upheaval, instability and war. They have influenced many of today's modern political institutions. Anthony Everitt, author of *Cicero: The Life and Times of Rome's Greatest Politician*, writes:

"Nearly two thousand years after his time, he became an unknowing architect of constitutions that still govern our lives. His big idea, which he tirelessly publicized, was that of a mixed or balanced constitution... the model is not so very distant from the original constitution of the United States..."

Cicero believed that each citizen's obligation was to participate in the preservation of the Republic. It was a principle he lived by

Cicero believed that each citizen's obligation was to participate in the preservation of the Republic. It was a principle he lived by. Convinced of the virtue of public service, he advanced quickly in his political career, which culminated in his election to the highest office – co-consul.

Crisis and exile

In his first year as consul, however, Cicero faced a crisis from which he never fully recovered.

Lucius Sergius Catilina, who'd stood against him in the consular elections, led a plot to assassinate him and overthrow the Republic. It was a crime Cicero could not forgive, and he had Catilina and his fellow conspirators killed.

Although he was named *pater patriae* for acting quickly to save Rome, his decision came back to haunt him four years later, when the tribune passed a law stating that no citizen could be put to death without a trial. From that time onward, Cicero lived in fear. In 58BC, he went into exile in Greece.

Recalled by a vote of the Senate, Cicero returned to Italy in 57BC and was greeted by a cheering crowd. But, vehemently opposed to the growing influence of Julius Caesar and his fellow triumviri, who flouted the rules for dictatorship, he had powerful political enemies in Rome.

After the assassination of Caesar in 44BC he began a valiant defense of the Republican state and its constitution. Everitt continues:

"Towards the end of his life, Cicero distinguished himself in his battle to save the Roman Republic. Through sheer force of character he took charge of the state... Cicero came to stand for future generations as a model of defiance against tyranny."

But, by now, he was swimming against the tide. A second triumvirate was formed by Caesar's great-nephew Octavian, Mark Antony and Marcus Lepidus at the end of 43BC, and, unlike the first, it had legal power, outranking the consuls. Cicero made a series of philippics, urging the Senate to overthrow Mark Antony. In so doing, he signed his own death warrant. Antony had Cicero's hands and head cut off – his hands because they penned the philippics against him, and his tongue because it had lambasted him.

Legacy

Cicero died for the Republican state. He stood up for what he believed in and he paid the ultimate price. Tragically, the great orator was, in the end, denied one of the principal freedoms of democracy – freedom of speech.

Today, Cicero is considered one of the fathers of the humanist movement, committed to intellectual integrity, democracy, and free inquiry in pursuit of the common good.

Edward Clayton, associate professor at Central Michigan University writes, "The politicians of his time, [Cicero] believed, were corrupt and no longer possessed the virtuous character that had been the main attribute of Romans in the earlier days of Roman history. This loss of virtue was, he believed, the cause of the Republic's difficulties. He hoped that the leaders of Rome, especially in the Senate, would listen to his pleas to renew the Republic. This could only happen if the Roman elite chose to improve their characters and place commitments to individual virtue and social stability ahead of their desires for fame, wealth, and power."

W.L. Gore & Associates
More than just a plastics company

Dave Myers had a feeling that his idea would work but he wasn't sure. He didn't play the guitar – he was an engineer. Nonetheless, he felt he understood some of the problems of the instrument. Natural oils and sweat from a player's fingertips can coat the strings and, over time, change how they vibrate and the sound they make. In theory, protective coatings helped; in practice, they changed the integrity of the strings and degraded the sound. Dave's idea was to try Teflon® – W.L. Gore & Associates' core product – and see what happened.

To try out the idea, Dave enlisted the help of his colleague, Chuck Hebestreit, a guitar player, and the two gathered together a team to develop and then test the Teflon-coated strings. Over a three-year period, involving trials with around 15,000 guitar players, they found that the tone of their new strings lasted three to five times longer.

Bill Connors, a Gore engineer, was so thrilled with the new product that he switched over to become one of the company's guitar-string product specialists. "One of the basic operating principles at Gore is that people will be most effective working on projects that they're excited about," he explains. "I was able to convince other associates that I was passionate about guitar strings, and I've been here ever since."

This is how, through the ingenuity and passion of one man's idea, a $2 billion engineering firm built the Elixir brand – the music industry's top-selling acoustic guitar strings.

Gore is an unusual organization. Like many engineering and R&D-based companies, it encourages employees to dedicate time at work to the pursuit of new ideas. But it does so within what, to the uninitiated at least, seems like a dangerously loose framework and fluid structure.

Gore flouts nearly all the rules of modern management. There are no titles and job descriptions, no spans of control, no reporting relationships, no updated organization charts – at least none of any great significance. There is minimal hierarchy. People are known as "associates." There's no set structure or reporting lines. All the offices are the same size. Work gets completed by small teams or clusters that emerge and dissolve based on the skills that are needed to get a project done. Team associates – regardless of their level – decide who gets hired, and they are compensated based on their peers' input.

The company proves that to be successful you don't have to live by the management book. It made more than $2.1 billion in 2008 and is a regular on the list of America's top places to work. Rather mystifyingly for a company that manufactures and sells plastic – polytetrafluoroethylene to be specific – and doesn't have that high a profile, Gore is a hot place. While most people will be familiar with GORE-TEX® – the waterproof, breathable and durable fabric that most of today's outdoor jackets and boots are made of – few will know its other products, which include electronic materials, filtration products, pharmaceuticals and medical products, and sealants.

Its unique organization is based on what founder Bill Gore – an ex-Dupont executive – called a lattice structure. He first presented this idea to Gore associates in 1967, but it wasn't formally written down and disseminated until 1976. A lattice organization structure, according to Bill Gore, is one where:

- lines of communication are direct, with no intermediary;
- there is no fixed or assigned authority;
- there are no bosses, only sponsors;
- natural leadership is defined by "followership";
- objectives are set by those who must make them happen;
- tasks and functions are organized through commitments.

Bill Gore firmly believed that leaders should be chosen by the people who follow them. Four principles lay the foundation of his company's culture: fairness, freedom, commitment, and "waterline".

The last principle encourages smart risk taking. It means that it's OK to make a decision that "might punch a hole in the boat as long as the hole is above the waterline so that it won't potentially sink the ship." It's vital to the spirit of innovation. Steve Shuster, a 27-year member of the enterprise communication team, says, "Gore asked me early on how many mistakes I've made so far. He then told me that if I'm not making mistakes, then it means that I'm not taking enough risks and trying to innovate as much as I should be."

How does Gore get the most out of its workforce? Walk through the company's halls and you'll see people who genuinely enjoy working for the company. Shuster adds, "You feel like you're part of a family. This creates a special bond between associates and a connection with the company. Everyone is an owner in the company and shares in the good times and in the bad times."

But Gore associates aren't run-of-the-mill employees. The only way that a company like this can be successful is if it's built on the principles of commitment and self-discipline, integrity, autonomy, and communication. This is a company where reporting lines are thrown out the window. Technically, no-one is anyone else's direct boss. "They understand the notion of empowerment," says John E. Sawyer, chair of the department of business administration at the University of Delaware. "They have established an environment where associates are able to have an impact. And it takes a tremendous amount of work to maintain it."

Another remarkable aspect of the culture is the ability to problem solve en masse. Associates don't get stuck in ruts working with the same people, mulling over the same problems, doing things the same way. Teams may change every few years, and an associate's first six months are usually spent getting to know the other team members.

Associates are passionate about discovering the next great idea. They're not instructed to take part and they don't report to any supervisor or boss; rather, they make commitments to their colleagues to work on projects and ideas that they are passionate about and that they believe will contribute to Gore's long-term success.

Most of the diverse product base has been produced during "dabble time," half a day each week that associates spend on an initiative of their own choosing. Once an idea is further fleshed out, other associates then join in, or are "recruited" to help develop it into something that may end up transforming the market.

Engineering teams often only have about three or four members, which makes them more efficient and flexible and speeds up decision making. Gore's manufacturing plants stay small, and don't go above 250 employees.

Leaders emerge naturally from the pool of employees based on the merits of their ideas – not on their tenure or experience. An engineer who made a significant contribution to the organization may reap a greater reward than the team's

leader. And anyone can rise to the top – provided, that is, that other associates want them to.

Current CEO Terri Kelly started out as a process engineer in 1983. One of the few associates with a title, she became CEO in 2005 – only the fourth person to hold the job in the company's half century history. What makes her remarkable is that she was elected by her peers. Associates were invited to nominate someone they would be willing to follow. "We weren't given a list of names – we were free to choose anyone in the company," Kelly says. "To my surprise, it was me."

That's a powerful process. It means that her peers will listen and follow her guidance because they respect her decision making and leadership, not because she's acting on behalf of an invisible senior executive team that holds all the power. "I'm a leader only if there are people who are willing to follow me," she says. "A project doesn't move forward unless people buy into it. You cultivate followership by selling yourself, articulating your ideas, and developing a reputation for seeing things through."

It seems that Kelly perfectly fits founder Bill Gore's original profile of a leader:

- The associate who is recognized by his or her team as having special knowledge or experience.
- The associate the team looks to for coordination of activities to achieve the agreed-upon objectives.
- The associate who proposes necessary objectives and activities and seeks team consensus on objectives.

At Gore, the real decision-making power is held by the group of associates or the team and not by any single leader. Each year, each team ranks their members by asking, "Who has made the biggest impact on the enterprise?" The open-ended nature of the question allows for associates to interpret "impact" in their own way. A separate committee reviews all of the associates to determine compensation levels. Everyone gets ranked.

Associates like the process because it feels fair, but it's not the easiest culture to adjust to. There are informal, but important, rites of passage. Kelly says, "To get ahead, you must first demonstrate that you can take ownership of a project and stick with it. Anyone can talk about going the extra mile. First, you've got to prove to everyone else that you can do it." When you're self-directed and empowered, there's no room for hitching a free ride. Associates are expected to be proactive and committed to the culture.

If there's any drawback to Gore's democratic environment, it's that processes can get confusing for both customers and associates. If there are no direct reporting lines and all associates are considered equal, who gets to make the final decisions and who takes the blame when things go wrong?

Kelly recalls a challenging incident that occurred in the late 1980s: "We didn't pay enough attention to accountability and decision making and who was actually leading. It was a good exercise for us to understand the need to distinguish between practices, which change with time, and who we really are, which doesn't. Otherwise you're paralyzed."

The company must be pragmatic, protecting traditions not out of a sense of nostalgia but because they've worked. The problem is providing the right amount of direction in an organization where formal structure and processes are emergent. "Some of the difficulties Gore faces involve how to systematize the culture, to put in the framework that allows it to continue to operate, even as it grows in size," the University of Delaware's Sawyer says. "But they're trying to be very careful."

However Gore balances structure, projects, and processes, it remains dedicated to the constant protection of one of its most valuable assets: its culture of innovation. For more than 50 years, the business has been one of the 200 largest privately-owned companies in the US. And while its actual number of products is difficult to pinpoint, the estimate easily rises above 1,000. Gore's medical products alone have been used in over 7.5 million patients around the world. Every aspect of its daily activities focuses on creating breakthroughs for the organization and its associates, providing new and exciting paths for innovation to emerge. Its biggest innovation, however, will always be its organization and leadership model.

Key characteristics of Senator & Citizens

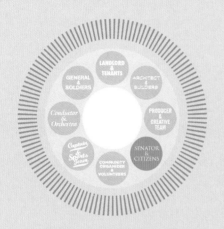

The Senator & Citizens archetype is a hybrid of the Producer & Creative Team and the Community Organizer & Volunteers models. There are elements of diversity, creativity and idea generation in the way the senator and citizens interact. Problems are tackled democratically through the sharing of opinions and the debate of differing perspectives. Solutions "emerge" from loose and fluid groupings; working together, the senator and citizens jointly decide their community's direction.

Citizens take their civic rights and responsibilities seriously and generally strive to act in the community's collective best interests. They join the community not only because they believe in personal freedom and democracy but also because they want to maintain its special character. Senators defend the values and constitution of the community, but ultimately hold little formal authority over the citizens.

 A "constitution" enshrines the principles and values that govern the citizens.

 Citizens voluntarily decide to join the community and agree to live by its values.

 Individual autonomy is a fundamental right of all citizens.

 Active participation is a core responsibility of all citizens.

 The community only functions if the structure is fluid and adaptive.

 Citizen communities can be either physical or virtual.

A "constitution" enshrines the principles and values that govern the citizens.

Founding members of communities usually create a constitution to ensure their values are upheld. Proud of the community's historical narrative, their descendants are pleased to abide by the rights and responsibilities the constitution defines. Senators are the guiding stewards of the community and the defenders of the constitution.

As with most organizations, upon arrival at Semco's offices in Brazil, you may expect a receptionist to greet you. But in fact the reception desk is empty. Despite all the attention and visitors Semco receives, they don't believe in receptionists. They also don't believe in secretaries or personal assistants because, they ask, "Why should people have those types of ungratifying, dead end jobs?" Everyone instead pitches in and does their share of the administrative work, even the top managers in the company.

Brazil's most famous company is really quite unique for many reasons. It currently employs about 3,000 individuals, but considering this number, Semco's organization has remained relatively flat with few formal titles. There are no vice presidents or chief officers for IT or operations, no HR department, and not even a fixed CEO (six senior managers trade the title every six months). In addition, there are no job descriptions at Semco. There is no formal structure at Semco. The bulk of employees are known as "coordinators" and "associates."

Perhaps even more interesting, every six months, all of the employees are invited to set their salaries based on information regarding what workers receive elsewhere – at Semco, all employee salaries, including the CEO's, are made public. Business units have full authority to spend their budget as they wish. Finally, employees evaluate their bosses every six months with the results displayed publicly – poor performers are pressured to improve or eventually leave.

Considering the degree of employee autonomy in the organization, how does any work get done at Semco? The company started off in the 1950s by manufacturing centrifuges for the vegetable oil industry. Over the years it began to branch out into various hydraulic pumps for ships and now makes a wide range of mechanical products including mixers, refrigeration equipment, food processors, and has most recently entered into a variety of new businesses such as engineering and mobile services.

But Semco wasn't always like this – satisfied employees working for a well-run, diversified organization. In the late 1970s, Ricardo Semler was originally hired by his father, Antonio, to work in the family business, Semler & Company. The two clashed over their management styles – Antonio favored a traditional hierarchical management style where Ricardo leaned towards a more participatory approach. In the early years, the father and son were in a constant state of disagreement and eventually, Ricardo threatened to leave the organization. But instead something amazing happened – in 1980, Antonio resigned as CEO and at the age of 22, Ricardo became Semco's new CEO.

Starting with small steps, Semler made changes to Semco by allowing employees themselves to drive the changes. Semler appealed to his employees' highest level needs: autonomy, freedom, empowerment, and passion. Some managers were worried that this approach would never work. However, employees themselves collectively arranged their schedules to ensure the operations could continue seamlessly. Instead of assembly lines, Semco puts teams together so they can assemble an entire product, not simply an isolated component.

Another example occurred during Brazil's economic downturn of the early 1990s. During that time, workers collectively agreed to wage cuts if profit sharing levels were increased. Management salaries were cut by 40 percent and employees collectively approved all expenditures and key business decisions. According to Semler, one factory committee leader came up with the plan: workers would voluntarily reduce their wages by 30 percent (in exchange for additional profit-sharing payments), give up subsidized meals, transportation allowance and other benefits. They would take over all the services at the plant provided by outside contractors and third parties, slashing the company's costs, including those of preparing the food in the cafeteria.

What's unique about Semler is that he, you could say, lets productivity happen rather than trying to make it happen. Basically, there's no-one in control. Semler guides the organization by empowering employees to do what's best for themselves and the organization. According to Semler, freedom is a prime driver for performance and only people who have respect for their followers can be leaders. He has a single vote on all activities just like his staff. In fact, a few years ago, the company even held a party to commemorate the tenth anniversary of the last time Semler made any decision at all.

In management terms, Semco operates with a philosophy of workplace democracy, combined with a bit of irreverence to managerial norms and absolute trust in the abilities of the employees. But every single employee that works there has bought into the idea of belonging to and defending that special culture community. Semco's employees don't need to be told what to do. Semco's website states, "A company full of crazy people? A group of nutters? If you think that Semco is something along these lines, you're not entirely wrong…"

The Semco Way follows ten principles which outline their view of how the business should be run, and how their employees should behave:

1. To be a dependable and reliable company.
2. Value honesty and transparency over and above all temporary interests.
3. Seek a balance between short-term and long-term profit.
4. Offer products and services at fair prices.
5. Provide the customer with differentiated services.
6. Encourage creativity.
7. Encourage everyone's participation and question decisions that are imposed from the top down.
8. Maintain an informal and pleasant environment.
9. Maintain safe working conditions and control industrial processes.
10. Have the humility to recognize our errors.

In addition to the ten principles, the company also has a "comic book-like" survival manual that outlines employee policies and values to ensure that "everybody speaks the same language." True to the Senator & Citizens archetype, they state that employees with opinions are important and they "expect their employees to … speak out and fight when something isn't right or does not fit their vision."

Nós temos 10 princípios, e fazemos um esforço especial para segui-los na prática. Torne-se um teimoso quando alguém quiser quebrar algum dos nossos princípios e defenda-os.

Miguel Pavia

How is this possible? Self-discipline and trust are key components. Semler states, "I have an added 30 percent faith in human nature." But the model only works if everyone is on the same page. The company continues to remain a business anomaly with Semco thriving since Semler became CEO.

Over 150 Fortune 500 companies have visited Semco in an attempt to discover the secrets of its success. It's been growing by double digits almost every year since Semler took control – from 1994 to 2008, revenues grew from $35 million to $240 million. And remarkably, employee morale is extremely high: the corporate turnover rate has remained around 1–2 percent over the past 25 years (compared with an industry average of approximately 18 percent.)

Semco is one of those unique companies that fall under the Senator & Citizens archetype. Its employees live and work by a set of both written and unwritten principles that center on the well-being and best interests of the organization while also meeting their intrinsic needs. There aren't formal rules and ways of working, but make no mistake, there is an informal "constitution" that all employees abide by and strive to uphold.

Driven by Semco's leader, Ricardo Semler, the values are a reflection of how engrained the constitution is within their community and culture.

Semler doesn't believe in writing out a formal "mission statement" but he's more than happy to say that the closest thing to Semco's credo would be: "Find a gratifying way of spending your life doing something you like that is useful and fills a need." For Semco, freedom drives performance. To make this work, Semler has removed the concept of top management "running the company" and instead empowers employees with key business decisions. Democracy is a "cornerstone of the Semco system."

———————

For organizations that fall under the Senator & Citizens archetype, the constitution represents the written cornerstone of the community. During the times of the Roman Republic, the Twelve Tables were created out of stone carvings and eventually etched into twelve bronze tablets. They represented the formal and public rules that governed the state to ensure that all citizens were aware of their collective obligations and responsibilities as being a part of the community.

Similar to the Twelve Tables, Senator & Citizens organizations live by a codified constitution that embodies its values and guides how the community and its citizens should behave and operate.

However, unlike the specific and scripted rules defined in Conductor & Orchestra that outline every detail of how a task should be completed, the constitution simply guides appropriate behavior and outlines expectations; it doesn't dictate what citizens must do but always ensures that the standards and principles of the community are upheld.

Citizens voluntarily decide to join the community and agree to live by its values.

People take an oath of citizenship to join the community, and thereby explicitly agree to abide by the constitution. Citizens accept that there will be differences of opinion among them, yet they are keen to protect the collective interest, and usually abide by the community's conflict-management process.

Every five years, an 11-mile parade of leather-clad, Harley enthusiasts make a five-day, 1,350-mile trek from the Harley factory in York, Pennsylvania to the company headquarters in Milwaukee, Wisconsin. Along the way they are cheered on by "thousands of well-wishers" and children waving American flags and Harley banners. Some even travel unbelievable distances, like the 300 bikers from Japan who chartered a plane for themselves and their Harleys to attend the 100th anniversary in 2003.

Clearly Harley-Davidson is much more than just a motorcycle or a brand – it is a way of life. Buying a Harley is like buying into a family; "a big rambunctious family whose members all have the same interests." It has reached iconic status to become a quintessential symbol of freedom, rugged individualism, excitement, and a sense of "bad boy rebellion."

There is a mystique surrounding Harley-Davidson which is difficult to explain. You either get it or you don't. It's about an "attitude, a feeling that because you own a Harley-Davidson motorcycle – you're special, you belong." A mystique continuously perpetuated through movies such as *Easy Rider* and through celebrities like Elvis Presley and James Dean firmly cement its place in pop culture.

The origins of the Harley-Davidson brand can be traced back to 1903, when two friends from Milwaukee, William Harley and Arthur Davidson, teamed up to develop a motorized bicycle that would eliminate the need for pedals.

Davidson's father built them a shed in the backyard, which became the first factory of the "Harley-Davidson Motor Company." This quickly became a family business, as Davidson's brothers, William and Walter joined shortly afterwards.

Harley-Davidson is now a US$1.3 billion business and has grown steadily, maintaining a rate of growth of at least 15–20 percent every year from 1987–2004. It held the majority of the market share in the US, reaching 53 percent in 2004 but has since slipped to 45.6 percent in 2009. The company's motorcycle club, Harley Owners Group, affectionately known as HOGs, boasts about one million members worldwide.

As Road Captain USA, one of the millions of Harley enthusiasts declares:

> The Harley mystique is all about attitude... In a society that worships at the altar of internal combustion, riding a Harley just may be the last pure expression of what it means to be American... the freedom to go somewhere, anywhere, just you and the road and the wind in your hair. The bar and shield has become a symbol of... the spirit of the open road, a slap in the face to mainstream sensibilities, a fantasy, a way of life, a noisy declaration of independence, an obsession, an escape, a revered American icon. Harley-Davidson represents adventure, freedom, individuality, and living life with all five of your senses. It is a legend.

What ties HOGs to the Harley brand and why is their community an example of the Senator

& Citizens model? In essence joining the Harley community represents taking a rebellious oath of citizenship. For Harley fans, the brand represents more than just a dedication to a specific lifestyle. HOGs fanatically support the brand's traditions, maintenance of the community, its members and the lifestyle.

Susan Fournier and Lara Lee, authors of the 2009 *Harvard Business Review* article, "Getting Brand Communities Right" state, "To solidify the connection between the company and its customers, Harley staffed all community-outreach events with employees rather than hired hands … Executives were required to spend time in the field with customers and bring their insights back to the firm. This close-to-the-customer strategy was codified in Harley-Davidson's operating philosophy and reinforced during new-employee orientations. Decisions at all levels were grounded in the community perspective, and the company acknowledged the community as the rightful owner of the brand."

HOGs really are a special breed; they are "much more than just a motorcycle organization. It's one million people around the world united by a common passion: making the Harley-Davidson dream a way of life." Part of being a HOG means that individuals have the ability to step away from their everyday lives, to break free from what society says is normal and accepted.

The background of individual HOGs doesn't matter, nor do any differences in their "everyday" lifestyle; they all recognize that they have one thing in common: the love of the open road and what their Harleys represent. As Road Captain USA says, "Today's Harley owner is more likely to be a dental hygienist, trucker, or coffee shop owner than a rebel without a cause. We are male and female, young and young at heart, but we all share a passion for the brand and everything that it represents." The members of the largest factory-sponsored motorcycle club in the world are basically like a big family where even between global HOG chapters there is a common bond and immediate connection.

———————

There's just something unique or special about the community with which citizens identify. Once citizens have agreed to join the community, they inherently agree to live by its rules and standards. In a sense, joining the community is almost like becoming part of a special group; a society of people that both look after each other as well as the community.

Compared with some of the other archetypes, citizens aren't homogenous. Although citizens come together based on the similarity of their beliefs and values with the community, by no means are they all the same. In fact, citizens are expected to voice their differing opinions. Similar to Cicero, who clearly did not always agree with how the Republic was governed, citizens use their voice as a means to ensure the best interests of the community are always maintained.

Autonomy is a fundamental right of all citizens.

Citizens have the freedom to choose their own activities. No-one tells them what to do or controls their behavior. They trust that the community – with the checks and balances inherent in the constitution – will naturally reinforce the appropriate norms.

The story of the Mondragón Corporación Cooperativa (MCC) can be traced back to a young Basque priest, Don José María Arizmendiarrieta. Don José María fought as part of the Basque resistance in the Spanish Civil War, and was subsequently captured and "narrowly escaped execution." He joined the priesthood after his release, and was sent to Mondragón by his bishop in 1941, to "look after the youth of the parish."

In 1959, the Caja Laboral Popular or the "Working People's Bank" was founded as a part of MCC. It represents an important part of MCC's history as it's a credit union that serves as the core of the financial system; a bank for co-operatives, run like a co-operative itself. The bank operates with the motto "Savings or Suitcases;" in other words, members can choose to invest in their own community or "watch their money leave their community to work elsewhere and enrich others."

What started as one firm and roughly 25 people in 1956 is now a major international business. Today, MCC is considered the largest and most successful worker-owned enterprise in the world with 264 independent co-operatives around the globe, 34,000 employees, and revenues of 16.8 billion euros in 2008. MCC develops an average of four new co-operatives every year, each with approximately 400 members; in its history, only two have ever failed – a remarkable statistic considering in Spain, 90 percent of business start-ups fail in the first five years. The

organization is built on the principles of social-ism, democracy, and grass-roots community development and applies them to the world of business.

From its humble beginnings as a paraffin stove manufacturer, MCC's businesses now span the manufacturing of automotive parts, domestic appliances, bicycles, and bus bodies, to the operation of supermarkets, travel agencies, and gas stations. Although these co-operatives are for-profit entities, they are also deeply committed to serving their community; a driving force behind this organization is the desire to create employment and education opportunities for the community.

It all started with a school, the People's Bank and a store but because of the decision making of the owners and their ability to take advantage of the available opportunities, the co-operative has branched out into many self-reinforcing and diverse businesses. The majority of workers are individual owners; each has an equal share and vote. And because these worker–owners cannot be fired, there is even more at stake in ensuring that the right types of owners are given the opportunity to join the co-operative. It's a very protective and protected community. For example, if an owner retires, though he or she can "cash out," their shares cannot simply be sold to anyone. They can only be purchased by a newly-joined owner within that specific firm.

Capital, resources, and knowledge are all shared across the various co-operatives, where capital is viewed as "a means to end" and the true goal for owners is for "a happy and productive work environment." As a result, the annual net profits from all co-operatives are pooled; 10 percent is donated to charity and 40 percent is retained in a collective account owned by all co-operatives and managed for the "common good"; the remaining 50 percent can be used at the discretion of the worker–owners of the independent co-operatives. In the end, this structure serves to ensure workers have a share in their firms' profits and enables owners to contribute to the group's ability to sustain the co-operative's long-term growth.

The Romans understood that freedom is comprised of three components: 1) national freedom: freedom from foreign domination; 2) political freedom: freedom to vote and choose one's leaders; and 3) individual freedom: freedom to live as one chooses without harming others. Liberty was the foundation of the new era once the Roman state had been released from the tyranny of the Roman monarchy.

MCC is not only democratic because the owners have equal say in all the significant business decisions but also because they have a large degree of participation and autonomy over the day to day activities, as well as the long-term vision of the co-operative. It is truly a business based on people and the betterment of its community. The autonomous decision making of the owners is the lifeblood of the business and the co-operative has been able to sustain a community where all feel the success is truly theirs.

Thus citizens are filled with the notion of freedom and pride in their work. Their behaviors are guided by the constitution and by their strong sense of belonging, thus they work hard to ensure that the community and what it represents are preserved.

Equally important, senators help create an environment where citizens can make autonomous decisions. No-one tells them what choices to make; they understand how their decisions impact the overall success of the community. They also understand that regardless of the strength of the constitution and its tenets, the community will not be successful without the civic virtue of its citizens. Even though citizens have the ability to make their own independent decisions, they strive to ensure that any decisions made positively impact the long-term outcomes and sustainability of the community.

Active participation is a core responsibility of all citizens.

Citizenship confers responsibilities as well as rights. Members uphold the values of the community and help to shape their environment. Since decision making is devolved, they have a duty to be well-informed and to participate actively. They have a say in how the community runs, but they respect other citizens' opinions by allowing them to contribute ideas.

Of all the extraordinary members of the founding father generation, it was Alexander Hamilton and Thomas Jefferson who together defined the course of the American political system in the 1790s. The two were contentious rivals who had very different visions of the promise of America. Hamilton favored a strong central government. By contrast, Jefferson, favored agrarian policies that would serve as an antidote to the corrupting influence of cities.

Hamilton and Jefferson achieved a meeting of the minds over the presidential election of 1800. Hamilton, although a bitter opponent of Jefferson, saw him as the better man and used his influence to persuade Federalists in Congress to cast their votes for Jefferson. This yielded two critical results: 1) Jefferson, the first President elected by a party other than the ruling Federalists, laid the foundations of the American two-party system, and 2) Hamilton, on a fateful day in July 1804, amidst continuing animosities against the Democratic-Republicans, would lose his life at the heights of Weehawken, New Jersey overlooking the Hudson River.

Copyright, 1876 by Currier & Ives, N.Y.

GEORGE WASHINGTON.
GEN+ HENRY KNOX, Secy. of War.
ALEXANDER HAMILTON, Secy. of the Treasury.
THOMAS JEFFERSON, Secy. of State.
EDMUND RANDOLPH, Attorney General.

WASHINGTON AND HIS CABINET.

How does the discourse between Hamilton and Jefferson represent the Senator & Citizens archetype? The dramatic interface between these two great adversaries produced a result that was clearly superior to whatever might have occurred had one or the other individually won. That they were able to co-operate for the good at a critical point in the process likely pre-served the nation from a political crisis. In fact, it was their responsibility as intellectual guides to ensure that the values of the constitution were created in the best interests of the nation. While Hamilton may have vehemently dis-agreed with supporting Jefferson, Hamilton ensured that he actively participated in deter-mining the positive future of the nation.

As a moral guide to the community, Cicero felt it was his obligation and duty to stand up for what he believed in and to protect his beloved Republic from the corruption that was threatening to overtake the state. Similarly, Hamilton also conceded to an ill-fated but enlightened decision to protect the nascent nation.

What distinguishes Senator & Citizens from other adjacent archetypes is the degree to which citizens have an ownership stake in maintaining the interests of their community. While Producer & Creative Team and particularly Community Organizer & Volunteers organizations may display aspects of accountability and responsibility, neither demonstrates true ownership to the extent of Senator & Citizens. The community would not exist if the citizens didn't actively participate in its growth.

———————

The importance of active participation of the citizens can be easily demonstrated with the popular business school case study of Jack Stack. Jack was a bright and energetic lad. In 1968 when he was 18, Jack got a start as a clerk in the mailroom at a 4,000-employee International Harvester plant. But it was not a happy place to work. Work was parceled into discrete functions. No-one ever saw the big picture. At 28, he became superintendent of machining, the least productive of seven divisions.

But Jack's plant manager, true to the company's close-to-the-vest theory of management,

said: "Numbers are power and the numbers are mine." It was after that conversation that Jack decided to make up his own rules. He set up a guerrilla statistics system and figured out how much his division was capable of increasing productivity. He offered to buy his division coffee if they exceeded their previous best numbers. And they did. The next week he said he'd invite them over to his house for pizza and beer if they improved on the previous week's numbers. For the next two weeks Jack and his wife entertained the 200 employees at their home and served them pizza and beer.

Jack's games worked. His workers became the top-performing division. Jack believed that if you appeal to employees' highest aspirations, you will elicit superior group performance.

This was definitely true in the case of the tractor near-disaster when International Harvester was about to fall into serious trouble. In 1979 with sales of $8.4 billion and earnings of $370 million, the company provoked a strike with the auto unions to renegotiate terms that were making them less competitive than John Deere and Caterpillar Tractor. The strike dragged on, costing the company $479 million in losses.

Putting his people skills to work, Jack went to the plant and begged the workers to give him a chance to make changes without bringing in the union. They believed him.

Stack and the new workforce transformed the plant. But they weren't out of the woods yet. Although they had begun to make $1 million profit a year, the parent company had been crippled by the 1980s recession. They told Jack to cut production by two-thirds. Appalled at the idea of laying off so many workers, Jack and 12 of his managers offered to buy the plant. Two years and a lot of angst later, both parties agreed to a $9 million deal.

Jack and his co-owners were now in debt up to their eyes, but not over their heads. They knew they had to do something. They promised employees that management would tell the absolute truth, so they'd build company-wide credibility that would ignite participation. They created an open-book management culture, making every aspect of the business visible to every employee and invested a substantial amount of time and effort training every employee in financial management so that they could understand in detail the financial reports. Finally, they offered employees a significant share in the equity gains they helped achieve through a participatory stock ownership program.

The results were practically unbelievable. In the second year of operations, sales increased by 20 percent to $15.5 million and the following year by 40 percent to $23 million. By 1992 sales were $70 million, there were 700 employees; and productivity and quality rose together such

that the defect rate dropped to 1 percent compared with the industry average of 6 percent.

On their tenth anniversary in 1992, the $100,000 investment of the original investors was worth $23 million.

Jack Stack is one of the most talked about examples of the "new kind of leader." As Kirk O. Hansen, who used Jack Stack as a Harvard Business School case study in 1993, writes, "The SRC employees did not just pull their company out of the ditch. They transformed themselves. They became self-styled entrepreneurs, venture capitalists and missionaries for a human, highly market-responsive kind of business management."

While citizens must actively participate in the decision making of the community, senators – the other half of the equation – need to remember that their role is to gently step back and allow the citizens to come to decisions on their own. As a successful senator, Jack shaped his community's values and principles but he wasn't heavy-handed in laying down the law. He had an idea of how successful the company could be and shared with employees the opportunity to own and create something special.

5

The community only functions if the structure is fluid and adaptive.

Since citizens are autonomous, the community allows them to form and disband groups at their own discretion. They have complete freedom of movement; they are not organized by a set or formal structure. Their direction emerges through collaboration with other citizens.

When certain molecules are put together and you add a little water, they will remarkably self-assemble – finding their own right place, at their lowest possible energy state, in the balance of the system. This action is driven by basic rules of science: attraction and repulsion, as well as size and shape.

These types of properties, however, can also be applied to larger organisms such as amoebas – which are nevertheless still the smallest life form that exists in nature. They freely change shape – expanding, dividing and disbanding as appropriate. Their ability to morph at will is a key factor in their survival. These fascinating characteristics inspired Kazuo Inamori – founder of Kyocera – to create tiny profit centers within the company, called "amoebas."

The word *amoeba* – from the Greek *amoibe* meaning change – was used to capture the concept of an entity at its smallest, most elemental level, as well as to describe its life-like capability to "multiply and change shape in response to the environment."

Like those in nature, amoebas within Kyocera quickly shape shift to meet market demand and conditions. They are made up of between 3 to 50 employees each with full responsibility for their planning, decision making, and administration. There are about 800 of these "creatures" within the Japanese portion of Kyocera.

Amoebas are essentially temporary working groups formed to perform specific tasks and produce specific products. As the nature of the tasks and products changes, so do the amoebas. Amoebas can change daily – each running with full profit and loss responsibility, but still held together by Kyocera's overarching strategy and goals.

The market flexibility of these tiny units has enabled Kyocera to become one of Japan's most successful companies. The company has quickly diversified its single product offering into a multitude of arenas such as industrial ceramics, solar power generating systems, telecommunications equipment, and electronic components across 189 companies worldwide. The enterprise may best be described as "a connected set of communities."

How do these corporate amoebas work? Amoebas aren't simply small separate subdivided units within the organization. Amoeba managers and their employees are encouraged to act like owners of a small, independent company. Inamori states, "Each amoeba unit makes its own plans under the guidance of an amoeba leader. All members of the amoeba pool their wisdom and effort to achieve targets. In this way, each employee takes an active role in the workplace and spontaneously participates in management. The outcome is 'management by all.'" Thus the amoeba system works in Kyocera because of Inamori's corporate philosophy that's based on the belief that "individuals are most satisfied when their abilities, talents, efforts are dedicated to the betterment of the human organization to which they belong rather than to their own individual interests."

Amoebas may be separate but they are fluid in structure, and able to divide into smaller units, move from one area of Kyocera to another or even merge with other amoebas to form a larger one. This fluidity is seen as a result of each individual that makes up an amoeba striving for the greater good of the organization. Several small amoebas make up larger amoebas which are grouped into even larger amoebas. Kyocera itself is a giant amoeba.

What is striking about Kyocera's amoebas is the outcomes that are produced because, in a sense, there isn't any pre-defined production line or organization of tasks. Individuals within an amoeba or even individuals from another amoeba can band together in the pursuit of a new opportunity, splitting away from existing amoebas and creating new ones. The production line within Kyocera emerges from the interactions between the various amoebas, in almost a domino-like effect. Each production line, as well as the amoebas involved, is unique.

Due to the degree of freedom that citizens have, they are free to work as they see fit to best contribute to the organization – collaborating with employees from different groups to see what new ideas can be created and implemented.

Because of the high degree of autonomy and independence, there is no set structure or direction that organizes the citizens. Instead, much of their strategy is emergent as they

"

Due to the degree of freedom that citizens have,
they are free to work as they see fit to best
contribute to the organization

"

gather ideas and create and disband teams that coincide with their work. These communities need not be physical organizations for collaboration to emerge. As self-sufficient and self-motivated individuals, citizens can readily decide how to most productively and effectively operate with the long-run goals of the community in mind.

For Senator & Citizens organizations, a fluid structure is key to supporting its citizens as well as the organization's long-term success. Senators must consider the impact of various structures not only on how work is completed but also on the needs and wants of the citizens.

Communities can be both physical and virtual.

Technology has allowed like-minded individuals to collaborate without face-to-face interaction. Citizens with a strong sense of shared identity can form virtual communities, connecting with each other across geographical distances.

Jamie Heywood is on a mission. While the MIT mechanical engineer was always ambitious, this time it was different and hit a little too close to home. Doctors said the first symptoms could be slight; barely noticeable. You may feel clumsier than usual. Perhaps trip once in a while or drop things occasionally. You may feel a little weak in your arms or legs, but perhaps you've been working too hard, haven't been getting enough sleep and are a little stressed.

For Stephen, Jamie's younger brother and a carpenter, he felt it first in his right hand. At 6 feet 3 inches, Stephen was a strong man with arms of steel. At the age of 29, he was building his dream home in California, when something didn't feel quite right. He couldn't quite place it but his right hand felt weak. Soon, the weakness had spread to his left hand. That's when he suspected something was terribly wrong. A trip to the hospital revealed shocking results. In December 1998, Stephen was diagnosed with amyotrophic lateral sclerosis (ALS) or Lou Gehrig's Disease. That day Jamie's life changed forever. His brother's disease was the impetus that spurred him to eventually create a very special company dedicated to making a difference in the lives of patients with life-changing diseases. It's called PatientsLikeMe.

In the dogged pursuit of a medical cure for ALS, Stephen Heywood's story and Jamie's dedication will always be remembered – through the autobiographical movie, *So Much So Fast*, and the book, *His Brother's Keeper* by Pulitzer Prize-winning author, Jonathan

Find Patients Just Like You ⊗

Do you have a life-changing condition? Learn from the real-world experiences of other patients like you.

Join Now! (It's free!)

" ...PatientsLikeMe is the most empowering place I could ever imagine, giving us all not just information, but courage enough to be proactive rather than sit back and hope the doctor is doing the right thing... "
—*Multiple Sclerosis Community Member*

CURRENT DISEASE COMMUNITIES

Prevalent Diseases

ALS/MND

Epilepsy

Fibromyalgia

Chronic Fatigue Syndrome/ME

HIV/AIDS

Mood Conditions

   Anxiety

   Bipolar

   Depression

   OCD (Obsessive-Compulsive Disorder)

   PTSD (Post-Traumatic Stress Disorder)

MS (Multiple Sclerosis)

Parkinson's Disease

Organ Transplants

Share your health data »

Answer simple questions to create a shared health profile to see how you're doing over time.

Find patients like you »

Search by gender, age, treatments, symptoms, and time since diagnosis to easily connect with patients like you.

Learn from others »

Learn from real-world treatment and symptom reports, forum discussions, health profiles, one-on-one conversations and more.

Want to know more about PatientsLikeMe?

Learn all about us. Ask us anything. Why do we embrace openness, and what about your privacy? How do we make money and who are our partners? Take a moment to read this and find out.

Work in the healthcare industry for a pharmaceutical, insurance or other company?

Looking for more innovative ways to learn from real-world patient experiences? You can find out more about our products and services on our **partners site »**

Weiner. These are both mementos of Stephen's life and his battle with the debilitating disease. Jamie even started ALS TDI (ALS Therapy Development Institute) – called the "world's most advanced research laboratory dedicated to ALS." But of all the shining stars resulting from Stephen's story, PatientsLikeMe has made a huge impact on the lives of millions of patients around the world by giving them hope, the ability to share information about their medical conditions, and a new way to connect to each other even from miles away.

When you are the one person out of 100,000 people that is suffering from an incurable disease, it can be difficult to gather information and find others – like yourself – to share your experiences or understand potential treatments. Patients want to know "how they're doing relative to the rest of the world? Is my disease progressing fast or slow? What treatments am I on relative to other patients? Am I taking medications at a dose higher or lower than other patients?" That information isn't readily accessible for many, but with it, they can immediately understand where they stand in the world.

PatientsLikeMe provides patients with serious life-changing illnesses a platform through which they can interact, and while doing so, enable vital information to be gathered that can help to accelerate the discovery of new, more effective treatments. Started by Jamie and his youngest brother, Ben, their belief was based on the fact that "the collective wisdom of hundreds of thousands of patients really is smarter than any one person, no matter how well researched you are."

PatientsLikeMe would not be successful without the open sharing of medical information. So when people create public profiles that list their symptoms, medications/treatments, and other pertinent details, they can also see how fellow patients are dealing with their illness. But the big picture impact is that PatientsLikeMe supports the medical community by establishing a database which collects detailed information from members – giving doctors the ability to collect and analyze data from around the world. In fact, regulators can receive drug side-effects information from patients without having to wait for the manufacturers, and drug companies can access the large network to recruit subjects for clinical trials. Heywood says, "We already have 5 percent of all ALS patients in the US on our site," he says. That's a larger data set on the disease than exists anywhere else."

Technology and the Internet have enabled PatientsLikeMe to accomplish something that would have been impossible 15 years ago. Patients from across the globe can take control of their lives and find others afflicted with the same illness. Now dozens of communities have formed through patients' initiative on PatientsLikeMe – all centered on various common or rare disorders, such as Chronic Fatigue Syndrome, Epilepsy, Fibromyalgia, HIV/AIDS, and Multiple Sclerosis.

———————

Technology has given citizens the ability to connect and create virtual communities from around the world. Considering collaboration is no longer constrained by geographic boundaries, autonomous citizens – by the hundreds, thousands or millions – can easily create virtual and fluid online communities – brought together by a sense of belonging and an affinity to a community's values. Citizens see the benefits of creating their own communities – whether virtual or physical.

Today, numerous online communities have appeared such as Flickr, YouTube, Facebook, Wikipedia, and Twitter but organizations and consumers have a different attitude – one that's a little more laissez-faire which enables communities to develop on their own. These communities are based and founded on the principles of self-organization, active participation and collaboration where the collective intelligence of the group is clearly smarter, stronger, and faster than any one person.

Is Senator & Citizens
the right model for you?

Is this archetype right for your current situation? And, if it is, how can you be the best senator you can be? The following sections will help you answer these questions.

Great if:

- You can invoke a strong historical narrative shared by all participants.

- Although made up of individuals with diverse views, your community shares a very strong commitment to a common set of operating principles or values.

- You can effectively and reliably interact with members through the Internet (or other communications network) if they're geographically dispersed.

Think twice if:

- Your participants differ widely in terms of core values.

- You have a significant number of participants who are uninformed, inactive or uncomfortable with ambiguity.

- You have a strong desire for efficiency and dislike how debate can slow things down.

- You don't have efficient systems for keeping citizens informed and for giving and receiving feedback.

How can you be a better senator?

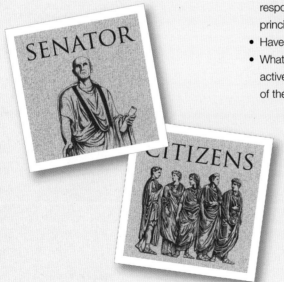

1. Is your "constitution" an accurate statement of the values of the community?

The constitution is the cornerstone of the community. It defines the rights and responsibilities of citizens. To join the community, citizens agree to abide by its principles but need to be aware of and keen to fulfill their civic responsibilities.

- Does your constitution define rights and responsibilities and clearly articulate founding principles and values?
- Have all citizens seen and read the constitution?
- What mechanisms do you use to increase the active participation of citizens in the preservation of the constitution?

2. How effective is your "citizenship test" at identifying whether people are a good fit with the community?

Citizens must have the best interests of the community at heart and willingly agree to abide by the constitution and its values. To fit in with the culture of the community, they must conform to a specific profile.

- What are the criteria for defining a "good fit" with the community?
- Do you have a citizenship test or other formal measures for deciding membership?
- How do you ensure that new citizens have the best interests of the community at heart?

3. How well-informed are your citizens about what's happening in the community?

If citizens are to reach independent decisions in the best interests of the community, they need to be well-informed. Information needs to be readily accessible to all.

- What efforts are you making to educate and inform citizens?
- Are all citizens able to access up-to-date information when making decisions?
- How transparent is the information that's shared amongst the citizens?

4. Do you provide a "strong why" or clear rationale for the desired behaviors?

Senators draw on the historical narrative of the community and the example of heroes and legendary figures to persuade citizens of their rights and responsibilities. People must be engaged in a discussion and understand the reasons for decisions before they commit to them. Storytelling, especially involving historical narratives, helps senators motivate and shape the behaviors of citizens.

- Do you ensure that you explain the reasons for decisions?
- Do you identify the themes where the explanation has been less clear and compelling and, therefore, the engagement less successful?
- How effective are you at using historical narratives to motivate and inspire citizens?

5. Do you provide citizens with effective means to express their opinions?

Freedom of speech is a given of participatory democracy, but citizens need to be able to contribute their ideas effectively. They need a means – for example, the ballot box – of getting their voices heard.

- What systems are there for canvassing citizens and collecting their votes?
- What are you doing to encourage the community "voice"?
- Do you act on the popular or majority opinion; is your democracy real or token?

6. Is your structure flexible enough to accommodate self-forming teams?

Citizens see freedom and autonomy as a fundamental right. They want the ability to create and disband teams in response to new opportunities, and the flexibility to move between working groups. The structure of the organization needs to support the mobility of citizens.

- What steps have you taken to encourage flexibility and mobility?
- Do the citizens have the power and authority to form and disband teams?
- Are the insights and experiences of teams recorded and used to build an "institutional memory"; do they inform future decision making?

7. How do you retain citizens' investment in the community?

Although citizens are given the autonomy to move, create, disband and reform teams, they need to retain a strong sense of allegiance to the larger community. Emerging factions can disrupt stable environments; mechanisms need to be used to preserve the community's integrity.

- How effectively do you balance autonomy and loyalty; how do you allow smaller groups to continue to participate in the wider community?
- What action do you take to prevent factions forming or to deal with them if they threaten to disrupt the community?
- What mechanisms are there to reinforce the stability and sustainability of the community?

Putting As One into practice

The eight As One archetypes can help transform the way leaders generate collective behavior in their organizations and communities, but putting them into practice is not a paint-by-numbers exercise. There is no precise wiring diagram or recipe book with detailed instructions for leaders to follow.

However, having said that, there is a proven method for applying the As One approach.

Our approach will guide you to ask the right questions and consider your options as you work through your collective leadership challenges. We have illustrated it using a number of case studies in order to bring the framework to life. The approach consists of the following three parts:

- Part 1: A **diagnostic** to assess the nature of your challenge and opportunity.
- Part 2: The formulation of a set of targeted and highly effective **interventions**.
- Part 3: A systematic way to broaden the **adoption** of As One as appropriate.

Part 1: Diagnostic

The diagnostic itself consists of three steps:

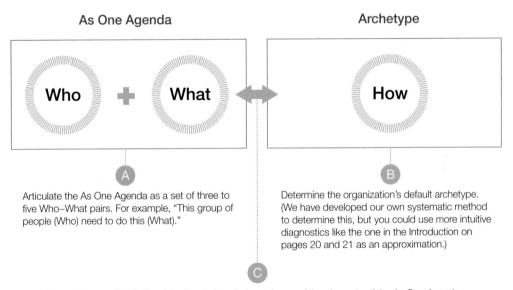

As One Agenda

Who ✛ **What**

Archetype

How

A

Articulate the As One Agenda as a set of three to five Who–What pairs. For example, "This group of people (Who) need to do this (What)."

B

Determine the organization's default archetype. (We have developed our own systematic method to determine this, but you could use more intuitive diagnostics like the one in the Introduction on pages 20 and 21 as an approximation.)

C

Assess how applicable the default archetype is to each one of the elements of the As One Agenda. Go through the three to five elements one at a time. (Please refer to the applicability sections that appear on pages 54, 88, 122, 156, 194, 228, 264 and 302 for where each archetype is a good fit and when you should think twice about its application.)

Let's use a real case study to illustrate how you can apply this diagnostic process.

In 2009, the CEO of a large wealth management firm with over $100 billion in assets under management (let's call it Wealthco) approached Deloitte to discuss the collective leadership challenges in his company. This leader had pursued a strong growth strategy but was also dealing with substantial challenges in executing this agenda across the organization. We began by asking him to think about his strategic agenda for Wealthco and to prioritize the top three areas where it was critical to get large numbers of his people to work well together. After some reflection, he identified the following three priorities:

1. Product innovation. About three to four years ago, the company had made a strategic decision to become more customer-focused. As a result, it had set up a new business unit to focus on customer segmentation and customer management. However, this new group had not yet succeeded in instilling a customer-centric culture within the organization. In particular, the insights gleaned from different customer segments were not being effectively channeled into the product development process. In effect, the two groups were working in silos, and consistent with the historic culture, it was difficult to get them to collaborate. The CEO's number one priority was to get these two groups to work effectively across group boundaries to achieve greater success in product innovation.

2. Regulatory compliance. The company had been under recent government pressure for past regulatory oversights; now regulatory compliance had become of the utmost importance. The organization simply could not afford another regulatory mistake. Failure to comply could result in significant costs and severely damage not only the organization's reputation but also its ability to engage in business. One of the key messages the leader had been trying to deliver was that of zero tolerance in this regard. Therefore, the CEO's number two priority was to ensure that employees always complied with these regulations; and that the company would not become the subject of another regulatory investigation.

3. Replicating best practice. Finally, the CEO explained that Wealthco had over 2,300 financial advisers who functioned largely as relatively independent, sole practitioners. One of the things that had become painfully apparent to him was that these advisers often reinvented the wheel when it came to the offers they tried to sell to clients. Instead of leveraging successful practices by other advisers, many were disinterested in seeing the bigger picture and never considered how they could work more productively together. The company had simply not been effective at convincing them to adopt proven practices. The CEO recognized the large missed revenue opportunity. Something needed to be done. Getting advisers to replicate each other's successful practices was thus his number three priority.

So, how could we use the As One diagnostic to help this CEO achieve his three collective leadership priorities?

Leaders tend to be very good at expressing their collective leadership priorities in terms of **Who–What** pairs. In the example above, the CEO described his agenda in terms of different groups of people who needed to achieve three specific goals. In essence, this list of Who–What pairs describes what we refer to as a leader's "As One Agenda."

As One Agenda

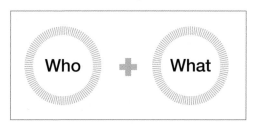

Priority #1	
To get people in product development and customer segment management…	…to work together to define and develop product offerings that tie closely to customer needs
Priority #2	
To get every employee…	…to abide by government regulatory requirements
Priority #3	
To get 2,300 financial advisers…	…to replicate each other's best practices

Collaboration is not an end in itself. It cannot be applied in broad sweeping strokes across an entire organization. The power of the As One approach comes from the focus on those few priorities where collaboration is critical and will have a disproportionately high impact on overall success. Our aim is to help leaders enhance collective leadership, *where it counts the most*. Essentially, the As One Agenda becomes an important and practical focusing device for leaders. However to get to the heart of the matter, we need to add a third dimension to our framework: namely, the **How**.

This third and most important dimension – what we refer to as the How – revolves around how people think about working with others. This is where our As One archetypes become invaluable, as most leaders have neither the language nor the frameworks to address this How dimension; a dimension that has previously been overlooked. The archetypes offer specificity in language around which of the eight different models leaders and followers intend to deploy.

Assess

Let's apply this assessment process to Wealthco. We already know the three priorities of the Wealthco CEO's As One Agenda so we need to identify the default archetype in the company and *assess* how well the archetype matches up with each of these priorities.

We ran our systematic diagnostic that established that over 57 percent of the organization perceived the default archetype of Wealthco to be Architect & Builders.

Archetype distribution at Wealthco

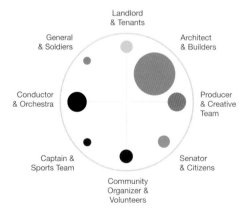

This is a very effective model for bringing together leaders who need to specify a top-down direction and vision, and for people, with innovative talents, who are committed to achieving it. The big question for Wealthco was whether this default archetype, Architect & Builders, was suitable for all three priorities in the CEO's As One Agenda.

Let's begin with the first priority: to get employees in both product development and customer segment groups to work effectively across their silos. The two groups were very different business units with different interests and incentives. The challenge had been that, in the past, they had always worked independently with little integration, but they needed to work together to develop a more "customer-oriented" product offering.

For them to achieve their objective of ensuring that customer insights were integrated into the product design processes, they needed to deliver on an "deliver a model of continuous innovation that requires people to push beyond normal boundaries." The Architect & Builders archetype is well-suited to achieving this objective. After all, it's an archetype that is all about groups of people with different capabilities working together toward a seemingly impossible goal. For priority number one, there was no mismatch between Wealthco's default archetype and their product innovation priority.

Now let's take a look at the CEO's second priority: to get every employee in the firm to abide by the regulatory compliance requirements. Due to the severe repercussions of non-compliance, all employees needed to follow the specifications of the regulations without question. There could be no leeway in interpreting or applying those rules. From an archetype perspective, the question for the CEO was, "Which archetype could best elicit adherence and compliance?" While the Architect & Builders archetype can be useful with its top-down approach and strong positive incentives for achieving the impossible, it is not as suitable in situations where leaders need to motivate and incentivize employees to avoid negative behaviors. There is a poor fit between the default archetype and Wealthco's second priority.

Finally, let's take a look at the third priority: to get 2,300 financial advisers to share each other's best practices across the group. Although Architect & Builders is very effective if there is a "a concept that needs to be refined by local experts to make it fit for expansion," a more granular review of the Wealthco diagnostic showed that the financial advisers were not actually part of the

57 percent majority. In fact, the Architect & Builders mode of working is simply not the way their part of the organization operated.

Instead, their group tended to operate in the Community Organizer & Volunteers archetype; they felt they were autonomous workers that should have a say in most decisions. Simply put, the CEO was finding himself in a mismatched archetype: Architect & Volunteers. Either the volunteers had to be transformed into builders (a very big ask), or as a leader, the CEO would need to develop more community organizer leadership tendencies himself.

To summarize the results of our assessment with the default archetype: Architect & Builders:

As One Agenda		Archetype
Who + What	↔	How ARCHITECT & BUILDERS

Priority #1			
To get people in product development and customer segment management…	…to work together to define and develop product offerings that tie closely to customer needs	✓	**Good fit** Needs to be better executed to be effective

Priority #2			
To get every employee…	…to abide by government regulatory requirements	✗	**Poor fit** The Architect & Builders mode doesn't work well when the adherence to strict rules is required

Priority #3			
To get 2,300 financial advisers…	…to replicate each other's best practices	!	**Archetype mismatch** The architect (CEO) was essentially working with a group of volunteers

Part 2: Interventions

Now, let's consider how to formulate targeted and highly effective interventions to address the opportunities uncovered by part 1. In essence, there are three classes of interventions but it's important to note that their application is dependent upon a specific situation:

1. If there is a good fit between the default archetype and the priority, leaders should *strengthen* the primary archetype.
2. When the default archetype is not a good fit or is a mismatch with a specific As One Agenda priority, leaders should *overlay* a secondary archetype.
3. When there is no clear default archetype, leaders must *narrow* down the field to develop a primary archetype.

Strengthen

In this situation, we need to consider how to enhance the default archetype's execution. If the organization is already performing effectively using the default archetype, we need to identify how to boost the organization's capability to function even better within that mode. However if an organization is struggling, then we need to consider interventions that effectively *strengthen* the execution of the default archetype.

Returning to the Wealthco case, the CEO needed to determine how his organization could operate more effectively in the Architect & Builders mode to achieve his first priority: to enhance collaboration between the product development and the customer segment groups. Some of the challenges that he may have been experiencing could have resulted from the possibility that a sufficiently inspiring goal may not have been communicated to the two groups. Or perhaps from an organizational perspective, the two groups may not have received appropriate and aligned positive incentives.

What are some of the ways that the CEO and his leadership team could become stronger architects?

After a good discussion with the leadership team that involved a review of the reflection questions in our Architect & Builders chapter, we discovered a few priority interventions for the CEO to boost the effectiveness of this mode at Wealthco.

We chose the following two reflection questions from the "How can you be a better architect?" pages reproduced above to get the discussion started with the CEO:

- Does the way you communicate your goals inspire and motivate people?
- How do you convince builders that every one of them has something special to contribute?

We then asked an additional and increasingly challenging set of questions to focus on the best opportunities for improvement:

- How do you ensure cross-innovation; how are different ways of solving problems shared by the different teams?
- Have you broken the project down into a coherent set of challenges that draws on different capabilities and experience?
- Are you using a systematic time pacing methodology to accelerate major releases of and minor upgrades to the blueprint?
- Are you using the best collaborative technologies to enable different teams to work off a single version of the blueprint?

231

Based on this discussion (and more detailed further analysis), the Wealthco CEO decided on three major interventions to strengthen the execution of the Architect & Builders mode and to drive better collaboration across the two silos:

1. Increase the transparency and granularity of Wealthco's performance management system.

This enabled the two different parts of the organization to understand how well each was performing and to create an increased sense of interdependence in their activities.

2. Deploy an intensive campaign methodology to link Wealthco's offers to market activities.

The group adopted a structured campaign methodology for taking new offers to the market and enabled them to evaluate their success using a disciplined approach. This heightened the sense of shared success across both groups.

3. Introduce stronger time pacing to Wealthco's project management process.

By shortening their reporting periods and building in weekly checkpoints for dependent outputs, the CEO was able to instill a stronger sense of collective urgency into both teams.

Interventions can take many forms. The most obvious are making adjustments to the operating model such as implementing structural changes, redesigning incentives, and reengineering business processes. A second type of intervention impacts people, leadership and cultural levers. Big changes to the information architecture and communications systems are often overlooked, but they can be powerful and successful in some archetypes. Finally, in some cases, adapting the strategy itself can be an appropriate response. After all, strategy is executed through people; and if the people are not in line, the strategy will likely be less effective.

Overlay

If the default archetype is a poor fit with a specific element of the As One Agenda, then we need to find a different archetype (ie, a secondary mode different from the default archetype) that is a better and more productive match with that specific priority. In this situation, the organization (and especially the leader) must learn how to *overlay* the secondary, more suitable archetype on top of the default mode in the same organization.

Let's return to the Wealthco case again. The CEO's second priority was to achieve full regulatory compliance across the entire organization. But the problem was, as we established earlier, that the Architect & Builders mode was not the most effective archetype for compliance purposes. Instead a much stronger match for enforcing compliance, with its strict rules, attention to detail and precision, is the Conductor & Orchestra archetype.

With such significant consequences for compliance breaches, Wealthco's CEO needs to dictate the processes that all employees must follow. Employees should not be allowed to freely interpret the regulatory requirements. The CEO needed to create a secondary mode that was better suited to achieve compliance in the whole organization. While overlaying a secondary archetype is no easy task, it can be done in a thoughtful and deliberate way. The trick is to enable large groups of people to distinguish when to use the default mode and when to shift to the secondary mode; and most important, to do it together.

To get a better sense of what this actually means, imagine being part of the most creative ideation session at IDEO when the fire alarm goes off. Everyone on the team looks to the fire warden and obeys the instructions given. The fire alarm triggers a Pavlovian reaction to switch from Producer & Creative Team mode into Conductor & Orchestra.

To create an equivalent in Wealthco, we developed a coded language around the words "blueprint" and "baton" to signal an archetype shift from Architect & Builders to Conductor & Orchestra. Employees are now being trained to collectively shift their behavior when told to be in "baton" mode, meaning that they need to follow the conductor's orders or face consequences.

To be perfectly clear, this is not a simple feat to achieve and the specifics of this intervention could be the subject of an entirely separate book.

However, we worked with Wealthco to successfully draw up and implement psychological and sociological techniques to craft new visual and verbal cues. They continue to practice and reinforce the right behaviors through repeated communications and tactical leadership signals. It takes systematic thinking and some time; but the results are so powerful that the use of these types of techniques is worth the dedicated effort.

Although poor fit is one situation that requires an overlay; another arises when leaders and followers have different perceptions or levels of awareness on how to collaborate to achieve a specific goal. This results in an archetype mismatch. This is a particularly challenging situation where usually the leader will have to adapt to the followers' archetype in order to connect with them; but sometimes, leaders can successfully and gradually transform their followers' archetype to better match with their own preferred one.

Returning to the Wealthco case, the CEO's third priority was to get the 2,300 financial advisers to replicate each other's best practices. As described earlier, the leaders were leading as architects while the followers were acting as volunteers. In other words, the situation presented an Architect & *Volunteers* mismatch.

In this case, the CEO needed to balance these mismatched archetypes by adopting some community organizer techniques. As part of the discussions to determine the most appropriate techniques, we consulted the reflection questions listed in Community Organizer &

Volunteers chapter, focused on the best opportunities for improvement and chose the following questions to pose to the CEO:

- Is your first call to action a reasonable request for volunteers?
- What tactics are you using to get dissenters to agree to do something (even if fairly small)?
- How rigorously are you assessing the success of different types of campaigns and different types of volunteers?
- How effective are you at building trust with your volunteers?

Based on this discussion and some further reflection, we identified a few important ways for the Wealthco executives to integrate a few effective community organizer tendencies and overlay them on their existing architect style.

For example, a community organizer would articulate very clearly why and how it would be in the volunteers' self-interest to adopt best practices from across the network. Also, community organizers need to field smaller requests that volunteers are more likely to accept. Therefore, the mismatched modes could be further balanced if the demands on the advisers were broken into smaller propositions (ie, leaders needed to choose a single best practice for people to adopt each week rather than expect advisers to implement all of the changes at once).

Single archetype

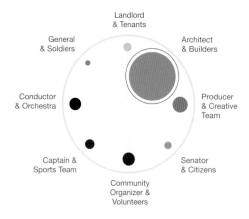

Split archetypes

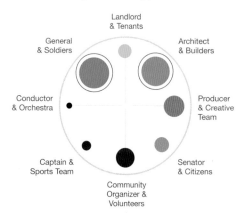

Narrow

While we've introduced our As One approach in a range of organizations in the private, public and non-profit sectors covering many different regions, we noticed an interesting pattern: there tended to be three different scenarios regarding how archetypes were concentrated in organizations. Specifically, some have a single clear default archetype, others have split archetypes with two that are equally popular, and finally, there are some organizations that have a spread archetype pattern with no clear default mode.

As you've already seen with Wealthco, it's relatively easy to decide what to do when a **single archetype** is dominant: you strengthen the ability of the organization to execute in that mode.

With **split archetypes**, such as the case shown on the left, your challenge is also relatively manageable, especially if you want to use both archetypes at different times. As previously discussed, you would simply overlay a secondary mode as required.

But what do you do if you are facing the third scenario with a highly-spread distribution of archetypes in your organization? How can you even conduct the assessment if there is no clear default archetype?

In this case, you need to consider your options and *narrow* the field by choosing a primary archetype and then building that default archetype over time.

Consider the case of a large global media company (let's call it Mediaco). This iconic company holds assets in television, radio, pro-

Spread archetypes

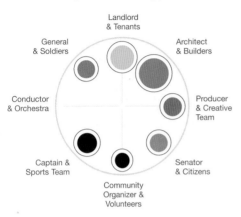

Landlord
& Tenants

General
& Soldiers

Architect
& Builders

Conductor
& Orchestra

Producer
& Creative
Team

Captain &
Sports Team

Senator
& Citizens

Community
Organizer &
Volunteers

duction studios, and publishing. Over the last few years, Mediaco was under significant scrutiny to reinvent itself, from both the external environment and its shareholders. Disruptive changes in the market were also forcing the media industry to adopt new digital technologies at a ferocious pace.

The diagnostic revealed no dominant archetype (see distribution in the **spread archetypes** figure.) In fact, it revealed a relatively even distribution across seven different modes. The top archetype registered only 29 percent, while the second largest represented 18 percent of the population. The remaining five archetypes ranged from 7 percent to 13 percent in size.

With the distribution so broadly spread, the employees were basically saying that they didn't feel the organization worked together in a single unified way. In fact, anecdotal feedback supported this conclusion; employees stated they did not always understand or agree with the way the leaders managed the organization. Given the scale of change that the organization is facing, the dilemma for the leadership team was: how can we deliver change more effectively in the future? Would a focus on a narrower field of archetypes help engage employees in more compelling ways going forward?

The best way to understand the optimal mix of archetypes is to go back to the applicability rules for the eight archetypes and determine which mode is most effective for delivering the As One Agenda of the organization. The leadership should then work to embed that particular mode within the organization.

In this case, Mediaco employees expressed a preference for the Producer & Creative Team archetype as well as support for the archetypes adjacent to it – which was not surprising given the company's long role in creating media content. In addition, the organization attempted to broaden the number of platforms on which their content is deployed; a goal that was also a good fit for developing creative solutions. Thus one potential intervention could be for Mediaco to form creative teams to work together to develop solutions to the platform challenge.

In Mediaco's case, the natural fit for their As One Agenda ended up being the Producer & Creative Team archetype because of the creative nature of their priorities. As with the other cases, the reflection questions served as a guide to focus the leadership team on identifying the most critical interventions to make the archetype changes stick.

Part 3: Adoption

Organizations are very complex entities. It is rare to find a large organization that is entirely homogeneous and not made up of many sub-cultures. These sub-groups are, in many ways, their own organizations with their own default archetypes. How then do you apply the framework if there are differences in archetypes across geographies or business units?

Embed

The answer is to *embed* the As One framework within and beyond the organization in a cascaded manner. This allows you to drive the broader adoption of a common language around collective leadership while retaining sufficient diversity across archetypes to enable collaboration.

Let's take a look at the story of a major global bank (let's call it Bankco). The new CEO of the wholesale division in Bankco was in the process of implementing a large-scale transformation program. He and his chief transformation officer had been working together for six months to develop a plan on how to communicate the new direction to the group.

It turned out that the bank's overwhelming default archetype was Architect & Builders. In fact, 74 percent of the employees felt that the bank on a whole operated in that mode. However within Bankco, there was a structural shift in archetype at different levels of the organization. While the organization demonstrated very high uniformity in the Architect & Builders archetype at the business unit level, we see a very different picture at levels above and below the business unit.

At the highest level, the global CEO tended to use a Senator & Citizens approach. He engaged the business unit leaders in a highly participatory collective effort to set the overall Bankco direction. In turn, those leaders used the Architect & Builders mode to share the set direction and vision with their own functional leadership teams and engaged their team's innovative talents to achieve the challenging goals. And finally when functional leaders engaged their own staff to deliver on expected performance objectives, they tended to be more scripted and used the Conductor & Orchestra mode for precise execution.

This is a clear example of how organizations can use the As One archetypes and embed them within their organization's levels and ways of working. For Bankco, these three archetypes integrate well within their structure and processes. There is no confusion for Bankco employees that the organization does not follow a single default archetype. Quite the opposite: it makes both cultural and operational sense for different archetypes to be used by different leaders as priorities shift up and down the hierarchy.

Hierarchy of archetypes at Bankco

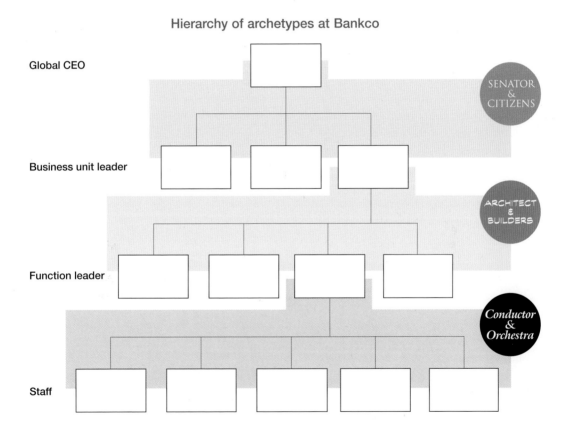

Global CEO

SENATOR & CITIZENS

Business unit leader

ARCHITECT & BUILDERS

Function leader

Conductor & Orchestra

Staff

Extending beyond boundaries

The As One concepts aren't just applicable to employees or individuals within an organization. The archetypes can be used to generate collective behavior within partner organizations in the supply chain – and even large groups of customers.

We have started to apply the As One archetypes to a variety of interesting contexts that are broader than the normal boundaries of the organization. Consider the following two examples.

The case of a popular sports franchise demonstrates how the As One approach could be extended outside the core team to impact the way the team played; to how they interacted with the coaches; to how management tried to create a successful franchise; and even to how the franchise is engaging and mobilizing their fan base.

Fans of this sports team were confounded when their team didn't make the playoffs. There was no reason they couldn't have won the championship. Expectations were high as the team had successfully recruited a large number of star players. But for some reason, teams with far less star power had been winning more games that season. The "dream team" just didn't play as one and thus didn't make the playoffs. The team embraced the slogan of "Stand As One," but rapidly realized that they had very few new ideas to implement this brand promise to their players, administration, management, sponsors, supporters and the community at large. Management decided to use the As One approach to gain a better understanding of how they could further align these diverse groups – who were both within and outside of the organization – around their core strategy.

The As One model for collective leadership applies to a wide variety of leaders in many diverse situations. In fact, to put this idea to the ultimate test, we decided to conduct the As One diagnostic across the largest private professional services network in the world: Deloitte. Diagnostics were conducted across the largest member firms to mid-sized and smaller firms each within very diverse geographies with unique cultures and different organizational priorities. What we discovered clearly supports the value of extending the use of the archetypes in a large diverse organization: one common language, but different archetypes for different priorities. The results of our member firm diagnostics can be found in the Appendix on pages 327–33.

The value of the As One approach is that the robust analytics behind the archetypes remove the guesswork by providing a very specific list of questions to consider for each archetype. They act as a key guide in helping leaders make important decisions on how to best apply the lessons learned from their archetypes to their unique situations. And more important, the specific and colorful descriptions of the eight archetypes allow a large group of people to talk about these issues using the same language.

The As One approach

Although the contextual factors may be unique, the As One approach is fairly universal in its application.

Part 1: Diagnostic

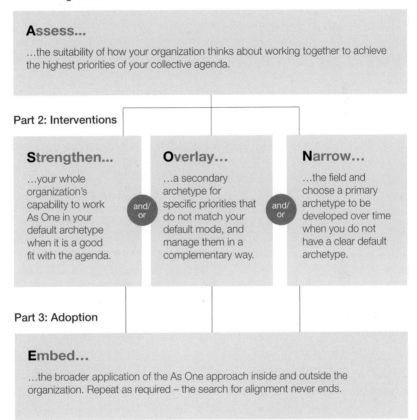

Assess...

...the suitability of how your organization thinks about working together to achieve the highest priorities of your collective agenda.

Part 2: Interventions

Strengthen...

...your whole organization's capability to work As One in your default archetype when it is a good fit with the agenda.

and/ or

Overlay...

...a secondary archetype for specific priorities that do not match your default mode, and manage them in a complementary way.

and/ or

Narrow...

...the field and choose a primary archetype to be developed over time when you do not have a clear default archetype.

Part 3: Adoption

Embed...

...the broader application of the As One approach inside and outside the organization. Repeat as required – the search for alignment never ends.

As One

Five letters that make all the difference between a group of individuals and a unified team.

Two words that transform individual action into collective power.

One idea that can help you realize the full power of your people.

The road ahead

We are just at the beginning of the As One journey and, for the first time, we have the components of a rigorous framework for leaders to understand and decide what it means to work As One. We have created both a common language for collective leadership as well as developed our first descriptions of eight different archetypes. This book is an initial contribution to this emerging body of thought, and we have learned a lot in the process.

Having said that, we recognize that collective leadership is very much a "next practice" domain. There is still a great deal of knowledge to discover, test and refine; that's why we see it as a collective action project in its own right. Real success over time depends on whether a growing group of collaborators will join us in this task and help to advance our work.

This book coincides with the launch of an important new global center that is entirely dedicated to the next practice of collective leadership. The Deloitte Center for Collective Leadership will draw on hundreds of practitioners and collaborators from academic institutions, the world of business, public administration as well as from many other walks of life.

A key aspect of the Center's work will be the ongoing development of a richer taxonomy for describing a broader array of As One archetypes. For us, the next leg of our research has already begun. We have already identified different levels within our preliminary model of As One behavior. For example, Architect & Builders can be further divided into three sub groupings: 1) achieving the "impossible dream" (as illustrated by the Tata Nano case), 2) matching the blueprint with local conditions to achieve geographic expansion (as illustrated by the Ecobank case), and 3) using employee empowerment for remarkable innovation (as illustrated by the GE Aviation case). In addition, we have discovered two sub-groupings for Senator & Citizens that exist as physical and virtual or technology-enabled communities.

We have only scratched the surface of understanding how leaders can take advantage of working As One. Around the world, examples of inspirational As One leadership continue to present themselves. The real power of As One happens every day, and in all kinds of settings as individuals come together and act as a collective.

Imagine the power of thousands of collaborators identifying and documenting these examples on a global scale. New iterations of our data analytics engine would undoubtedly give rise to the discovery of many new modes of As One behavior. Our collective effort would make a big contribution to the ability of leaders and followers to transform their organizations and effectively address all kinds of societal challenges.

Therefore, we seek to attract a community of like-minded individuals to help us identify and catalogue a growing library of cases in order to further our collective understanding of this topic over time. We are calling this effort "Project 10K" because our goal is to gather over 10,000 examples of As One behavior from around the world. We intend to re-run our analytic model when we reach 1,000 cases (a big advance over our current 60-case model) and to refine and enhance our preliminary taxonomy of collective leadership on an ongoing basis.

To support the project, we are launching an online community where collaborators who encounter powerful and interesting As One examples can contribute them to a central repository. The stories can be simple such as one individual igniting a movement, or complex such as those that involve multiple organizations working together across the planet. But each must demonstrate how individual action can be transformed into collective power.

As we increase the number of case studies in our repository, we will continue to glean further information on the different forms of collective leadership. We are just beginning to unlock the potential of this approach; and are using our common language to launch the "next practice" in understanding As One behavior and enhancing leaders' ability to improve their organizations' performance.

Please register online and begin to share your As One experiences with us, and the rest of the community. You can upload your stories to our website **www.asone.org**. Or to make it even easier, you can use our free app for iPhones, iPads and Android phones. It only takes a few minutes to potentially make a big difference.

Together, let's continue our collective journey. Join us to help more and more people discover the power of working As One.

The Deloitte case study

As Deloitte Touche Tohmatsu Limited CEO, Jim Quigley's challenge has been to lead a large and diverse organization in the highly competitive professional services market. Deloitte's global organization is both legally and substantively a network of individual member firms with separate profit pools distributed to national partners. The member firm business model is the product of history, regulatory requirements and legal precedent. Through the member firm business model, country partnerships are both empowered and accountable for market-focused behavior in their individual markets. The market focus, accountability and focused reward structures are all strengths of this business model.

Some strategic activities are much more effectively executed at scale, with strong control and direction from the center. For example, vision, values, strategy and brand are all directed from the center. The marketplace for professional services has been highly influenced by the globalization. Global clients have little respect for national boundaries, as they work to globalize their operations and structures. Their expectations of a professional services organization are for borderless, seamless service. For many years, the Deloitte strategy, and the strategy of other professional services organizations, has been to provide borderless, seamless client service excellence. While that is very easily said, consistently executing to that standard with over 170,000 professionals in 147 countries, through 53 individual member firms is no small challenge.

Deloitte has remained committed to its member firm business model, as well as the market focus and clear accountability the model provides. By rejecting the structural integration approach taken by other organizations, Deloitte has maintained very strong member firms, which operate as part of a global network with a strong client-centric culture. This approach has paid off handsomely as Deloitte has climbed from the number eight position in the original Big 8 to an organization that is ascending to the leadership position today. Deloitte has achieved market-leading growth in each of the past five years. Although proud of this achievement, Jim was never content; he knew more could − and must − be achieved in a rapidly evolving marketplace.

Deloitte's global strategy

Jim and his leadership team have believed that the primary way to retain their number one position was to excel at working across geographic and functional boundaries. The key source of competitive advantage has come from being better than the rest at working "As One." This belief formed the basis for Deloitte's new global strategy, fittingly named the As One Strategy.

This strategy was finalized with input from senior member firm partners attending the 2010 World Meeting of Deloitte. A diagnostic survey of 550 Deloitte member firm leaders in advance of the meeting provided excellent insights into the perceived archetypes within Deloitte. The survey also measured as the degree of commitment by the Deloitte leadership team to each key element of the proposed strategy. This pragmatic and realistic understanding of our current position informed the strategic planning process.

The diagnostic at the global level revealed a split archetype pattern. The primary archetype was Architect & Builders with nearly 45 percent of the top leadership comfortable with working creatively to deliver a strong and inspiring top-down direction. But that was not the full story.

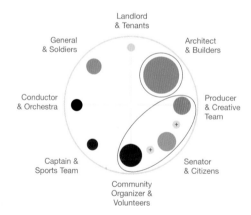

Closer analysis revealed a second large group comprised of the lower right quadrant archetypes, specifically Producer & Creative Team, Senator & Citizens, and Community Organizer & Volunteers. These three archetypes share characteristics such as a preference for democratic processes as well as individual independence and autonomy. In general, the members of this group don't respond as well as others to being handed a firm top-down direction. This second group, which matched the first in terms of size, represented a preference toward a highly participatory mode of direction setting.

The challenge for Jim and his team was to balance these split archetypes and run a strategy process that engaged and satisfied both populations. The strategy process involved a mix of top-down analysis and direction setting, with ample opportunities for thousands of member firm partners to meaningfully contribute to the overall process. The culmination, at a Deloitte World Meeting, saw hundreds of the Deloitte network's most senior leaders spend hours in small groups discussing the As One archetypes as well as the network's commitment levels to different parts of the strategy in order to refine and prioritize the key elements of the global strategy.

Jim has strongly advocated the Deloitte As One Strategy, and he is confident that with the common language and clear understanding of the As One Agenda, Deloitte's competitive advantage is within reach. There is little doubt that the active involvement of the Deloitte leaders in the strategy development process has strengthened the overall ownership and commitment to its implementation. However, the value of the As One approach has not been limited to the global strategy process. It is being embedded in many other parts of the global organization. The Australian firm provides a good example.

Deloitte Australia

It was only six years ago that the Deloitte Australia firm was considered the "sick puppy" of the Australian accountancy services sector. Compared with its three big rivals, Ernst & Young, KPMG and PricewaterhouseCoopers, it was the clear laggard of the Big 4. Voluntary staff turnover was at 36 percent, and the firm had trouble filling positions, with 400 open jobs in a firm of 2,000 employees. People used to joke about the Big 4 being, in reality, the Big 3 or the Big 3-and-a-half.

Back then, the organization's culture was different. Deloitte was an organization where each partner had the authority to make changes in their practices as they saw fit. There was little coordination across groups and each member firm partner settled into their own silos. In essence, it was a strong Community Organizer & Volunteers culture and partners would have felt they had the choice to independently opt in or out of policies and programs as they wished.

Giam Swiegers took over as Deloitte Australia CEO in 2003 and wasted no time in making changes. One of the first programs he implemented was to instill a culture of accountability and individual commitment to delivering the expected collective performance. Another critical aspect of the transformation was to implement a culture of innovation and profitable growth aligned to a deliberate strategic vision.

In short, Swiegers wanted to drive a shift in firm archetypes from Community Organizer & Volunteers to the directive/creative mix embodied in Architect & Builders. He felt that an Architect & Builders archetype could help the firm become more strategically focused to identify coordinated growth opportunities, improve cross-selling, improve implementation of defined strategic initiatives and lower costs. At the time the firm was described as "having the freedom to implement," not "having the freedom from all constraints."

By recasting the Deloitte Australia change journey in terms of archetypes, we used the diagnostic to take a read on the progress made through 2009. Analysis of the data indicated that there were three predominant modes, specifically 37 percent in Senator & Citizens, 35 percent in Architect & Builders and 18 percent in Community Organizer & Volunteers.

The remaining five archetypes registered less than 5 percent each. During the six years with Swiegers at the helm, a significant change in culture had already been accomplished with one-third of the firm being squarely in the Architect & Builders archetype.

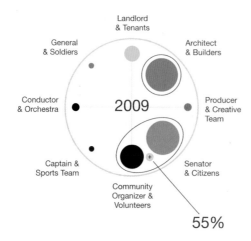

The 2009 diagnostic revealed that Deloitte Australia's journey was well under way. The leadership team thought long and hard about how to bring along the 55 percent of the organization who were in Senator & Citizens and Community Organizer & Volunteers mode. They began a concerted effort to have messages delivered in a way that communicated a strong "why" in order to aggressively shift the individuals' mindsets that were still progressing through the Deloitte journey. They also introduced innovative communication techniques such as videos, the art of storytelling and embracing social media as a key catalyst to allow people to recognize the sense of ownership of ideas.

Not surprisingly, in 2010 the partnership elected Swiegers to continue as CEO for another five years. Operating more emphatically in Architect & Builders mode, Swiegers and the firm's leadership formulated a more specific and inspiring vision for 2015 by engaging the entire partnership in the effort. We have just received the results from their 2010 diagnostic as we go to press with this book. The percentage of the organization in the Senator & Citizens and Community Organizer & Volunteers archetypes has halved from 55 percent to 26 percent. The journey continues. With a strong As One vision and commitment, Deloitte Australia has become the growth leader in Australia; in fact they are within striking distance of number 2 today and are now one of the most admired firms in their marketplace.

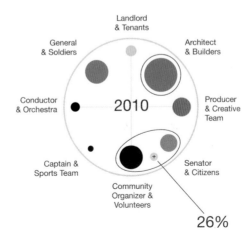

Other parts of the Deloitte network

We have worked hard to embed the As One methodology throughout the Deloitte network. To date, nearly 20 diagnostics have been or are in the process of being conducted by member firms within the Deloitte network. It is part of our ongoing work to continue to refine and embed As One lessons within our own organization. To get a sense of the breadth of our effort as well as the diversity of the results, consider the following four additional examples with accompanying archetype distribution diagrams:

1. Large member firm

This large member firm has been focused on regulatory and process compliance goals. It is not surprising that General & Soldiers – which is consistent with a compliance focus – is the most widely perceived archetype. The challenge that this firm's leadership is grappling with is how to overlay the Architect & Builders approach – well-suited for developing creative solutions to client issues – on top of the dominant General & Soldiers archetype, which is used to ensure compliance with internal and external requirements.

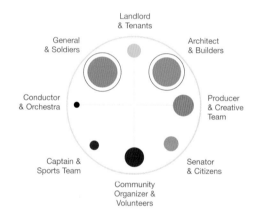

2. Partner group in a small member firm

This view shows one of the small Deloitte member firms as seen by its leadership – the partners in the firm. There is unanimity in this group on a Senator & Citizens model. The partners all know each other and view each other as a group of committed colleagues who gather as equals to decide how to run the firm. This firm is small enough to pull off this kind of participatory democracy to great effect.

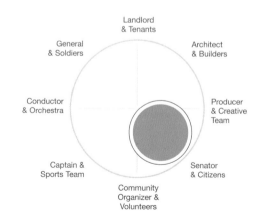

3. Single function within a member firm

In this firm, the Consulting practice perceives a clear single dominant archetype in Architect & Builders, which also happens to be the preferred archetype of that group. The archetype fits the goals of the organization to grow through more innovative client solutions. The challenge is to find ways to continually strengthen the archetype, especially given sub-populations with very different default archetypes.

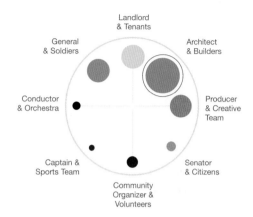

4. Director group in a large member firm

The data from this large firm about their Director group (one level below partner) suggests an interesting pattern in what people would prefer: the most common preference is Producer & Creative Team. However what's striking is that it represents a desire for independent creative work somewhat detached from top-down strategy. The firm's personnel strategy is "What Are You Famous For?" and leading a creative team may be seen as just the right path to achieve that.

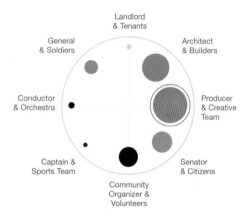

Jim, with the support of his leadership team, strongly believes that As One behavior can lay the foundation for Deloitte's competitive advantage: As One in client service; As One in talent development; As One in brand management; As One in risk management; not to mention the specific global initiatives to deliver that aspiration frames the Deloitte global strategy. We will continue to be committed to further embed the As One approach into Deloitte and to bring more people across our organization and member firm clients around the world to discover the varied ways to collectively work As One.

This book is a true collaboration of many people whom we recognize in the acknowledgments.

That being said, we owe a great deal of gratitude to our lead writer Katherine Lee, whom we would like to single out for special thanks, and who for all intents and purposes, has been a co-author of this book.

Kat has been instrumental in the development and refinement of our ideas. From conducting detailed research on all our cases to finding inspiring stories that bring our ideas to life, Kat has done it all. We cannot thank her enough for helping us to express our ideas, findings and stories through a more accessible and flowing narrative than we could have ever hoped to create by ourselves.

We would also like to recognize our "internal publisher" Pom Somkabcharti, who has managed the entire research and writing effort. She has been a terrific source of inspiration, drive, persistence, and hands-on assistance to us as well as our lead writer Kat. She is a fountain of wisdom and experience in publishing and has always demanded the highest standards of quality. We are indebted to her help.

Finally, we would like to thank Roya Baghai who has played the lead design role in this project. She has the amazing ability to pay attention to the most nuanced details while ensuring that everything fits into the big picture in a seamless and integrated manner. We are so appreciative of the time she has dedicated to creating the look and feel of this book and the As One brand.

Quite simply and honestly, there would be no book without our brilliant trio Kat, Pom and Roya.

Acknowledgments

This book is the result of a true "As One" effort by many people over the past two years. Our colleagues, clients, friends and families have all made major contributions to this work.

First, and most important, we acknowledge the support of Deloitte for funding our two-year research project. Our colleagues from different member firms in Deloitte have contributed enormously to the refinement of our ideas as well as applying them in real organizations. Without their intellectual challenges, and the ability to "beta test" our ideas, our thinking would simply not have coalesced.

Deloitte is the largest private professional services network in the world with over 170,000 member firm professionals in 147 countries. The challenge of getting that many people to work "As One" is, quite simply, a mammoth undertaking. We have made every attempt to apply our ideas and frameworks to this leadership challenge. We have learned a great deal as a result. We are absolutely confident that our ideas can similarly benefit other organizations.

While literally scores of Deloitte partners from member firms around the world have contributed to this "Flagship Project," we single out and recognize specifically Margot Thom, Jeff Watts and Brett Walsh who have been part of our leadership team. They have worked tirelessly to promote the As One ideas and approaches inside their practices and regions within Deloitte.

We would also recognize the significant contributions of several country leaders who provided the team resources and applied the emerging thinking with their clients over the course of the project: Andy Garber (United States), Allan Gasson (United Kingdom), David Brown (Australia), Leon Pieters (Netherlands), Gert De Beer (South Africa), Milton Da Vila (Brazil), Jorge Castilla (Mexico) and Verónica Melián (Uruguay).

We also specifically recognize Giam Swiegers, CEO of Deloitte Australia, and his whole team. Not only did they offer our teams a fantastic home base in Sydney, but they also gave us access to a set of world-class resources in the analytics, online and creative arenas. We thank Andrew Barrow, Lisa Barry, Belinda Bushby, Frank Farrall, Justin Giuliano, Rob Hilliard, James Hillier, Matt Kuperholz, Renny Nanaiah, Chris Nunns, David Redhill, Jonathan Rees, Chris Russell, Ben Shields, Jason Smale, Anthony Viel, Heiko Waechter and Pete Williams for applying their craft to our special initiative. Giam signed up as our very first alpha test and dedicated his four-day leadership team to our as-yet-unproven work. It is difficult to overstate the impact Giam's retreat had on accelerating the development of our ideas.

Second, we thank the clients of member firms who have contributed meaningfully to our work. We know that realizing the full power of all the people in a multibillion-dollar corporation, an entrepreneurial company, a big government department and other large institutions is an enormous leadership and management challenge. Our thoughts and ideas derive principally from our work with clients confronting this challenge. Their encouragement and success convinced us to undertake the challenge of writing this book and gave us the courage to share our ideas with a larger audience.

Third, we recognize the enthusiastic, dedicated and creative work of our teams over the life of the project. We divided the project into seven "sprints" each consisting of three to four months of work. We recruited the most promising talent from across the Deloitte world and combined them with experts from outside the organization to drive the research and development activities. To a person, they have advanced the thinking and ensured that a breadth of perspectives was reflected in the ultimate result. Interestingly, we experienced each of the eight archetypes described in this book at some point in the project.

The objective of Sprint 1 was to survey the knowledge landscape through twelve different lenses ranging from science, technology and nature to politics, history and psychology. The Deloitte team included David Price-Stephens, Jane Hallam, Ruchika Bhalla and Annie Tobias. They were joined by Keith Berwick, the legendary Aspen Institute guru as well as renowned Australian scientists Ron Sandland and Vijoleta Braach-Maksvytis. The team, which operating in Senator & Citizens mode, was exceptionally prolific and produced over 200 memoranda covering an exceptionally broad range of themes related to collective behavior. By the end of the sprint, we had landed on a distinctive "big idea."

The objective of Sprint 2 was to establish a rigorous analytic fact base in order to validate and develop the core idea. Keith, Ron and Vijoleta were joined by new Deloitte team members Blair Carlson, Nassim Behi, Mike Silverberg, Kim Haifer and Blake Woodward. Working with military efficiency, the team operated in General & Soldiers mode to produce 60 case studies of successful collective action. With help from our analytics gurus Matt Kuperholz and Anthony Viel, we ran sophisticated data analytic models to identify the archetypes described in this book.

The main objective of Sprint 3 was to apply our emerging thinking to a real organization and to validate its value to a leadership team. Fred Miller took the helm and was joined by Mike Silverberg, Irwin Liu, Dan Johnston and our analytics team, who worked together in Architect & Builders mode to develop and test an As One diagnostic for Deloitte Australia. Their resounding success gave us courage to accelerate our efforts.

The challenge in Sprint 4 was to validate our approach with lighthouse organizations. Irwin Liu and Elissa Liu were joined by our analytics and online experts to operate in Producer & Creative Team mode under the leadership of Kate Huggins. Together, and working under incredible pressure, they were able to validate and refine our approach in a number of client situations. By the end of Sprint 4, we could feel that we were on to something really valuable.

Known internally as the "mother of all sprints," Sprint 5 involved a very large ensemble working in Conductor & Orchestra mode for four months. Fred Miller rejoined the team and, with lots of help, reworked all our cases and the data analytics in order to generate a new "gamma" version of our archetypes, which are described in this book. The other team members, Pete Miller, Nobuyuki Kimura, Hebe Boonzaaijer, Lungile Mahluza, Belinda Bushby and Elena Shalygin, worked tirelessly to systematize our approach and support teams around the world who were running diagnostics. By the end of Sprint 5, we were ready to scale up.

Sprint 6 involved a return to Architect & Builders mode to support our rollout to organizations in different countries and involving different cultures. Fred Miller worked with new team members Verónica Melián, Orlando Mejia, Joanne Coll, Will Yell and Lynn Gonsor-Anvari as well as an all-star cast from prior sprints to deliver the results from our global diagnostic to the Deloitte World Meeting. A large gathering of several hundred senior member firm partners from around the Deloitte world, the meeting was designed around the theme of As One and featured ten parallel breakout sessions that dived deeply into our ideas and the diagnostic results. The massive logistics challenge demanded a switch to Captain & Sports Team mode for that whole week.

Finally, Sprint 7, which was a prelude to our external launch, involved the establishment of business processes for the rollout of the As One offerings as well as the preparation of hundreds of people for the launch. The key new addition to the team was Steve Langton who now leads our new Deloitte Center for Collective Leadership, which we specifically have created to advance this work. Steve was joined by the very talented duo of Joanne Coll and Will Yell. With respect to our algorithms and diagnostic products, we operated in Landlord & Tenants mode setting the rules of engagement and access. With respect to rallying support from partners around the world however, we operated in Community Organizer & Volunteers mode selling each person on the benefits of joining the group.

Over the past year, Fred Miller has played a grand master role in our project, with supposed emphasis on coordinating our research. However, he has been so able in that work that he has become the key firmwide resource on "As One behavior." From leading our case research analytics, to responding to literally dozens of enquiries, to leading client workshops, Fred has been a critical bulwark.

We also make a special acknowledgment to Leigh Jones, David Redhill, Carlton Lamb, as well as Bill Bovopoulos and his team at Aqua Media, who have helped us to synthesize our thinking and express things more clearly and elegantly. Gifted thought partners as well as communication and design specialists, they have been an invaluable source of ideas for creative expression, and indeed, have played a real role in the refinement of our ideas. We also thank Jim Prior and his team at The Partners as well as Michael Broadhead and his team at The Folk for their creative contributions.

We appreciate all the guidance and support from Adrian Zackheim, Joel Rickett, Will Weisser, Allison McLean and the whole team at Penguin. They have been encouraging and provocative at the same time; and they have made invaluable contributions to shaping this book.

And, of course, none of this would have been possible without the professional assistance of Nichole Brien, Beverley Dean, Terry Kidd, Ava Sloane, Karen Thiess, Noela Fowler, Anthony Johnson and Patricia Webb who have helped us through the many ups and downs of this project. We are thankful for their very hard work and patience.

Finally, we thank our families for their help. From Naysan Baghai's support on whale taxonomies and the *Star Wars* case study, to Nathan Quigley's case on LiveTV, we appreciate the flow of ideas and the moral support.

We especially thank our wives, Roya Baghai, Bonnie Quigley, Suzie Aijala, Abir Challah and Elizabeth Vorster for their unconditional support, understanding, and patience during this extended effort. They have cheerfully made sacrifices greater than ours so that we could focus on completing this labor of love. We owe them everything.

Index

Ainar D. Aijala, Jr. leads Deloitte Touche Tohmatsu Limited's global Consulting group, which is comprised of 30,000 member firm consultants serving clients in 147 countries. He has been with Deloitte since 1982 and was the founding leader of DTTL's Global Human Capital group; his immediate past role was National Managing Director-Services for the Deloitte US Consulting practice. He specializes in human resource and benefits issues particularly as they relate to the execution of the business strategy. He is also a member of the board for JA Worldwide™ (Junior Achievement) and its former global chairman. He is active in many charities, including the Central Park Conservancy in New York, NY.

Sabri Challah is Vice Chairman of Deloitte UK and a partner in the Human Capital practice. He has been advising large global companies and government departments on strategy, organization and transformation for 25 years. He is a board member of Deloitte Touche Tohmatsu Limited and has previously led the Human Capital group globally. He trained as a doctor and practiced for a number of years.

Gerhard Vorster is Chief Strategy Officer for Deloitte Australia and the Regional Managing Partner for Deloitte Touche Tohmatsu Limited's Consulting group in Asia Pacific and has lived, advised leading organizations and led teams of professionals in South Africa, Southeast Asia and Australia over the past 27 years. He is responsible for the Innovation program in Deloitte Australia, and he has published widely on the topic of innovation in organizations as well as the impact on individuals. He is actively involved in the national innovation agenda of Australia.